Blue Paper on Data Protection

A Data Breach Accountability Framework: How to reduce the risk of GDPR sanctions (Professional edition)

Guido Reinke

London – Brussels – New York

GOLD RUSH Publishing 2020

A Data Breach Accountability Framework:
How to reduce the risk of GDPR sanctions (Professional Publication)
Copyright © 2020 GOLD RUSH Publishing®
All rights reserved.

ISBN-10: 1-908585-14-5
ISBN-13: 978-1-908585-14-1

For further information or if you wish to submit any comments or ideas for future publications, please email to the email address below.

GOLD RUSH Publishing® books are for educational, business, or sales promotional use. We are an independent publishing house promoting innovative publications.
For more information please email: info@GoldRushPublishing.org.

© Guido Reinke, 2020
A Data Breach Accountability Framework:
How to reduce the risk of GDPR sanctions (Professional Publication)
Includes text, diagrams and tables. First Printing, edition for professionals, 2020.
978-1-908585-14-1 (ISBN 13) paperback.
Available for sale in bookshops, online at Amazon.com, and other channels worldwide.

European *Data Breach provisions* are about: –

1. empowering data subjects over those who possess and process their personal data

2. mandating a proactive approach to safeguarding personal data

3. assuring the integrity and confidentiality of personal data

4. notifying data subjects and regulators when a data breach is likely to result in high risks to a natural person

5. holding data controllers and data processors more accountable

6. transferring data only when its safety can be assured

7. implementing technical and organisational measures that assist with monitoring of and speedy response to breaches

8. conducting, as required, risk assessments of the data protection impact of new technologies and processes

9. arming regulators with power to sanction offenders

10. establishing a data protection regulatory regime to exercise oversight in an ever more complex data environment.

– Guido Reinke (2020)

FOREWORD

by

– Professor Ian Walden –
Data Breaches and information security provisions provide ongoing challenges for organisations

The GDPR has made data protection a boardroom issue for business, from multinational companies to SMEs. Such enhanced awareness and concern is in part due to increased fines and enhanced enforcement powers of data protection authorities, but also to the new provisions for controllers and processors concerning information security and data breaches.

The GDPR provides three categories of regulatory enforcement: notices, criminal penalties and administrative fines. As the *Morrison Supermarkets v Various Claimants* case shows, even if the regulator takes no enforcement actions, organisations still have the risk of civil litigation individually or as a group (*i.e.* representative actions), which may lead to higher pay-outs than a regulator's likely administrative fines. Enforcement of the GDPR across the EEA is inconsistent, which is a challenge for international organisations that have to deal with multiple regulators and jurisdictions. As a member of the European Commission's multi-stakeholder expert group supporting the application of the GDPR, I have seen how complex it is to identify issues from the perspective of competing stakeholders, from global businesses and private citizens. In the area of security compliance, for example, the notion of what is 'appropriate' presents challenges for all. Organisations often need external advice on developing a defensible position that will protect them from pecuniary and reputational risks. Many organisations still see compliance as an administrative burden for which they struggle to see the benefits.

The *Data Breach Accountability Framework* presented in this Blue Paper is a good starting point for organisations seeking to develop a robust compliance regime in light of the integrity and confidentiality principle of the GDPR. It can raise organisations to a higher maturity level and facilitate demonstrating to the regulator – not always an easy task – the sufficiency and proactiveness of their approach to safeguarding personal data. A Framework of this kind can furnish Data Protection Officers a toolkit for developing a defensible position, but ultimately, it is up to senior management to determine how much they invest in safeguarding personal data *versus* the risk and expense of liability of being held to be non-compliant.

Professor Ian Walden

Professor Ian Walden, Queen Mary University of London

Dr Ian Walden is Professor of Information and Communications Law and Director of the Centre for Commercial Law Studies, Queen Mary, University of London. His publications include Media Law and Practice (2009), Free and Open Source Software (2013), Computer Crimes and Digital Investigations (2nd ed., 2016) and Telecommunications Law and Regulation (5th ed., 2018).

Ian has been a visiting professor at the universities of Texas, Melbourne and KU Leuven. He has been involved in law reform projects for the World Bank, European Commission, Council of Europe, Commonwealth and UNCTAD, as well as numerous individual states. Ian was a 'expert nationaux détaché' to the European Commission (1995-96); Board Member and Trustee of the Internet Watch Foundation (2004-09); on the Executive Board of the UK Council for Child Internet Safety (2010-12); the Press Complaints Commission (2009-14), a member of the RUSI Independent Surveillance Review (2014-15) and a member of the Code Adjudication Panel at the Phone-paid Services Authority (2016-). Ian is a member of the Commission's Expert Group to support the application of the GDPR. He is a solicitor and Of Counsel to Baker McKenzie. Ian leads Queen Mary's qLegal initiative and is a principal investigator on the Cloud Legal Project.

ACKNOWLEDGEMENTS

Data Protection brings together professionals from across multiple areas. I am grateful to all the Chief Compliance Officers, Chief Operating officers, Chief Risk Officers, senior managers and legal counsel who have been telling me for years how complex and mystifying the legal and regulatory framework for data protection is.

I would like to extend my gratitude to all the professional colleagues and friends I met on the journey to writing this Paper, and the forerunners with whom I have previously published my regulatory compliance works and practitioner papers.

I am thankful to Prof. Ian Walden, Director of the Centre for Commercial Law Studies at Queen Mary University, who helped me to frame the issues for this Paper and lent focus when discussing my research at the Centre. His reviews and suggestions helped me deepen my research in crucial areas.

I could not have written this Paper or made it relevant and useful for practitioners in the field without the challenges posed by my professional friends who brought their decades of experience in data protection to bear, notably Jack Nagle, Noriswadi Ismail, Thanas Loli and Dr Klaus Meyer. I am indebted to Mikko Niva for the opportunity to gain invaluable experience in implementing GDPR for Vodafone, and to Steve Collins for entrusting me with the lead data protection role at William Hill. I am grateful too for the intellectual stimulation of Jerry W. Bains, whose legal background in particular helped me understand the multi-dimensional complexity of the legal landscape and gave me a US-perspective.

In my career, and prior to becoming a Data Protection Officer, I audited and advised dozens of organisation on privacy matters. I discussed with many colleagues and clients how to comply with the data breach provisions, with which the most security-aware organisations and finest DPOs are struggling with. I am pleased that many of my professional friends responded to the Data Breach Survey you will find in this Paper, which furnishes first-hand insights from data protection experts in the field. As I promised to keep the respondents anonymous, I can't name them here, but they should know how grateful I am for their support.

Above all, I am thankful for my friends and family who have supported and encouraged me, particular in dark moments when I felt like I would drown in the deluge of empirical data I gathered for this publication. At the peak of the coronavirus pandemic, when I spent long hours working on the GDPR Sanctions Directory and translating data on administrative fines from unfamiliar European languages in order to compile the most comprehensive GDPR sanctions inventory and analysis to date, I began to call this "the Beast" as the battle to pull it together began to feel Titanic and endless.

My parents provided me endless inspiration on this topic, how cookies and privacy notices affect their lives, and the wonderful technology that helps them to decide what to buy online next though adverts popping up which seem to be able to read their minds. This Blue Paper is dedicated to them, and to all who have supported me in this endeavour, and who have given me their advice, but more importantly, their enthusiasm.

Guido Reinke

TABLE OF CONTENTS

LIST OF ACRONYMS

The following acronyms are used in this Blue Paper:

AEPD	Agencia Española de Protección de Datos [Spain]
Article 29 WP	Article 29 Working Party
CIA [triad]	Confidentiality, integrity, and availability
COE	Council of Europe
DBAF	Data Breach Accountability Framework
DLP	Data Loss Prevention
DPA 2018	Data Protection Act 2018 [UK]
DPIA	Data Protection Impact Assessment
DPO	Data Protection Officer
DSAR	Data Subject Access Request
DPSA	Data Protection Supervisory Authority [national]
ECtHR	European Court of Human Rights
EDPB	European Data Protection Board
EDPS	European Data Protection Supervisor
EEA	European Economic Area
CJEU	Court of Justice of the EU [*a.k.a.* the European Court of Justice (ECJ)]
GDPR	General Data Protection Regulation [Regulation (EU) 2016/679 of the European Parliament and of the Council of 27 April 2016]
ICO	Information Commissioner's Office [UK]
MFA	Multi-factor authentication
NIS Directive	Network Information System Directive 2016
PbD&D	Privacy by Design & Default
PECR	Privacy and Electronic Communications Regulations 2003
PETs	Privacy Enhancing Technologies
ROPA	Record of Processing Activities
SDLC	System Development Life Cycle
SBNL	Security Breach Notification Law
VPN	Virtual private network

LIST OF FIGURES

EXECUTIVE SUMMARY

Although the GDPR was passed by the European Parliament in April 2016 and entered into force across the EEA in May 2018, many organisations are still struggling to implement and maintain the measures required for information security. From the outset it seems that the 173 Recitals and 99 Articles provided sufficient clarity about what is expected from data controllers and processors. The GDPR demands "appropriate technical and organisational security measures" are implemented, but leaves it up to organisations to choose their state-of-the-art technologies and organisational processes based on their risk assessment. The law omits to define clearly some key terms, such as accountability, responsibility, risk and high risk. Organisations are to do their own risk assessments and develop "appropriate" data protection frameworks.

This Blue Paper presents a Data Breach Accountability Framework (DBAF), which was developed by using data sources and methodologies covering legal analysis, the practical experience and insights of professionals, advice from regulators, and other primary empirical research, plus secondary research. The three key sources used were:

(1)   *The Data Protection Law*

An in-depth analysis of the General Data Protection Regulation and its provisions for information security and data protection, which include:

- the integrity and confidentiality principle (Article 5(1)(f)),
- the legal definition of security of processing personal data (Article 32),
- the importance of risk assessments (Article 25),
- the relevance of data breach notifications (Article 33 and 34),
- cooperation and prior consultation with regulatory authorities (Article 31 and 36),
- how to "demonstrate" compliance with the law to the regulator, and
- important considerations when demonstrating compliance with risk prevention and damage mitigation provisions of GDPR.

(2)   *The Regulators' decisions, collected in*

- the GDPR Sanctions Directory, a comprehensive inventory and analysis of primary quantitative and qualitative data on the sanctions by national regulators in the EEA, covering the 30 months since the coming into force of the GDPR (25 May 2018 to 24 November 2020).

- case law based on Data Protection Supervisory Authorities investigations, decisions and court rulings.

(3) *Organisations' responses, known from*

- insights gained through attendance of data protection events with thought leaders and professionals.
- a survey which targeted Data Protection Officers (DPOs), data protection lawyers, and distinguished specialists in the field of privacy.
- the author's personal experience in data protection and regulatory compliance.

From triangulation methods based on the foregoing, from legal and compliance experience, as well as from implementing elements of the Data Breach Accountability Framework for various business organisations, it becomes clear that Data Protection Frameworks can be structured around a number of key domains. Each domain can be broken down into certain key compliance controls (or deliverables). The following table shows how organisations can demonstrate compliance with the GDPR.

Figure 1: Data Breach Accountability Framework:
A legal framework for demonstrating compliance

Ref.	Requirements per GDPR Article	Design and implementation of organisational controls to demonstrate compliance
1.	**Privacy Governance – DPO function and reporting**	
1.1	**Article 38(3)** [*DPO position*] – "report to the highest level of the controller or processor".	<ul><li>Appoint a DPO (where necessary).</li><li>Define the privacy governance structure that enables the DPO to report data breaches to senior management.</li></ul>
1.2	**Article 29** [*Processing under the authority of the controller or processor*] – the controller must instruct the processor.	<ul><li>Clearly define the responsibilities of the data controller and processor in legal documents (contracts, work orders and SLAs) as well as in process guides and playbooks (*e.g.* communication lines for reporting incidents/ breaches).</li></ul>
1.3	**Article 5(2)** Controllers' responsibility for principles and for demonstrating compliance (with data security).	<ul><li>Review and update the six accountability measures regularly.</li></ul>
2.	**Policies and Processes for Privacy by Design & Default**	
2.1	**Article 13** [*Information to be provided to data subjects*] – provide	<ul><li>Design and implement policies, processes, procedures and guidance to safeguard the</li></ul>

Ref.	Requirements per GDPR Article	Design and implementation of organisational controls to demonstrate compliance
	details of when data is collected. **Article 25** [*Data protection by design and by default (PbD&D)*] – design and implement data-protection principles and safeguards even when not legally obligatory.	processing of personal data. ■ Be transparent: provide a clear and plain privacy notice at collection point. ■ Deploy PbD&D to cover the entire data lifecycle from collection to destruction, and implement measures to contain the risk of breaches at each stage of data processing.
2.2	**Article 35** [*Data Protection Impact Assessment (DPIA)*] – Conduct assessments of the impact of new technologies and processes if likely to pose high risks to natural persons.	■ Complete DPIAs to better understand the risks of data processing and the harm that could be caused to data subjects in case of a data breach.
2.3	**Article 30** [*Records of processing activities (ROPAs)*] – Controllers and processors shall maintain a detailed ROPA containing the obligatory information listed in the GDPR.	■ Maintain a ROPA to document which personal data are processed to help develop a data security strategy with speedy investigation after a data breach.
2.4	**Article 5(1)(c)** – "*data minimisation*" principle. **Article 5(1)(b)** – "*purpose limitation*" principle. **Article 5(1)(e)** – "*storage limitation*" principle.	■ Enforce the Data Retention Policy and Retention Schedule to contain the risk that no-longer-needed personal data might be breached.
3.	**Individual Rights**	
3.1	**Article 5(1)(f)** – "*integrity and confidentiality*" principle. **Article 15(3)** – "*secure transfer*" of personal data to data subject by electronic means.	■ Securely transfer personal data when responding to Data Subject Assessment Requests (DSARs) to assure the data's integrity and confidentiality.
4.	**Security for Privacy and Data Breach identification & notification**	
4.1	**Article 32(1)** [*Security of processing*] – implement appropriate technical and organisational measures assuring a level of security proportionate to the risk. **Article 32(3)** – Implement an approved code of conduct or certification mechanism.	■ Design and implement technical and organisational controls to safeguard personal data from "accidental or unlawful destruction, loss, alternation and disclosure" (Article 32(2)). ■ Implement technologies for encryption (*e.g.* of laptops), pseudonymisation and anonymisation of data, and data management (*e.g.* data retention, data cleansing, data destruction). ■ Adhere to relevant codes of conduct and

Ref.	Requirements per GDPR Article	Design and implementation of organisational controls to demonstrate compliance
		obtain formal certifications through third-party attestation.
4.2	**Article 33** [*Breach notification to DPSA*] – notify without undue delay and provide details, including likely consequences. **Article 31** [*Cooperation with DPSA*] – Support the DPSA in performing its tasks. **Article 34** [*Breach communication to data subject*] – notify without undue delay if the breach could pose a high risk.	▪ Establish an incident response plan, including a process for a speedy breach investigation, with internal/external reporting and remediation/ mitigation to meet the 72 hours or "without undue delay" requirements. ▪ Act transparently and timely, giving evidence-based information, when dealing with the DPSA. ▪ Engage with data subjects where possible, and start planning remediation/mitigation actions *immediately*.
4.3	**Recital (85)** – demonstrate that the breach is unlikely to result in risk to the data subject.	▪ Keep a record that includes non-notifiable incidents, as well as evidence of assessment of notifiable breaches.
5.	**Procurement and Third-Party Management**	
5.1	**Article 28(1)** – Data controller shall only use processors who provide sufficing guarantees of being competent to implement appropriate technical and organisational measures.	▪ Do data protection due diligence (*e.g.* by using a supplier questionnaire) when onboarding new suppliers to assure that they can implement due measures to safeguard personal data.
5.2	**Article 28** [*Processor*] – Processing should be covered by a contract and comply with Article 32 requirements. **Article 33(2)** – Processor shall notify the controller of a breach without undue delay. **Article 82(2)** [*Liability*] – Processors shall be liable for damage caused by processing.	▪ If suppliers are data processors, the supply contract and data processing agreement must include clear instructions about data transfers to third countries, as well as responsibilities and reporting timelines for data breaches.
6.	**Approach to Consent and Direct Marketing**	
6.1	**Article 5(1)(f)** – "*integrity and confidentiality*" principle. **Article 21** [*Right to object*] – data subject can object to direct marketing and profiling.	▪ Build-in appropriate security when using personal data for marketing purposes to avoid unintended disclosure of personal data (*e.g.* disclosure of email addresses, sending personal data to the wrong person). ▪ Protect spreadsheets that contain personal data and passwords, and centralize records-keeping of personal data where possible.

Ref.	Requirements per GDPR Article	Design and implementation of organisational controls to demonstrate compliance
		▪ Provide the data subject a user-friendly opt-out process.
7.	**Training, awareness, and communications**	
7.1	**Article 39(b)** [*Tasks of DPO*] – assign awareness-raising and training of all staff involved in data processing.	▪ Provide regular privacy and information security training, as "human errors" contribute the most to data breaches. Keep an attendance record and follow-up non-attendees.
7.2	**Article 47** [*BCR*] – adequate training of staff with permanent or regular access to personal data.	▪ Offer specialised training for functions that process large amounts of personal data or special data categories.
8.	**International Data Transfer**	
8.1	**Article 46** [*Transfer to third countries*] – set up adequate safeguards with enforceable rights for data subject, including effective legal remedies.	▪ Pre-set up legal safeguards: data processing agreements, inter-group agreements, and other mechanisms. ▪ *Prioritise* data subject's rights in case of breach.
9.	**Monitoring compliance**	
9.1	**Article 32(1)(d)** – implement a process for regular testing, auditing, and assessing risks and the security measures' effectiveness.	▪ Conduct regular internal and external information-security and privacy audits.
9.2	**Recital (85)** – demonstrate that the breach is unlikely to result in risk to the data subject.	▪ Maintain an incident and breach register.
9.3	**Article 38(3)** – [DPO post] – "report to the highest level of the controller or processor".	▪ Include incidents and breaches in metrics / Key Performance Indicators to provide senior management with the oversight ability needed to take strategic decisions, and provide enough budgeted and other resources for mitigating information security risks.

This Blue Paper provides best practice guidance for professionals who need more insight into how to develop a robust compliance framework for handling data breaches. It will empower them to translate into practical action the GDPR and recommendations from Data Protection Supervisory Authorities.

When designing and implementing the Data Breach Accountability Framework (DBAF), it is important that this is not left to the DPO alone, but that senior management sponsors this initiative and a number of key stakeholders actively support compliance efforts. In larger and medium-sized organisations this should involve the following functions:

- *A formally appointed DPO, Privacy Officer or Data Protection Manager*, who engages with the identified stakeholders; coordinates specialist input where needed; is hands-on involved in designing / reviewing policies, processes and procedures; and signs off on the design and implementation of the DBAF. As the main custodian of personal data, and as the person responsible for notifying data subjects and regulators, the DPO should maintain the ROPA, – the central register of all processes involving personal data.

- *The legal department*, which provides input about local breach notification requirements, including data protection clauses in vendor contracts, employment contracts, client agreements, work orders, and SLAs.

- *The risk and compliance department*, which evaluates and assesses data breach risks with the support of other stakeholders; understands their likelihood and impact; and, where needed, can identify risk-mitigating or -compensating controls.

- *The information technology (IT) department and information security team*, who assure that the required technical and organisational measures are implemented to prevent or detect accidental or unlawful destruction, loss, alteration, or disclosure of personal data. IT also should regularly review and update their own Incident Management Process and Disaster Recovery Process, and include the names and contact details of the incident management group to be notified in case of an information security breach.

- *Senior management* (CEO, COO, CIO, CCO and others) who sign off on the risks management controls and provide sufficient budgeted and non-budgeted resources to design and implement a DBAF. Senior management must also define a governance structure which will allow the DPO to efficiently notify data breaches and swiftly respond to regulators, as required, to reduce the risks for data subjects arising from incidents or data breaches.

- *The procurement team*, who should cover data breaches and information security as part of their due diligence when on-boarding new suppliers. The procurement team must assure that all suppliers processing personal data sign the data processing agreement and report any breaches in less than 48 hours.

- *The training department*, who raise awareness, provide information security and data protection training, and keep an attendance record. Non-attendance to training must be followed-up and escalated, if necessary.

- *The audit team*, who should perform annual reviews to assure that the controls work as designed. Any audit-of-design walkthroughs and operation effectives testing must include access controls, a processes review, and a review of the incident management process and testing.

- *All functions that process personal and sensitive personal data*, which include human resources, marketing and sales, should be aware of their responsibilities for safeguarding and avoiding unintended disclosure of personal data, and should understand their roles in identifying a data breach.

PART I

Overview of the Blue Paper – the legal position on data security and breaches

The knock-on effect of a data breach can be devastating for a company.

When **customers** start taking their business

– **and** their money –

elsewhere, that can **be** a real body blow.

– Christopher Graham
(UK Information Commissioner 2009-2016)

Chapter 1

INTRODUCTION

In the 30 months since the General Data Protection Regulation (GDPR) EU 2016/679 began to be enforced, that is, from 25 May 2018 to 24 November 2020, a total of 503 sanctions in the form of administrative fines, totalling €298,916,013 in costs,[1] have been imposed by the national Data Protection Supervisory Authorities (DPSAs) in the EEA[2]. The highest number of infringements was for violations of the "integrity and confidentiality" principle (also called the "information security principle") under Article 5(1)(f), and for violations of the "security of processing" provision under Article 32, which accounted for 70 cases (or 10.4%) and 113 cases (or 11.7%), respectively (Figure 5 and Figure 12), amounting, in total, to 22.1% of all infringements.

The GDPR has strengthened the enforcement powers of DPSAs across the EEA significantly. Six of the ten highest administrative penalties ever imposed for data breaches under Article 32 are:

- H&M Hennes & Mauritz Online Shop for unsecure storage of sensitive personal data (fine of €35,258,708);
- the Italian Telecom Provider Tim (fine of €27,802,946) for unlawful data processing and a data breach;
- British Airways (fine of €22,046,000) with more than 500,000 website users affected;
- Marriott hotel (fine of €20,45,000) for compromising 30 million EU residents' data;
- Vodafone for a lack of customer resource management security and telemarketing (fine of €12,251,601) and
- 1&1 Telecom GmbH for an violation in protect processing of personal data (fine of €9,550,000).

---

[1] This total includes all fines published by DPSAs and were available in legal and data protection databases. Please note that there is a lack of transparency by some DPSAs, and those in Germany publish their fines only in *annual* reports.

[2] Toolkit 5 presents an inventory of all EU Data Protection bodies and Toolkit 6 lists details of all the EEA DPSAs.

The remaining four top-ten fines include:

- Google Inc. in France (fine of €50,000,000) for violations of transparency (Article 5) and legal basis (Article 6),

- the Austrian Post (fine of €18,000,000) for selling details of three million customer,

- Merlin for unsolicited marketing-communications (fine of €16,700,000), and

- Deutsches Wohnen SE for unlawful storage of personal data (fine of € 14,500,000).

A survey conducted for this Blue Paper revealed that data protection professionals believe that data breaches are most likely to incur sanctions from the DPSAs (Figure 8). This is a clear correlation between actual enforcement actions by regulators and data controllers' awareness of it, which raises the complex question of how these professionals can reduce their organisations' liability? The question of liability for breaches is also examined in the Morrison case study (Section 3.5.3). The Supreme Court's ruling on vicarious liability for a breach by an employee sets a precedent protecting the employer from a pay-out for future actions by rogue employees, that is, one acting beyond the scope of his employment.

1.1   Key objectives, assumptions and value for data controllers

The objective of this empirically oriented Blue Paper[3] is to critically analyse the legal requirements in the GDPR for information security and data breaches, as well as guidance issued by the EDPB and other official bodies; to review GDPR sanctions by analysing administrative fines and recent cases; and to assess the responses by organisations to meet their legal requirements and the expectations of the regulators.

As information security principle infringements and data breaches combined make up the highest percentage of cases and of administrative fine totals among all EEA countries (Figure 12), organisations have a strong interest in understanding how they can demonstrate compliance with the GDPR.

This Blue Paper's thesis is that organisations will not avoid sanctions for data breaches unless they are proactive and smart in the way they design and implement the

---

[3]   A "Blue Paper" is neither a *White Paper*, an official government report giving information or proposals on an issue, nor a *Green Paper*, a preliminary UK Government or EU proposal that has been published in order to stimulate debate. I am introducing the novel term *Blue Paper* to designate an analysis and guidance paper that reviews the *legal options*, in this case to guide organisations how to respond to the legal and regulatory requirements for information security and data breaches. The content of a Blue Paper, however, is not theoretical nor pitched to lawyers, but to the laity. It strikes a practical balance for professionals working across functions, giving them a robust range of recommendations to design and implement appropriate technical and organizational measures to reduce the risk of administrative fines by regulators and legal actions by individuals in case of an information security infringement or data breach.

obligatory compliance framework. Companies should be shooting for more than adequate security and confidentiality of personal data, such that it will also enable them to demonstrate to the regulator's satisfaction the GDPR compliance of their processing data activities.

The objectives of this Blue Paper are:

(1)   to deepen understanding of the law in regard to Article 5(1)(f) and Article 32 infringements, and provide clarity and an interpretation of the regulator's understanding of "appropriate technical and organisational measures";

(2)   to analyse regulators' enforcement actions for failure to secure the processing of personal data; and

(3)   to offer a legal and regulatory compliance framework that can assist organisations with the GDPR's mandate to demonstrate compliance by implementing "appropriate technical and organisational measures to ensure a level of security appropriate to the risk", as provided by Article 32(1), in order to protect data subject's personal data "against unauthorised or unlawful processing and against accidental loss, destruction or damage", as provided by Article 5(1)(f).

To be able to demonstrate the implementation of a framework to meet these legal requirements at organisational level can reduce administrative fines. But it also will lead to better protection of data subjects against breaches resulting "in physical, material or non-material damage [...] such as loss of control over their personal data or limitation of their rights, discrimination, identity theft or fraud, financial loss, unauthorised reversal of pseudonymisation, damage of reputation, loss of confidentiality of personal data [...] or any other significant economic or social disadvantage to the natural person concerned" (Recital 85).

It is assumed that compliance with the GDPR's principles and provisions is applied consistently. The empirical research conducted for this Blue Paper has shown that the number of cases and amount of fines can vary significantly across countries; however, as long as the administrative fines in each individual case are "effective, proportional and dissuasive", these variations are in line with the Regulation (Article 83(1)). If the number of cases and the number of fines exists shows a wide divergence across countries, the question is: Does this not violate proportionality after all? Section 3.3 investigates this further.

1.2   Scope of this Blue Paper

In-depth analysis of regulatory enforcement actions on all seven principles set out in Article 5 and other key provisions would be too voluminous for this Blue Paper; therefore, the scope of this Blue Paper has been confined to enforcement actions on the "integrity and confidentiality" principle (Article 5(1)(f)) and the relevant provisions related to security of processing (Article 32).

The GDPR provides for three categories of enforcement: (1) a notice in the form of a *reprimand* to a controller or processor for minor infringements of the GDPR (Article 58(2)(b) and Recital 148); (2) *prosecution* of criminal offences and execution of criminal penalties which include prevention of threats to public security (Article 2(2)(d) and Recital 149); and (3) *administrative fines* (Article 83). This Paper only covers the last. The author acknowledges that private claims, in particular US-style class actions (see *Morrisons* and *British Airways*) have an impact on law enforcement. Organisations have to fear not just regulators' administrative penalties, but also their responsibility in civil court to the complaints of data subjects, in other words they are exposed to civil liability, not just regulatory liability. The *Morrisons* case below shows that there has been a discrepancy between the UK's ICO and the English courts' decisions, and the question arises if a wide divergence possibly exists also between private claims and regulators' enforcement actions. If so, this could mean that the "proportionality" requirement in Article 83(1) is out of sync. Clearly, this would require a comprehensive separate analysis, and so private claims have been excluded from this research.

The primary interest herein is GDPR enforcement by the national DPSAs and EEA supervisory oversight within the EU; therefore, excluded are comparisons to jurisdictions outside the EEA.

Also excluded from this Blue Paper are penalties for non-compliance with the Privacy and Electronic Communications (EC Directive) Regulations 2003 (PECR), and the continuing enforcement, under Member State domestic law, of the Data Protection Directive 95/46/EC (*e.g.*, in the UK the DPA 1998). EU Directive 2016/1148 on "a high common level of security of network and information systems across the Union" (NIS Directive), which aims to address cybersecurity threats, is excluded as well (EU Agency for Cybersecurity, 2020)[4]. Finally, excluded as well from the scope of this Blue Paper are a number of other security breach requirements which are overseen by other regulators, such as financial services or communications regulatory authorities, and apply to specific industry sectors, *e.g.* to the telecoms industry and for payment services.

It should be noted that new technologies and therefore new threats are constantly emerging, which requires operators to patch operating systems and implement new "defence systems" to deal with the threats. This Blue Paper will review the standard technical and

---

[4]   It should be noted that the UK ICO has power to issue fines similar to the GDPR (up to £17 million) (ICO website – What is NIS, 2020). NIS applies only to operators of essential services and relevant digital services providers yet violations carry similar fines as the GDPR.

organisational measures already available and recommended in the GDPR and other legal texts. This Paper intends to avoid political debate, focussing solely on mechanisms that will help companies be compliant by meeting their legal and regulatory obligations under data protection law. The objective is to take up a lawyer's and/or a data protection professional's standpoint to help organisations minimise liability when processing personal data.

The ultimate objective of this Blue Paper is to assist organisations with legal liability to achieve compliance. Organisations have different structures, different levels of complexity of internal and third-party data processors, and process different types of personal data, depending on the nature of their activities (*e.g.*, employee data, customer data, sensitive data, and/or high volumes of data); therefore, there is no one-size-fits-all solution, and so each organisation ought to implement those specific measures under the provided Accountability Framework which best fit their situation.

1.3   Structure of this Paper

This Blue Paper consists of three parts after this introduction, and a conclusion. The first part is a legal analysis of the GDPR on the topics of data security and data breaches. The second is a survey of the enforcement actions on data breaches. The third is about how organisations can demonstrate that they comply with the law to reduce the risk of being sanctioned.

Chapter One provides background on the topic, defines its objectives, basic assumptions, the multiple research methodologies used, and its scope.

Chapter Two explores the legal position of the GDPR on data security and breaches thereof. It analyses the relevant principles and provisions in the Regulation which may be breached and may subject the breacher to administrative sanctions. It reviews the opinions of legal scholars and professionals, and tries to discover the operation of these legal obligations.

Chapter Three analyses the data yielded by primary research; in particular, an annexed compendium of all the known GDPR enforcement actions across all EEA countries from 25 May 2018 until 24 November 2020 (hereinafter "GDPR Sanctions Directory", see Figure 17 in Toolkit 4), plus the results of a targeted survey. These data enrich our understanding of the national DPSAs' regulatory focus, and their possible differential treatment of industry sectors and of violations and sanctions. The case studies of *Doorstep Dispensaree, Cathay Pacific, WM Morrison Supermarkets, British Airways,* and *Marriott International* which are an Article 32 violation from the UK, give supplementary insights into mitigating factors *etc.* in what organisations should do in order to reduce administrative fines.

Chapter Four inquires into organisations' self-protection from sanctions for data breaches, presenting legal and regulatory compliance toolkits which lawyers and compliance professionals can use to assist in demonstrating compliance. It analyses the survey results and the authors' participant observation in privacy events, and draws conclusions about a better approach to take in implementing security measures and expected actions following a data breach.

Chapter Five critiques national DPSAs and the European Regulator, and makes some key recommendations for developing a defensible legal and compliance position for minimising the risk of data breaches. This new model is called the *Data Breach Accountability Framework* (DBAF).

The following diagram illustrates how the different parts of this Blue Paper contribute to the development of the model.

Figure 2: Logical flowchart of the Blue Paper

1. Problematization	Why does it matter? What are the objectives, methods and scope?
2. Legal analysis	What does the GDPR say? What do scholars and legal professionals think?
3. Understanding sanctions	Analyse empirical data from the GDPR Sanctions Directory. Lessons leaned from five case studies.
4. Organisational development	Practical relevance Contribution of survey respondents and authors' participant observations.
5. Conclusions	Data Breach Accountability Framework: A legal framework to demonstrate compliance.

1.4   Methodology applied and resources used

The data sources used and methodologies applied for this Blue Paper cover substantive empirical research, legal analysis, and secondary research.

This includes:

a)   Primary research, which consisted of

    i)   a review of relevant laws, EU and national regulatory guidance, and case law;

    ii)   a comprehensive collection and analysis of primarily quantitative data on the sanctions that have actually been imposed by national regulators, covering the 30 months since the coming into force of the GDPR (25 May 2018 – 24 November 2020);

    iii)   a qualitative analysis of regulatory enforcement and organisational response, by reviewing data obtained through a closed survey which targeted Data Protection Officers (DPOs), data protection lawyers, and distinguished specialists in the field of privacy to learn insights about the DPSAs' focus of enforcement actions and the triggers for penalties; and

    iv)   the author's participant observation (Becker, 1970) for more than two years, which provides further qualitative data collected through involved participation in events with DPOs and privacy professionals; personal attendance of presentations at conferences and events at law firms about this subject; and development of personal relationships (as described by Burgess, 1984:92-96; Delbridge *et al.*, 1994:50-59) in order to gain acceptance, to win trust, and to develop co-operation, rapport and friendship (Jorgensen, 1989:69-81); allowing in-dept insights into regulatory behaviours.

b)   Secondary research, which included:

    i)   reviewing academic literature on the GDPR; and

    ii)   digesting articles and *thought leadership* on this topic by law firms.

Triangulation was used to doublecheck the soundness of data and inferences. Triangulation means, according to Cohen and Manion (1986:254), an "attempt to map out, or explain more fully, the richness and complexity of human behaviour by studying it from more than one standpoint". O'Donoghue and Punch (2003:78) define it as a "method of cross-checking data from multiple sources to search for [ir]regularities in the research data". The sheer multiplicity of data-collection acts, especially the Sanctions Directory, made it unfeasible to triangulate discrete observations; triangulation was deployed at method- more than at data level, the main instance being *triangulation of perspectives*. The first perspective is legal (Chapter Two). The second perspective is the regulator's, expressed through its GDPR sanctions (Chapter Three). The third perspective is the organisation's, expressed through the responses to the data breach survey and the author's participant observation (Chapter Four).

Chapter 2

THE LEGAL POSITION OF THE GDPR
ON
DATA SECURITY AND DATA BREACHES

This Chapter begins with an overview of why data breaches occupy a unique position in the General Data Protection Regulation. The following sections analyse the integrity and confidentiality principle in Article 5(1)(f) and the provisions for data breaches made in Article 32. As breaches are an inherent risk, the law provides additional provisions which mandate prevention of security incidents, or when they occur, following a structured approach to identification, notification, and mitigation. The following sections analyse these instruments, such as DPIAs, PbD&D, notifications, cooperation and consultation with DPSAs, all which form an important part of the Regulation which enables controllers to demonstrate compliance with the law.

2.1   Why data breaches occupy a unique position

Security breaches occupy a unique position in the GDPR. Unlike other provisions, the Regulation requires notifying incidents to both the DPSA (Article 33) and the data subject (Article 34), even if it could lead to an investigation that the data controller would like to avoid. DPSA investigators may even levy fines for late reporting if the data controller does not report within 72 hours.

The duty to report breaches to the regulator is new in EU law, but in some jurisdictions it has existed for more than a decade. California enacted the first security breach notification law (SBNL) in September 2002 (California Senate Bill 1368). After South Dakota and Alabama passed their SBNLs in 2018, now all 50 States have enacted legislation to notify individuals of security breaches of personal data (NCSL website).

The effectiveness of SBNLs in improving how organisations safeguard personal data has been subject to much debate. Winn argues that, while it has brought to the attention of

[American] consumers their inadequate information security, the focus on disclosure and not on reinforcing the underlying right to privacy has not helped consumer rights (Winn, 2009a). Winn chides the American law for also providing no right of compensation for breaches (Winn and Wright, 2009b). In contrast, the GDPR was drafted with the aim of empowering data subjects by defining and vindicating their individual rights, safeguarding their personal data, and holding data controllers and processors fully accountable and liable for damage caused; and it guarantees that "data subjects should receive full and effective compensation for the damage they have suffered" (Recital 146, Article 82).

While the EU Privacy and Electronic Communications Directive 2002 required providers of publicly available eCommunications services to inform subscribers of the risks of breach, it did not require subscribers to be notified in case of breach (Article 4(2) ePrivacy Directive). The impact of the GDPR is much wider, as every organisation in the EEA has to comply with the law or is threaten with punitive and dissuasive administrative fines.

The GDPR has not only redefined how organisations must respond to data breaches, it has also made data controllers and processors alike liable for the damage caused by malprocessing (Article 82(2)). The new regime recognises the "accountability principle" (Article 5(2), Recital 39 and 74) as central, and makes controllers responsible. Embedding accountability for employees' and suppliers' acts may be difficult, but building a top-down privacy culture can help achieve this aim. For such third parties, contractual arrangements that define the data processing relationship are necessary (ITGP Privacy Team, 2017:116-117).

GDPR accountability means that (1) organisations are responsible for complying with the GDPR, and that (2) controllers must keep records of some kind ("accounts") that can demonstrate compliance not only to the regulator, but also to data subjects, in court if necessary (ICO website – Accountability and governance). In matters of information security, accountability means controllers are expected to keep records demonstrating the "appropriate technical and organisational measures" they have installed (Article 32(1)).

Article 4 neglects to define *accountability*, and other terms such as *responsibility*, *risk* and *high risk*, but legally accountability implies that controllers need to generate clear evidence (*viz.*, ROPAs and DPIAs and other documentation) that is presentable on lawful demand to the regulator in case of investigation and to data subjects in case of litigation.[5]

Liability is a legal concept, and once controllers are singled out as accountable, they become the first point of contact in case of an infringement. Controllers are held ultimately

---

[5]   Accountability is defined as "an obligation or willingness to accept responsibility or to account for one's actions" (Merriam-Webster online dictionary, available at https://www.merriam-webster.com/dictionary/accountability) and as the "responsible for and having to explain your actions" (Cambridge dictionary website, https://dictionary.cambridge.org/dictionary/), while responsibility is "to be in a position of authority over someone and to have a duty to make certain that particular things are done" (Cambridge dictionary website).

responsible for notifying DPSAs and data subjects of breaches, but they are also responsible for managing their processors, employees, and sometimes other suppliers (see Morrisons case study below).

2.2   The integrity and confidentiality principle (Article 5(1)(f))

Article 5 defines seven principles governing the processing of personal data, among which the "integrity and confidentiality"[6] (or "security") principle in Article 5(1)(f) and Recital (83) require assuring appropriate protection of the security of personal data through technical or organisational measures "against unauthorised or unlawful processing and against accidental loss, destruction or damage" (Article 5(1)(f)). A certification such as ISO 27001 Information Security Management Systems can provide reasonable assurances if joined up with DPIAs or risk assessments to meet the requirements of this principle (ITGP Privacy Team, 2017:116).

The GDPR provides that infringements of these seven basic principles for processing, and conditions for consent (Articles 5-7 and 9), data subjects' rights (Articles 12-22), and transfer to third countries (Articles 44-49) all fall under a second tier of administrative fines which is double the first tier's (Article 83(5)). The fines can be up to €20,000,000 or 4% of global annual turnover, whichever is higher (Article 83(6)). While both controllers and processors must comply with this principle, controllers are responsible for demonstrating to the regulator and interested parties that they have implemented appropriate security; therefore, for controllers, it is important to understand the full scope of the security principles and to be able to "demonstrate compliance" with them per the *accountability principle* in Article 5(2)). Section 2.7 will explain the concept of "demonstrating", while the case studies and other empirical data in the following chapters explain the DPSA's understanding of "compliance".

To comply with the "[information or data] security principles", first, it is important to understand what security means in the GDPR. A security principle was of course already there in the GDPR's predecessor, the Data Protection Directive 95/46/EC (Section VIII: Confidentiality and security of processing, Articles 16-17) and in national regulations, such as the UK DPA 1998 (Part I of Schedule 1, principle 7). Information Security is defined as the practice of protecting the confidentiality, integrity, and availability (the "CIA triad") of data in general (including commercial data such as financial and business-related data) and personal data in particular (Sheldon, 2016:5-8). These well-established information security principles were already defined by Article 29 WP long before the GDPR was enacted

---

[6]   ISO/IEC 2700:2016 defines confidentiality as "property that information is not made available or disclosed to unauthorised individuals, entities, or processes" (Clause 2.12) and integrity as the "property of accuracy and completeness" (Clause 2.40).

(Article 29 WP, 2014).[7]

The principle is, as the ICO put it, "a fundamental building block for good data protection practice"; however, "they don't give hard and fast rules, but rather embody the spirit of the GDPR" (ICO website – The principles). As the principles do not clearly define what is expected of controllers and processors, it is important for organisations seeking a "compliance haven" to bring together interdisciplinary teams with technical, compliance, business assurance, and legal backgrounds for developing a compliance approach, – *not* just lawyers. This will also provide organisations some flexibility in customising a solution based on inherent and specific risks. The DBAF presented in this Blue Paper aims to assist these efforts.

2.3 The legal definition of security of processing (Article 32) and DPIAs (Article 35)

The GDPR defines "personal data breach" as "a breach of security leading to the accidental or unlawful destruction, loss, alteration, unauthorised disclosure of, or access to, personal data transmitted, stored or otherwise processed" (Article 4(12)). Article 32 requires that controllers and processors consider "the state of the art, the costs of implementation and the nature, scope, context and purposes of processing", and conduct a risk assessment which takes into account the likelihood of incidents and the level of their impact on the "rights and freedoms of natural persons posed by the processing". This is to help determine the "appropriate technical and organisational measures to ensure a level of security appropriate to the risk".

The GDPR uses the word "appropriate" 115 times, stressing that organisations have the liberty to define technical and organisational measures "appropriate" to, that is, *befitting* the risks presented by the processing of personal data. Article 32 furnishes a few examples of what this might mean; *viz.*, pseudonymisation and encryption, process controls, resilience plans, backups, disaster recovery plans, regular testing, and process effectiveness reviews. It also recommends demonstrating compliance *via* approved codes of conduct and certification mechanisms. Smedinghoff acknowledges that there is no "one size fits all" approach, and based on his review of US SBNLs, identifies a number of criteria for appropriate security measures, such as the probability (or likelihood) and gravity (or impact) of a threat materializing; the company's size and capabilities; the nature and scope of the business; the sensitivity of the data; the state of art regarding technology and security; and the costs of implementing the security measures (Smedinghoff, 2015:14). Section 4.3 below provides a

---

[7]   Art. 29 WP Opinion 03/2014 defined "confidentiality breach" as an unauthorised or accidental disclosure of, an "integrity breach" as such an alteration of, and an "availability breach" as such a loss of access to personal data.

summary of *practical* appropriate measures.

Appropriate measures can be established through risk assessments. It is obligatory to conduct a risk or Data Protection Impact Assessment (DPIA) when new technologies and processes are likely to pose high risks and to concern the rights and freedoms of natural persons (Article 35). The assessment must be (a) "systematic", (b) consider the proportionality of processing, (c) assess the risks, and (d) consider security measures to protect personal data (Article 35(7)). It must also gauge the likelihood and impact of the risks (Article 25(1) and 32(1), Recital 76). Where risks exist, they must be identified and best practices to mitigate them described (Recital 77). As failure of cybersecurity and data loss are inherent risks to all organisations, at least a basic assessment should be conducted by all data controllers. Article 29 "Guidelines on Data Protection Impact Assessment" (Article 29 WP, 2017a) offers further guidance for determining whether processing is "likely to result in a high risk" for GDPR purposes. It stresses the importance of a risk assessment first (p. 8), as a DPIA is obligatory only for operations "likely to result in high risk" (for examples see Article 35(3)). The Guidelines also offer nine criteria governing assessment of risk, which is an indication of its importance.

Based on the assessment, controllers are obligated to develop a procedure that builds "the necessary safeguards into the processing" and is capable of compliance with GDPR provisions. The appropriateness of security measures is determined on a case-by-case basis, and may include pseudonymisation and encryption (FRA *et al.*, 2018:131-134). It must be reviewed on a regular basis. This includes *e.g.* "Guidelines on Data Protection Officers" (Art 29 WP, 2017b), which recommend that DPOs take a risk-based approach so as to "prioritise their activities and focus their efforts on issues that present higher data protection risks" (p. 18).

It is also important to understand the meaning of "state of the art", referred to in Articles 25(1) and 32(1). This is a dynamic concept that implies that organisations stay up to date on technological advances in protecting personal data (Claridge, 2020), which is also an expectation that the regulator expressed in the Cathay Pacific case study below. Importantly, processes must be regularly tested and evaluated to assure conformity with these technical and organisational measures (Article 32(1)(d)).

Interestingly, the GDPR prioritises prevention over cure. The GDPR is written so that some cases could fall in either category of fine, the full 4%/€20 million tier or only the 2%/€10 million tier pursuant to Article 83(4) and (5); for example, if you lose an unencrypted work laptop, the controller could be fined for the data breach (Article 32), as well the failure to have the necessary encryption software installed (Article 5(1)(f)). It seems that the GDPR punishes "systematic inadequacies in data security" more severely than inadequate reactions to breaches (Cellerini and Lang, 2018:10).

2.4   Safeguarding the rights of data subjects through PbD&D (Article 25)

The EU Data Protection Regulation has dual objectives which are intrinsically linked: protecting the fundamental rights and freedoms of natural persons, and ensuring the free flow of personal data between Member States (Orla, 2019:46-88); therefore, safeguarding personal data is essential to the whole regime. Article 25 further clarifies how organisations are to demonstrate to the regulator that they have embedded the security principle in the "development and design of products, services and applications" (Recital 78); however, the meaning of Privacy by Design and Default (PbD&D) is not spelled out in the legally obligatory text of the GDPR; therefore, organisations are obligated to go beyond the four corners of the Regulation in order to stay compliant. PbD&D was developed by Dr. Ann Cavoukian, former Information and Privacy Commissioner of the Province of Ontario (1997-2014). It was formally adopted in Article 25. PbD&D is based on 7 Foundational Principles[8] (Cavoukian, 2011a, 2011b, 2012, 2013). These are now widely accepted as basic to the protection of individual rights and interests throughout the data lifecycle and obligatorily applicable to business processes, specific technologies, system architectures, and networked data systems. Privacy should be incorporated by default from the design phase through the whole development cycle, which covers project objectives, design processes, and operational priorities. Like information security, privacy should be embedded in every process, standard and protocol (Cavoukian, 2011a, 2011b). The European Data Protection Board (EDPB, 2019) and national regulators such as Britain's ICO (ICO website – PbD&D) have fully endorsed this concept. Even so, some critics have questioned whether PbD&D is more a high concept than the silver bullet, which only patches up the conflict between privacy and security (Leese, 2015:271-287). In the author's view, PbD&D furnishes just another piece of the Privacy jigsaw puzzle.

The GDPR mandates the following:

Firstly, Article 25(1) [Data Protection by Design] requires that the "technical and organisational measures" are appropriate "taking into account the state of the art, the costs or implementation and the nature, scope, context and purpose of [data] processing" (Article 25(1)).

Secondly, Article 25(2) [Data Protection by Default] makes data controllers accountable to "implement appropriate technical and organisational measures [...] for each specific purpose of processing". These provisions are applicable to all stages of the design

---

[8]   These are: (1) Proactive not reactive, preventive not remedial, (2) Privacy as the Default, (3) Privacy embedded into the design, (4) Full functionality – positive sum, not zero sum, (4) End-to-end security – lifecycle protection, (6) Visibility and transparency, and (7) Respect for users.

and development of all relevant business processes, including those in the supply chain. The concept of PbD&D even covers applications of processing activities across an industry sector (Recital 92). It should be considered for each phase of the classic System Development Life Cycle (SDLC), which may be broken down into five phases: − (1) design and development, (2) testing, (3) implementation, (4) operation and maintenance, and (5) retirement a.k.a decommissioning (Agarwal, 1990:172).

Thirdly, Article 25(3) makes organisations responsible for demonstrating that they have followed the legal requirements under Article 25(1) and (2). It recommends use of approved certification mechanisms (under Article 42) as one way of doing this; however, alternatives are an internal or external data protection audit and a formal certification accredited by an independent assurance.

The European Union Agency for Cybersecurity (ENISA) has published a guide titled "Privacy and Data Protection by Design − from policy to engineering" (ENISA, 2014) which focusses on Privacy-Enhancing Technologies (PETs), *e.g.* encryption, protocols for anonymous communications, etc., developed especially for IT security staff to help assess technical elements of PbD&D. The whole concept could be applied to information security. Practitioners as well scholars are attempting to assess practical ways of implementing this new concept (Rubinstein and Good, 2012).

Professional associations, the collaborative efforts of industry, and standards institutes have all developed a number of risk management and control frameworks that assist organisations in implementing their regulatory compliance obligations more effectively and consistently. Governance and IT security frameworks and guidance establish a common terminology; provide standards against which organisations can assess their control and compliance systems; and give guidance in deciding how to improve them.[9]

Although some IT and governance standards apply to various information security

---

[9] Examples of standards and compliance frameworks that support the implementation of information security controls include:
   (i)   the Control Objectives for Information and Related Technology (COBIT), developed by the IT Governance Institute of the Information Systems Audit and Control Association (ISACA) provides guidelines for IT controls for 34 processes (IT Governance Institute website, 2020; ISACA website – COBIT, 2020), ISACA, 2019);
   (ii) Standards developed by the International Organization for Standardization are also relevant (ISO website, 2020); such as: ISO/IEC 27001:2017 *for Information security management systems*; ISO/IEC 27701:2019 *for Security techniques for privacy information management*; and ISO/IEC TS 19608:2018 *Guidance for developing security and privacy functional requirements*, which in Section 6.2 defines security functional requirements for implementing the Privacy Principles of GDPR;
   (iii) the IT Infrastructure Library (ITIL), developed by the UK Office of Government Commerce, improves IT service management, including problem and incident management;
   (iv) Payment Card Industry Data Security Standard (PCI DSS), an information security standard for organisations which process credit cards, covers security incidents; and
   (v)   Generally Accepted Privacy Principles (GAPP), developed by accountants (AICPA and CICA, 2007), is defining ten principles to implement global privacy frameworks.

matters, they can nonetheless be "mapped up" to specific data protection requirements. COBIT have the major advantages of being globally accepted and promoted as open standards available to all organisations (Williams, 2006:26-28). Owing to global corporate-governance and cybersecurity regulation, and to the increasing number of new regulations at all governance levels, compliance frameworks have been widely used by organisations in recent years. The more widely these frameworks are used, the more likely it is that the regulator, or bodies that work closely with the regulator, will endorse their use for implementing compliance.

2.5   The relevance of data breach notifications (Articles 33 and 34)

The Article 29 WP described breach notification as "a tool enhancing compliance in relation to the protection of personal data" (Article 29 WP, 2018:5), and it recommends implementing processes able to detect breaches, assessing the risk, and developing a DPSA/data subject notification process. It also states that "the failure to notify a breach could reveal either an absence of existing security measures or an inadequacy of the existing security measures" (Article 29 WP, 2018:5). In case of a personal data breach, the controller must, without undue delay, but not later than 72 hours after becoming aware of it, notify the DPSA. If there are delays in notifying the DPSA, reasons for this delay must be provided (Article 33(1) and Recital 85). The GDPR also makes processors responsible for notifying controllers (Article 33(2)). The GDPR takes a descriptive approach when listing as per Article 33(3) what the notification must include at the least: a description of the breach, an estimate of the number of data subjects and records affected, likely consequences of the breach, and remedial and mitigating actions. Data breaches should be recorded, including even non-notifiable incidents.

If the data breach is likely to result in high risks to the rights and freedoms of a natural person, Article 34(1) and (2) requires that the controller shall also communicate with the data subject and "describe in clear and plain language the nature of the personal data breach" without undue delay. Individuals may be exposed by reputational, psychological, or financial harm caused by a breach (Burton, 2020:642). Article 34(3) provides exemptions from this requirement.

Data breaches that lead to the disclosure of sensitive, confidential or personal data are a major concern of information security; therefore, the obligation to report personal data breaches without undue delay, and where possible not later than 72-hours after becoming aware of it, demands that DPOs have a clearly delineated process ready for timely response. It is important to note that data controllers must design and implement a process for data breach identification and notification which complements the IT [major] incident management process, as the DPO must be able to provide the DPSA with specific information.   This includes the nature of the incident, the number of data subjects and records affected, the possible consequences, and the remedial and mitigating actions taken (Article 33(3)).

2.6   Cooperation and prior consultation with the DPSA (Articles 31 and 36)

Both the data controller and -processor are required to cooperate with the DPSA (Article 31).   This requires that the controller consults with the DPSA if the DPIA indicates that processing could lead to high risks to data subjects that cannot be mitigated (Article 36(1)). Risk mitigation and breach prevention are key objectives of GDPR, but it is left up to individual organisations to develop a solution appropriate to the risk.   Although cooperation and consultation should be a given, as the empirical data and the *Doorstep Dispensaree* case study below shows, organisations have different approaches and some may be less forthcoming when dealing with regulators.   It is impossible to quantify how much DPSAs might add to an administrative fine if an organisation is less cooperative, but as shown by the Sanctions Directory (Toolkit 4), throwing away evidence or closing a business ahead of an investigation will be punished by a higher fine.

2.7   The concept of "demonstrating" compliance with the Regulation

Data controllers and processors are responsible for implementing "appropriate and effective [technical and organisational] measures" *and* must be able to "demonstrate the compliance of processing activities" involving personal data with the Regulation.   Article 24 and Recital 74 make the controller accountable for demonstrating the compliance of its processing activities with the GDPR.   This new term "demonstrate", which is mentioned 26 times in the Regulation, requires demonstrating in particular:

- accountability for the seven principles of processing personal data (Article 5(2)), and for keeping evidence of data breach assessments regarding the risks to data subjects (Recital 85);
- adoption of internal policies and measures to fulfil PbD&D (Recital 78), maintaining ROPAs (Recital 82), and carrying out risk assessments through DPIAs (Article 35(7)(d), Recital 84); and
- assurances of compliance with GDPR provisions in the form of audits or inspections (Article 28(3)(h)), certifications, and codes of conduct (Articles 24(3), 25(3)) and 32(3), Recital 81).

2.8   Demonstrating risk prevention and damage mitigation

The GDPR requires organisations to identify best practices for mitigating risks, and suggests approved codes of conduct, certifications, and guidelines by the EDPB[10] or a DPSA to address such risks (Recital 77). Controllers should in particular assess and mitigate inherent processing risks through encryption and other data loss prevention measures (Recital 83). If necessary, and where no mitigation actions can be identified, the controller should consult with the DPSA (Article 36, Recital 84). Mitigating activities must also be part of breach notification to data subjects (Recital 86) and of a DPIA if high processing risks have been identified (Recital 94). When notifying a breach to the DPSA, controllers must report "remedial actions" (Article 33(5)). Interestingly, a study by Kapoor found that there is often an overemphasis on technical remediation measures, yet many survey respondents believe paying more attention to the human element is equally vital (Kapoor *et al.*, 2018:16).

There is a clear incentive for controllers to make "mitigating activities" a central part in their PbD&D approach, which goes beyond protecting organisational assets. In the event of a breach, organisations can reduce or even avoid sanctions by demonstrating to regulators that they have implemented mitigating and remediating measures to reduce the consequences of infringements (Article 83(2), Recital 148 and 150). At a minimum, organisations must implement measures and be able to demonstrate compliance with the minimum legal requirements noted above, at least.

2.9   Conclusions of the legal review

Although the security-principle approach leaves organisations some flexibility in complying with GDPR provisions, the spirit of this far-reaching data protection law is about demonstrating to the national DPSAs how compliance is to be *and* has been achieved, both. To elucidate the regulator's intent, this chapter interprets key terms such as "appropriate" and "state of the art" (Section 2.3), "demonstrate" (Section 2.7), and "mitigating measures" (Section 2.8). Furthermore, it rigorously analyses the legal provisions most relevant to demonstrating compliance with Article 5(1)(f) and Article 32. In sum, by conducting data protection risk assessments to understand the impact and risks of data processing for natural persons; following the PbD&D approach when developing new applications, services and products; and keeping records of processes and maintaining logs of incidents, organisations put themselves in a strong compliance position. Lawyers are instrumental to defining the

---

[10] By the end of 2019 the European Data Protection Board had adopted 67 documents (of which 16 originated with the former Art. 29 WP (EDPB website)), including 10 new guidelines and 43 opinions (European Commission, 24 June 2020:6).

legal approach to security for privacy under GDPR compliance; however, managing the risk should not be left up to them alone. The following chapters analyse how to develop a defensible compliance position. This requires not just legal competence, but also the technical competence to analyse empirical evidence compiled from breaches which have been investigated.

PART II

———

Insights from regulators
and
data protection practitioners

It's very important to have the comfort of the regulator
in every geography where you operate.

— *Chanda Kochhar*
(Former executive director of ICICI Bank)

Chapter 3

THE EMPIRICAL DATA: ANALYSIS OF DATA BREACHES

The IAPP-EY Annual Privacy Report 2019 asked which specific privacy topics have been reported to the board of directors. At the top of this list were data breaches (68%), followed by "status of compliance with GDPR" (64%) and "privacy KPIs" (58%) (IAPP and EY, 2019). This highlights the importance of breach risk management, which should start with an understanding of the legal requirements for being compliant. The empirical data collected and analysed for this Blue Paper support the conclusion that *security for privacy* is the most important provision in the GDPR, judging by enforcement action by the regulator and the opinion of privacy professionals.

This chapter analyses the empirical data collected *via* the Sanctions Directory, from the survey respondents, and out of the three case studies. It also investigates the consistency of sanctions enforcement across the EEA. All these insights from the regulatory perspective allow us to understand the regulator's expectations for data controllers and processors.

3.1 Sanctions by national DPSAs

This section analyses the sanctions imposed by national DPSAs. Spain leads the pack in numbers of fines imposed, with 175, followed by Romania with 46, Italy (35), Hungary (34), and Germany (33). These five countries alone account for 64.21% of all GDPR sanctions in the EEA in the first two years after the Regulation entered into force (see Figure 3).

Figure 3: Total cases by country

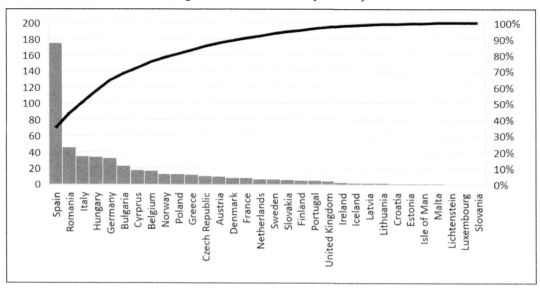

The 175 administrative fines imposed by the Spanish regulator, the Agencia Española de Protección de Datos (AEPD), since May 2018 amounted to 34.79% of the total *number* of GDPR fines so far. 17 fines have been for Article 32 infringements and 29 for Article5(1)(f) principle violations (Sanctions Directory). In its latest annual report of 2019 AEPD revealed that breach notifications had tripled in 2019 and that the total value of fines collected from security breaches had increased by 664% compared to 2018 (AEPD, 2020:118). Although practitioners are aware of the very high number of fines (see Cazalilla and Martín, 2020), the exact reasons for this high volume remain unclear. Judit Garrido Fontova, Spanish privacy lawyer at Kemp Little, believes that "the AEPD's smaller fines aim to encourage a wide-spectrum of organisations to comply to the GDPR" (2020). The author's surmise that the Spanish DPSA has more effective administrative sanctioning and investigation procedures is shared by Spanish privacy lawyer López-Lapuente as well. Andrea Romano, privacy lawyer at EUIPO in Alicante, confirmed that "the GDPR and the Spanish law gives the DPSA more instruments to prosecute, investigate and fine organisations". She also noted that "the GDPR received a big publicity among the Spanish citizens, which led to a higher number of complaints" (Romano, 2020). Interesting to note is that Spain enacted a law supplementing the GDPR that implements three categories of infringements – minor, serious, and very serious – to the GDPR's two (López-Lapuente and Bosch, 2019), which implies the AEPD is punishing offenders based on the degree of harm they cause under this stricter law.

The evidence that I was able to collect is inconclusive and this issue cannot be fully resolved herein, but questions for further research do suggest themselves:

(1)   Does the AEPD in fact fund at least some of its operations from the proceeds of its own fines (giving rise to a moral hazard)?

(2)   Why has such an activist regulator never taken on the American tech giants, following Sweden (€7 million fine for Google) and France (€50 million fine for Google)?

(3)   If the AEPD's strategy is to impose many small fines as a teaching device, this would imply that the volume of cases should have declined in tandem with the learning curve, yet the volume has been increasing: 47 cases in all of 2019 and 127 cases till 24 November 2020. Why is the number of fines still increasing?

The lack of transparency is something that can cover up conflicts of interest such as subsidising oneself on the proceeds of sanctions. An ultimate answer to this puzzle is currently out of reach due to the AEPD's lack of transparency (see Section 3.3).

Interestingly, the most prolific finers were not the highest-value finers. The gap by country between the number of fines and the total value of fines is notable (see also Figure 13 in Toolkit 3). The countries imposing the highest fines in terms of total value were Italy (€69,651,897), followed by Germany (€62,860,291), France (€54,400,000), United Kingdom (€44,221,000) and Austria (€18,075,100). See Figure 3. The subtotal of €249,916,013 for sanctions by these five countries makes up 83.93% of all the value of GDPR fines.

Figure 4: Total value of fines by country

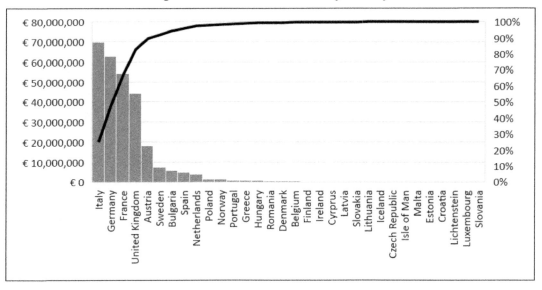

It should be noted that the UK has imposed one of the highest administrative fines by value to date. But the UK has now exited the EU. Data collected in primary research for this Blue Paper also suggested, but could not prove that the Spanish regulator may be funding itself partly out of the monies collected in fines. If true, this would explain the high number of fines, but simultaneously constitutes a moral hazard (Unnamed source interviewee, January 2020). It was queried whether Spain or the UK (or France) were statistical outliers, and whether the subtraction of these two countries (or just the outlier fines) from the data set would yield a significantly more consistent enforcement pattern. Taking this approach, France, Germany, and Italy are revealed by the Sanctions Directory (Toolkit 4) to be more suitable candidates for having the strictest DPSAs in the EEA.

3.2 Sanctions for data breaches *vs.* other GDPR provisions that carry liability

Out of the 503 sanctions counted in the Sanctions Directory in Toolkit 4, 113 cited Article 32 in their enforcement notices. Please note that the average DPSA notice cites 1.91 violations, which is why the total number of administrative fines for Article 32 infringements is difficult to determine exactly; however, fines explicitly citing Article 32 added up to €146,929,282 in value, which is 49.15%[11] of the value of all sanctions.

Figure 5 lists the total number of fines by GDPR Article, identified in the Sanctions Directory.

---

[11] Please note that the average DPSAs notice cites 1.91 violations, but a significant number of Article 32 fines also cite Article 5(1)(f) violations. The total value of administrative fines related to data breach and information security infringements is still the highest compared to any other fines.

Figure 5: Total number of fines by provision (GDPR Article)

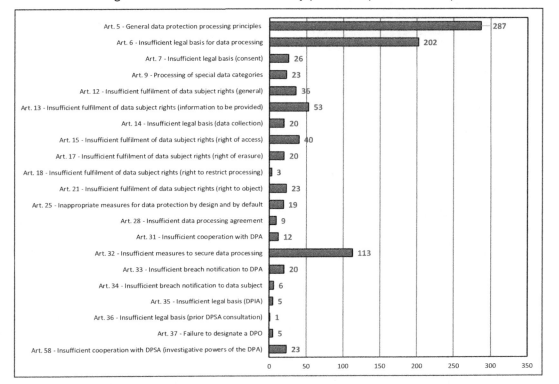

Non-compliance with the "integrity and confidentiality principle" in Article 5(1(f), which is also called the "security principle", together with the "lawfulness, fairness and transparency" and "data minimisation" principles, attracted most of the fines. Figure 5 comparatively totals the number of administrative fines sanctioning the seven data protection principles.

Figure 6: Total number of fines by provision (GDPR Article 5)

GDPR Article	Principle	Total cases	In %
Article 5(1)(a)	"Lawfulness, fairness and transparency"	74	11%
Article 5(1)(b)	"Purpose limitation"	30	4.4%
Article 5(1)(c)	"Data minimisation"	73	10.8%
Article 5(1)(d)	"Data accuracy"	13	1.9%
Article 5(1)(e)	"Storage limitation"	14	2.1%
Article 5(1)(f)	"Integrity and confidentiality" (or "security")	70	10.4%
Article 5(2)	"Accountability"	18	2.7%

From 25 May 2018 to 27 January 2020 within the EEA, a total of 160,921 personal data breaches were notified by organisations to their national DPSAs. The UK Information Commissioner's Office (ICO) alone received 22,181 personal data breach notifications (DLA Piper, 2020:4). Taking into consideration the number of these self-notifications, the number of administrative fines seems relatively low. Furthermore, the question arises whether and to what extent DPSAs have been using their powers of investigation to initiate their own inquiries, or whether and to what extent they have been relying on self-reporting and other forms of notification such as customer complaints or referrals of cases from other public authorities.

Most enforcement notices do not provide many details about what breaches of which GDPR Articles triggered the administrative action. Due to mandatory breach notification, it might be expected that in most cases self-notification would lead to the DPSA investigating, insofar as self-notification gives away to the DPSA free information about actual or potential breaches. Interestingly, a majority of the survey respondents believed that self-notification is the *least* likely scenario to trigger an enforcement action, while customer complaints and enforcement by the CJEU or the domestic courts are the most likely to trigger the DPSA to impose administrative fines. Figure 7 presents the results of the survey.

Figure 7: What is most likely to trigger enforcement actions following a breach? (Q5)

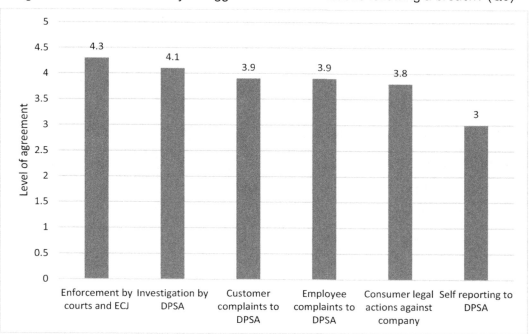

3.3   The consistency of enforcement across the EEA

The GDPR demands that each DPSA shall ensure that fines are "proportionate" (Article 83(1)), sanctions for infringements are "equivalent" (Recital 11), and that there is "consistency of application and enforcement" (Article 57(1)(g)). At the same time, it gives national DPSAs discretion to carry out audits and investigations of alleged infringements (Article 58(1)) and to use corrective and advisory powers (Article 58(2) and (3)). It is important, then, to distinguish between theory, as defined by the law, and what can be observed in practice in the implementation of the law.

The data does allow discernment of patterns within the various national enforcement efforts, which may or may not reflect the influence of a national sanctioning regime. A cross-country comparison of GDPR sanctions over 30 months revealed that the number of cases and the value of administrative fines of different DPSAs differs significantly; which raises the question whether this does not violate proportionality after all. Furthermore, one may wonder if DPSAs are more lenient in some countries than others, an explanation of the disproportionality of which is attempted below.

Interestingly, the European Commission's biannual GDPR report, required by Article 97, comes to the same conclusions on the performance of the cooperation and consistency mechanism, stating that "further progress is needed to make the handling of cross-border cases more efficient and harmonised across the EU" (European Commission, 2020:5). The report also acknowledges that, although the roles have been harmonised, there is still a degree of fragmentation and divergent approaches to how the GDPR is adopted at Member State level, in particular through the extensive use of facultative clauses, such as the age of children, exceptions, and different approaches to the implementation of derogations (European Commission, 2020:6-7).

As customer and employee complaints have been identified by the survey respondents as a significant factor triggering enforcement actions, the question is whether the number of enforcement cases is higher in countries with higher GDPR awareness. As the FRA survey shows, although countries like Germany and Spain have a higher GDPR awareness than average, there is no correlation across all EEA countries (FRA, 2020:12). Therefore, the reasons for inconsistency of enforcement are likely institutional.

Professionals in the field of data protection agree that enforcement across EEA countries is inconsistent. Of the data protection professionals responding to the data breach survey, a clear majority (21) answered "no" to the question of whether data breaches are sanctioned consistently across the EU; 2 responded "yes", while 9 were unsure. To the question which countries are the strictest enforcers (plural answers were possible) 13 responded Germany; 11 France; 3 UK; 3 Spain; and 2 Belgium (Figure 10). Asked for the reasons for this inconsistency, they opined that DPSAs have not agreed among themselves criteria for fines, have different enforcement cultures, different compliance priorities for certain GDPR provisions, variations in guidance and standards, administrative maturities, and resources available. Interestingly, respondents also mentioned that DPSAs can be subject to different political pressures and policy agendas. The respondents intuitively singled out France and Germany as the strictest, but perhaps they are only the most celebrated. Germany and France have a long history of tough data protection law enforcement. Together with Sweden, they introduced the first data protection legislation in the 1970s, which may explain why these two countries are near-universally seen by the survey respondents as the strictest (see Lynskey, 2019:47). The objective data tell a counterintuitive story. These show Spain and Romania, for example, to have the most activist regulators in terms of volume of cases. In terms of total value fined, France and Italy topped the list (Figure 3).

Max Schrems, privacy activist, also confirmed that DPSAs' reactions to the CJEU Privacy Shield decision were inconsistent. Yet the bureaucracies and consensus of 27 countries have blocked an EEA-wide approach, and thus the DPSAs press ahead each with their own approach. Schrems also pointed out that the Irish Data Protection Commission is a "bottleneck" to GDPR enforcement, and raised the issue that, if certain rules do not apply in Ireland *de facto*, then an unfairly unlevel playing field will have been created that impacts competition (Schrems, 2020).

Patrick van Eecke, chairman of DLA Piper's international data protection practice, stated, "Ask two different regulators how GDPR fines should be calculated and you will get two different answers. We are years away from having legal certainty on this crucial question, but one thing is for certain, we can expect to see many more fines and appeals over the coming years" (DLA website – Newsroom). The drafters of the GDPR foresaw the difficulty of getting 27 Member States to act in harmony, that is, consistently in the sense of legal certainty across the EEA, and so they established a "consistency mechanism" in Articles 63-67 of Section VII on "Cooperation and consistency", to prevent the very situation above-complained-of. The primary data leads to the conclusion that consistency in matters of enforcement is indeed a long way from being achieved.

3.4   GDPR sanctions by DPSAs (Sanctions Directory)

A comprehensive review of all administrative fines of which any record was found and entered into the GDPR Sanctions Directory in Toolkit 4 evinced some common themes which are summarised in this section. The analysis is complicated by important differences in how national DPSAs process administrative fines, some of which appear to be more transparent and consistent than others; raising issues of non-transparency and inconsistency across the EEA space.

(1)   Publication is the responsibility of national DPSAs.   Therefore, decisions are published (if at all) only on national DPSA websites in the corresponding official languages.

(2)   The publicly available legal justification of decisions in some cases is incomplete; *e.g.*, some DPSAs' notices are just a few sentences long, like most of the German Federal State (*Bundesländer*) DPSAs'; often without referring to any legal basis in the GDPR; while others publish lengthy legal rationales (*e.g.* the Spanish, Romanian, and UK regulators).

(3)   Anonymisation of entities fined is at the DPSA's own discretion; thus, for some of the larger, six-figure fines, the entities are anonymised to avoid damaging business reputation (*e.g.* in April 2020 the Netherlands fined an unknown organisation €725,000), and in other cases to protect vulnerable individuals (*e.g.* in March 2020 Germany (Nordrhein-Westfalen) fined a truck driver €229 who streamed videos on his YouTube channel).

(4)   The timing and frequency of the DPSAs' announcements vary significantly. Germany's administrative jurisdiction is divided between its 16 Federal States, whose DPSAs publish information on fines only in annual reports; whereas, the Irish DPSA's first fine was reported in the Irish Times and other private outlets long before being published officially.

(5)   Incompleteness of records is a problem for researchers.   Not all DPSAs maintain a log, and even when they do, the author found that decisions may be (re)moved from their website after just a few months (*e.g.* Belgian regulator).

(6)   Lack of transparency at European level is an issue too, surprisingly.   In the national news section on the EDPB website (EDPB website – National News, 2020), only 114 sanctions in all of two years and a half have been disclosed, which is less than a quarter (just 22.66%) of the 503 sanctions identified by the author.

The analysis of the primary data revealed notable inconsistencies across Member States as to the likelihood of being fined and the severity of the fines in respect of –

(1)   differing volume (number) of fines for different industries and public services.   The most fines fell on the Utilities sector (112 fines), followed by Public services & administration (65 fines), and Financial services (43 fines) (see Figure 14);

(2)   size (amount) of fines.   Some entities have received enormous fines, *e.g.* Austrian Post [€18m]; Eni Gas, Italy [€11.5m]; 1&1 Telecom [€9.55m] and Deutsches Wohnen [€14.5m], Germany; Google, Sweden [€7m], while others have been singled out for multiple fines for the same kind of violation (*e.g.* Vodafone has received 42 fines for a

total of €14,086,351).

(3)   delayed or defaulted enforcement. It is notable that some DPSAs take longer to enforce their fines than others. DPSAs also may use their discretionary powers, as laid out in Recital 150. The Irish DPC, which is the Lead Supervisory Authority for many global tech-firms such as Facebook, WhatsApp, Google, Twitter, and Instagram, has been investigating these tech giants so interminably long as to draw widespread and loud criticism. The DPC imposed its first fine of only €75,000 in May 2020, two years after GDPR went into force.

(4)   use of *referrals by national DPSAs to the CJEU* (under Recital 143). This causes long delays and in effect redelegates responsibility. The Irish DPC and the High Court (Ireland) handed over a case to the CJEU on 16 July 2019 (see *Data Protection Commissioner v Facebook Ireland Limited and Maximillian Schrems* (Case C-311/18)). The CJEU ruled that the Privacy Shield does not provide adequate protection, and invalidated the agreement on 16 July 2020.

3.5   Case studies: Lessons to be learned for after the data breach

Lessons about expectations for information security, breach prevention, and mitigating factors may be gleaned from three case studies which the UK's Information Commissioner's Office (ICO) has investigated. These cases are important for offering a second perspective, *i.e. the regulator's perspective*. Data controllers and processors can learn important lessons from these cases about reducing potential administrative fines.

Case One, a breach under special data categories, is a physical breach case handled by the ICO that has a final disposition. Case Two, about a cyberattack, illustrates a maximum fine under the UK's Data Protection Act 1998, a predecessor of GDPR. Case Three concerns vicarious liability for a breach also under the DPA 1998. Case Four and Five did carry the biggest administrative fines so far; however, due to COVID-19 and other factors, these fines were significantly reduced by the ICO after more than 15 months of administrative appeals and informal negotiations. Each study summarises the breach event, its severity and data subjects affected; its significance is reviewed; lastly, recommendations follow. The insights offered can help organisations implement appropriate technical and organisational measures.

3.5.1   Case One: *Doorstep Dispensaree Ltd.*

Doorstep Dispensaree Ltd. provided pharmaceutical dispensary and delivery services to customers and thousands of care homes. It was fined €320,000 (£275,000) on 17 December

2019 under GDPR Article 32 for taking insufficient measures to secure special category data. Between January 2016 and June 2018 the company had stored on site in unsealed containers nearly 500,000 paper documents involving 78 care homes, with names, addresses, birthdates, NHS numbers, medical and prescription information. The company neglected to protect the documents from weather, resulting in water damage; in any case, the storage was not secure, and waste was never marked as confidential. The ICO began investigation after being alerted on 24 July 2018 by the Medicines and Healthcare Products Regulatory Agency ("MHRA"), which had been carrying out a separate enquiry into the allegedly unlicensed and unregulated storage and distribution of medicines by the pharmacy (ICO, 2019a; ICO website – *Doorstep Dispensaree*).

Case review

Steve Eckersley, ICO Director of Investigations, faulted the "careless way" special data was stored, which "failed to protect it from accidental damage or loss" (ICO, 2019c). The fine was imposed for two breaches:

Firstly, the data controller failed to securely store data that fell under the "special data" category (medical information). In its enforcement notice, the ICO found breaches of Article 32 (security of processing), Article 5(1)(f) ("integrity and confidentiality" principle), and Article 24(1) making data controllers responsible to "implement appropriate technical and organisational measures to ensure and to be able to demonstrate that processing is performed in accordance with this Regulation".

Secondly, the company did not adopt an appropriate privacy notice. The policy that it did post did not name *Doorstep Dispensaree* as the data controller; did not state the legal basis or the conditions for processing "special data"; did not list the categories of personal data to be processed (Article 14(1)(d)), nor specify their legitimate interest in retaining the data long-term to serve patients whom they supply with medicines long-term; and did not inform data subjects of their rights (Articles 13 and 14).

An earlier ICO Notice of Intent and Preliminary Enforcement Notice (ICO, 2019d; ICO, 2019e) proposed a fine of £400,000; however, it omitted exact details on the calculation methods and the rationale for the subsequent fine reduction. The ICO explained that the financial information about *Doorstep Dispensaree* available on the Companies House website as well as representations made by the data controller relating to their financial position were used to calculate the fine. GDPR Article 83(2)(a-k) required the ICO to consider the nature, gravity (deemed *"very serious"*), duration, number of data subjects affected, and damage caused by the breach, as well as any mitigating actions and other factors (Penalty Notice, paragraph 48-66). The ICO never made clear how it weighted each of these criteria in calculating the fine. The company's last-filed accounts as at 30 December 2018 showed no turnover (only a loss of £559,024) (Companies House website). The calculation seems to be based on the Companies House's annual turnover threshold for SMEs, as defined by the Companies Act 2006, Section 382(3) to be not more than €10.2 million turnover with not more than 50 employees. This means that the fine is around 2% of its threshold annual revenue. Although it seemed small, considering the size of the company and its revenue, this fine constitutes a significant penalty.

Conclusions and recommendations

The ICO found Doorstep Dispensaree's violations of the GDPR to be "extremely serious" and noted in particular the failure to communicate, let alone implement an appropriate privacy policy. Having considered all the circumstances, and that penalties must be effective, proportionate, and dissuasive, the ICO in its initial notice proposed a fine of €468,000 (£400,000), which was reduced to €320,000 (£275,000), a significant 31.25% reduction, after the company's submission to the ICO, and taking into account the remedial work it had done since the MHRA visit (Cordery, 2020; Penalty Notice, paragraph 48). It can be argued that the regulator used this large fine as a whip to discipline the data controller into cooperating, and adjusted the fine after cooperation was forthcoming. Such a large reduction is not really a surprise, even though during the initial phase of the investigation in August 2018 the company was in denial and refused to answer any questions, until the ICO Commissioner issued its Information Notice under DPA 2018, Section 142(1)(a) on 25 November 2018. The data controller persisted in delaying the investigation until 1 March 2019 (Enforcement Notice, paragraphs 23-29).

This Blue Paper can suggest recommendations based on the measures listed in the Enforcement Notice. These are organisational measures to be implemented to secure personal data sufficiently to comply with the GDPR standard of information security.

(1)   Effective measures must be implemented to protect the storage of hard-copy (not just electronic format) personal data against unauthorised access. Personal data must also be protected from exposure to the elements and accidental destruction such as by water damage (Penalty Notice, paragraph 37 and 40).

(2)   "Utmost care" must be given to categories of special data, such as health data, according to GDPR. The ICO has made clear that health data and other special data categories must receive enhanced protection. Controllers of such sensitive data *"ought to be well aware of its data protection obligation and be taking them far more seriously"* (Penalty Notice, paragraph 49).

(3)   Data protection policies and supporting procedures must be regularly updated. Meaningful documentation should include the controller's and staff's responsibilities, clear advice on data processing and destruction, and instruction on how to respond to a breach (Enforcement Notice:13).

(4)   A DPO or an Information Governance Lead must be appointed who is accountable

for data security and incident investigations (Enforcement Notice:13).

(5)   Mandatory training must be provided for all staff, with regular refreshers once every two years. Attendance should be monitored and recorded, and enforced in case staff would not complete the training (Enforcement Notice:14).

(ICO, 2019a and 2019b; Hart, 2020; Ronco *et al.*, 2020).

3.5.2   Case Two: *Cathay Pacific Airways Ltd.*

Cathay Pacific Airways Ltd., the Hong Kong airline, experienced a brute force attack on its database in March 2018. A brute force attack submits a torrent of passwords and phrases to the server in hopes of guessing the valid password correctly and getting access to the target system. An external cybersecurity firm was called in after the breach was detected (Fox, 2020).

Case review

As the breach took place prior to GDPR being in force, Cathay Pacific was fined the maximum of £500,000 (€590,000) under the DPA 1998. Under GDPR Cathay would have faced a substantially larger fine. The fine was imposed for failure to secure customers' personal data, which exposed personal details of 9.4 million customers worldwide, of whom 233,234 were from the EEA and 111,578 from the UK; when the airline's systems were hacked via a server connected to the internet, into which data-harvesting malware was installed (ICO, 2020).

Conclusions and recommendations

Here is the regulator's review, which the author has converted into technical recommendations that would be of interest to any company in the same position as Cathay Pacific.

(1)   Use *state-of-the-art encryption* technologies. Although Cathay Pacific's information security policy required encryption of data backups, the company failed to follow through (Enforcement Notice 24(1)).

(2)   Execute *regular vulnerability scans* of computers, networks, and communications devices through penetration testing. Cathey Pacific had a vulnerability in an Internet-facing server that had been publicly known since February 2007, but had failed to remediate it, which allowed unauthorised persons "to bypass authentication and gain administrative access" (Enforcement Notice 24(2) and 24(11)).

(3)   Implement *access controls for employees and third parties* and give or withhold privileges to authenticate and authorise them as appropriate. In order to identify risks, carry out

risk assessments on a regular basis; for example, Cathy Pacific failed to implement the least-privilege principle and multi-factor authentication (MFA) for VPN network users. It also created 90 accounts in the administrator-group domain, which allowed the hackers to take control (Enforcement Notice 24(3), Enforcement Notice 24(6) and 24(10)).

(4) Assure adequate *system-patch management* to perform regular security updates in support of systems. This practice reduces the likelihood of system crashes and security breaches. It is recommended to patch all operating systems, servers, laptops, and mobile devices within a month of release. Cathay Pacific was running an OS which was no longer supported with security updates, and one server had no anti-virus software installed due to compatibility problems (Enforcement Notice 24(4), 24(7) and 24(8)).

(5) *Harden systems* by using the latest tools and techniques to reduce vulnerabilities in systems, applications, and infrastructure. This can be achieved e.g. by removing user permissions and access, deactivating unused ports, and removing superfluous applications. Cathy Pacific had installed unnecessary applications that were usable as attack points (Enforcement Notice 24(5)).

(6) *Segregate critical networks* connected to the Internet from internal and less sensitive networks. This can be achieved through firewalls, virtual local area networks (VLANs), and intrusion prevention. Cathay Pacific had installed an admin console which was publicly accessible via the Internet. A risk assessment (such as a DPIA) would have detected this (Enforcement Notice 24(5)).

(7) Implement *a data retention policy* and enforce retention periods. Mechanisms to comply with this requirement include a document classification scheme, automated deletion of files (available in MS Office 365), and an email archiving policy. Cathay Pacific's data retention policy was not granular enough and data was kept for too long (Enforcement Notice 24(12)).

(8) *Preserve digital evidence* following a data breach in order to support internal and external investigations. Cathay Pacific decommissioned its servers after its own investigation and was unable to provide evidence as requested by the ICO (Enforcement Notice 24(9)).

(ICO, 2020; Dittle, 2020)

3.5.3   Case Three: WM Morrison Supermarkets plc

WM Morrison Supermarkets plc was fined under UK law (DPA 1998). This case study analyses employer vicarious liability for acts done by its employees which cause violations of

GDPR, such as misuse of personal data and breaches of confidence.

Case review

Morrisons employed an internal auditor (Andrew Skelton), who in November 2013 was asked as in the previous year to transmit payroll data for Morrisons' entire workforce to its external auditors. He kept a personal copy of the data of nearly 100,000 employees, including date of birth, salaries per person, bank details and National Insurance numbers, which he uploaded in early 2014 to a publicly accessible file-sharing website. Skelton also sent the file anonymously to three newspapers, pretending to be a member of the public who found the file online. One newspaper contacted Morrisons, which promptly responded by removing the data from the Internet and alerting the police. Skelton was arrested and prosecuted and was sentenced to eight years in prison in July 2015. Morrisons has spent more than £2.26 million in dealing with the aftermath of this breach. The employee's motive was a grudge he held against management following a disciplinary procedure (The Supreme Court, 2020a). 5,518 Morrisons employees brought before the High Court a *group litigation* against the company for compensation for violation of their statutory rights under DPA 1998, Section 4(4), which covers misuse of private information and breach of confidence. The High Court found Morrisons liable under the common law principle of vicarious liability, by which employers may be liable for the acts of their employees (The Supreme Court, paragraph 11 and 12).

On appeal, the Court of Appeal affirmed the High Court, but gave Morrisons leave to appeal to the Supreme Court (PrivSec, 2019), which reversed both lower courts and found that, although the DPA 1998 did not exclude vicarious liability, the facts of the case did not support the vicarious doctrine in the first place, as Skelton had acted beyond the scope of his employment; indeed, directly contrary to his employer's authorisation (The Supreme Court, paragraph 13). Therefore, on 1 April 2020 the Supreme Court found Morrisons not liable (*WM Morrisons Supermarkets Plc (Appellant) v Various Claimants* (Respondent), [2020] UKSC 12).

Conclusions and recommendations

The employee committed the breach out of working hours, using his own computer and from his home. The ICO had investigated the case and dismissed the complaint against Morrisons, finding it not responsible for any failure of security controls (Blair *et al.*, 2020). The judgement sets a precedent whereby employers cannot be held vicariously liable for rogue employees' acts who are deliberately endeavouring to damage the employer.

Another important conclusion from this case is that the law courts may well come to different decisions than the ICO. The ICO decided that a rogue employee committing a breach did not implicate the employer and closed the case against the latter. It should be noted that, even though, ultimately, the Supreme Court effectively affirmed the ICO's finding, the ICO is in no position to define vicarious liability and has no power to declare the law or set legal precedent. The ICO's judgements are administrative proceedings merely. Plaintiffs are free to disagree with ICO decisions and try their luck in the courts. This case highlights that two separate systems of sanctions exist in parallel which may reach contrary decisions: – the administrative acts of regulators, and court judgments under common law and/or statutory law. (Administrative acts, moreover, are subject to judicial review but not *vice versa*.)

Employers are still on the hook for vicarious liability generally, and must take a pro-active approach to manage it. Organisations should adapt three lines of defence (Chartered Institute of Internal Auditors, 2019). Note that a similar approach could be adopted to manage threats of data breaches by insiders, covering onboarding, access controls, and monitoring of staff.

(1) *First line of defence*: strengthen the vetting process ("hold management accountable"). When recruiting staff for positions that provide them access to large volumes of personal data or sensitive personal data (special data categories), organisations must do enhanced background checks.

(2) *Second line of defence*: restrict access to external devices or open networks ("enforce compliance"). In the Morrisons case, besides the disciplinary actions against Skelton, there was no history of breaking the law or overriding internal procedures. Data loss prevention (DLP) software can often detect and block the transfer of confidential and sensitive data. It has the capability to track the movement both over the network and on mobile and removable storage devices, such as the USB data key that the rogue employee used in the Morrisons' case (Rogowski, 2013). Although the author's review of this case found no information about how the personal data was uploaded from the data key to the Internet, using DLP software might have prevented it. Even if the DLP had failed, the fact that the controller had a DLP strategy would have strengthened its case in court.

(3) *Third line of defence*: implement a monitoring processes ("conduct frequent audits"). Insider Threat Detection software can detect unusual data movements, alert as to anomalies, and monitor user behaviour. Even if a breach occurs, timely detection and speedy remediation can reduce the impact on data subjects. Internal audits should also perform manual checks, which may include spot checks of personal data on shared drives and unsecured folders on desktops.

3.5.4   Case Four: *British Airways*

British Airways (BA), the flagship airline of the United Kingdom, with its main hub at Heathrow Airport, suffered a sophisticated, malicious cyberattack on their website in August 2018. The hackers data breach affected approximately 429,600 customers and staff, which compromised personal data including payment card numbers and CVV numbers of 244,000 BA customers. BA notified the ICO on 6 September 2018 and in July 2019 the ICO fined BA £183.39 million (which equalled 1.5% of BA's turnover). This was the highest-ever fine handed down by the ICO and the highest issued by any EEA DPIA for a GDPR infringement. Subsequently, in the final decision on 16 October 2020 this fine was reduced to £20 million (€20,460,000). This case study analyses the ICO's reasoning for imposing such a fine and its subsequent reduction of it. This case is documented in detail in the 114-pages Penalty Notice. (ICO, 16 October 2020a; ICO, 16 October 2020b).

<u>Case review</u>

Between 21 August 2018 and 5 September 2018, malicious hackers gained access to BA's internal system via a Citrix Access Gateway, by using the login details of an employee of Swissport, a third-party provider of cargo services to BA. On 5 September the breach was discovered after another third party reported to BA that data was being re-directed to a third party website. Within 90 minutes, BA contained the vulnerability, and 20 minutes later all re-directs were blocked.

The hackers managed to find a pathway from the Citrix environment to access a file that contained the username and password of a privileged-domain administrator account which gave relatively free access to the wider BA infrastructure. They found files containing code for the BA website, which they manipulated to redirect customer payment card data to a different website owned by the hackers. During this cyberattack, the hackers were able

- to access log files in plain text containing payment card details from approximately 108,000 customers, including CVV numbers, for BA redemption transactions going back 95 days.
- to automatically redirect to their website for 16 days a copy of every transaction in which a customer used a credit / debit card on the BA website.

The reason why it took over two years to get from BA's breach notification to the final decision is because this was the ICO's first GDPR case, four sets of representations were made under complex circumstances, and the facts of COVID-19 caused the case to be newly considered, leading to a significant reduction in the administrative fine.

   In calculating the length of the breach, the ICO deemed that it lasted from 25 May

2018, the day GDPR was enforced, until 5 September 2018 (103 days). ICO determined £30 million as an appropriate fine, but agreed to a 20% (£6 million) reduction due to mitigating factors, and a further reduction of £4 million due to the impact of COVID.

Conclusions and recommendations

The ICO found that BA breached its obligations under GDPR Article 5(f) and Article 32. In its initial ICO Notice of Intent (4 July 2019) BA had also been found to have breached Article 25 (privacy by design and default); however, following BA's representations by BA's legal counsel, this was removed from the final decision. BA maintains that the security measures at the time of the cyberattack were "appropriate" and therefore complied with the requirements of the GDPR.

The ICO's investigation showed the following failures in BA's technical and organisational measures to lower cyberattack risk or mitigate its impact, which the author has translated to practical recommendations for organisations that suffer similar cyberattacks.

(1)   Limit *access to applications, data and tools*. These should be restricted to the need of users to fulfil their roles.

(2)   Conduct *regular and rigorous testing for vulnerabilities*. Simulations of cyberattacks or firewall penetration tests on business systems could have revealed some vulnerabilities in BA's security settings.

(3)   Implement *robust access controls to protect employee and third party accounts*. This can be achieved, for example, through multi-factor authentication, which is a common practice for online banking nowadays.

(4)   Implement *detection and notification systems*. BA was unaware of the attack for far too long, not detecting the attack when it commenced on 21 August 2018 but having to be alerted by a third party more than two weeks later. Only then did BA act promptly and notify the ICO. To the ICO it was not clear whether or when BA would have detected the attack themselves, which, had it been delayed further, could have caused much more significant harm to data subjects.

(ICO, 16 October 2020a)

Further key lessons from this case, which are likely to be applied to other DPSAs, are that:

▪   an ICO investigation can require significant resources and be lengthy.

▪   aggravating and mitigating factors, such as illicit financial gain, intent, response time to mitigate and notify the ICO, and whether special categories of data were affected, can help reduce fines. In this case the combination of names, addresses and payment card details with CVV numbers was treated as "sensitive financial data".

▪   when determining what measures against data breaches are "appropriate" by GDPR, the ICO will consult multiple information security bodies and guidance. The final decision in this case contained around 100 pages of detail.

- engaging the ICO by being co-operative and providing detailed information in the organisation's representations to the ICO is key, and can reduce fines significantly. The ICO can issue fixed penalties ranging from £400 to £4,350 for non-cooperation.

- downplaying the impact of the breach is not appreciated by the ICO.

- the ICO seems to take into account no financial losses by BA and its customers arising from data breaches.

- most of the measures that the ICO recommended would not have entailed excessive costs or technical difficulties, some of them being available through the Microsoft Operating System that BA was already using.

(McLean, 3 Nov 2020; Dittel and Dunphy-Moriel, Nov 2020)

3.5.5   Case Five: *Marriott International*

Marriott International suffered a malicious cyberattack, which when it was discovered, was notified to the ICO. The personal data of 339 million guests globally were exposed to hackers a result of a breach of Marriott's IT systems, of which 7 million were UK residents and 30 million residents of 31 other EEA countries. The attack took place over a period from 25 May 2018 to 17 September 2018. This case is similar to the BA case above and is documented in a 91-pages Penalty Notice. (ICO, 20 Oct 2020a; ICO, 30 Oct 2020b)

Case review

The vulnerability began when Starwood Hotels and Resorts Worldwide Inc ("Starwood") IT systems were compromised in summer 2014. A hacker installed a web shell on a Starwood device and gained remote access to the system via an application used to request changes to content on the Starwood website. The hacker used this access to install Remote Access Trojans to enable remote administrator control of the Starwood system. Marriott acquired Starwood in 2016, but the customer data breach was not discovered until 2018. On 7 September 2018, the hacker performed a "count" on a file, triggering an alert to Accenture which was managing the Starwood IT system for Marriott. Accenture notified the alert to Marriott's IT team on 8 September 2018, who investigated the breach before notifying the ICO, finally, on 22 November 2018.

The ICO ruled that Marriott had done insufficient due diligence when acquiring Starwood and could have done more to secure its IT systems. The final decision two years later, on 30 November 2020, reduced the fine from £99,200,396 to £18.4 million (€20.45 million) because of Marriott's full cooperation with DPSA plus the economic impact of the

COVID-19 pandemic. (ICO, 30 Oct 2020a)

Conclusions and recommendations

The ICO found that Marriott breached its obligations under GDPR Article 5(1)(f) and Article 32. Marriott did not admit liability, arguing that the measures implemented were in line with industry standards. However, the ICO found in its Penalty Notice that Marriott failed to process personal data in a way that assured appropriate security of personal data, which included "protection against unauthorised or unlawful processing and against accidental loss, destruction or damage, using appropriate technical and organisational measures, as required by Article 5(1)(f) and Article 32 GDPR". (ICO, 30 Oct 2020a:p3)

Some key lessons from this case useful to all organisations finding themselves in a similar situation are as follows.

(1)   Implement *appropriate technical measures that can detect cyberattacks*. The ICO acknowledged that the attack began before Marriott acquired Starwood and that the level of due diligence that would have been required to have detected the breach pre-acquisition was unrealistic. However, post-acquisition, Marriott should have done more to implement appropriate security measures to detect such a cyberattack.

(2)   Be aware that *controllers cannot make processors accountable for data breaches*. Marriott's responsibility for data breaches was not reduced by appointing Accenture to manage the legacy Starwood system.

(3)   Be aware that *the administrative fine calculation does not depend on the actual harm caused to data subjects*. The ICO has no obligation to investigate what, if any, financial harm has actually been suffered by data subjects.

(4)   Be aware that the administrative *fine calculation does not depend on the number of complaints received*. Marriott's dedicated call centre only received 57,000 calls out of potentially millions of affected customers. The ICO concluded that this was not persuasive and did not provide any real indication of the extent of distress or harm suffered.

(McLean, 3 Nov 2020a)

Chapter 4

HOW CAN ORGANISATIONS PROTECT THEMSELVES FROM DATA BREACH SANCTIONS?

While the previous chapter exhibited the regulator's stance on how to comply with Article 5(1)(f) and Article 32, this chapter gives an *organisational perspective* as expressed by respondents to a data breach survey and by the author's participant observation of views expressed by professionals at industry events on privacy. Conclusions drawn from this field research, and insights gleaned from the case studies, are summarised in the final sections of this chapter.

4.1 Insights obtained by survey respondents who are professionals in the data protection field

I received 32 responses out of 60 Sanctions and Data Breach Survey questionnaires sent (Toolkit 2). 17 of the responses were from the UK, while the rest were scattered across the Continent. Questions 6 and 7 garnered some interesting insights into how data breaches might be addressed from an organisational perspective. Tables analysing the results of the survey are presented in Toolkit 1.

This section 4.1 summarizes the key themes developed from the survey and provides a synoptic view of the 32 respondents. The themes are categorised in three domains: governance and policy, processes and procedures, and technology.

4.1.1 Governance and policy

Several respondents mentioned the "accountability principle" (Article 5(2)) as a cornerstone of the data protection compliance framework. If required, a DPO should be appointed with reporting lines to relevant committees and groups agreed. Survey respondents highlighted that documentation and record-keeping (accountability procedure) is essential to demonstrate that adequate controls to safeguard personal data have been implemented.

Concerning data breaches, survey respondents mentioned the importance of conducting a risk assessment with clear assessment criteria about what constitutes a data breach and how these might arise. Respondents gave examples of organisational practices that conduce to breaches: fraudulent procedures, unlawful basis for processing, implied or assumed consent, unlawful cross-border transfer, and lack of transparency.

Organisational measures should include segregation of duties, which could mean anything from a separation between business functions that need access to personal data and IT functions that grant access ("access control") to an indented internal or external audit function that conducts regular information security and privacy reviews, then reports its findings to senior management or in larger organisations to the Audit Committee. Survey respondents from larger organisations stressed that formal ISO certifications like ISO/IEC 27001 "Information Security Standard" and ISO/IEC 27701 "Privacy Information Management", or privacy certifications as per Article 42 can strengthen an organisation's defensible compliance position.

Organisations can have world-class reporting systems and technology, but if employees are not using these as required, data breaches will occur. This is why training and awareness campaigns were mentioned by many respondents as an essential ingredient.

Other recommendations included monitoring of the DPSAs' and EDPB's recommendations, and even obtaining cyber-liability insurance. Lawyers recommend amending existing insurance policies, then ascertaining with insurance companies if these are sufficient expressly to cover regulatory fines. Some EEA countries prohibit insuring against regulatory fines as a matter of public policy (Jones Day Lawyers, 2018). Although it seems that some insurance companies cover damages, defence costs, even fines arising from data breaches, the question remains if these promises are actually enforceable in court, especially as the policy will likely contain onerous stipulations like continual audits and external certifications (Crendon Insurance Brokers website). The UK's ICO told Out-Law.com that there was "nothing in the GDPR which either permits or prohibits" insurance coverage; nevertheless, "the insurability of fines and penalties has remained a grey area for some time" (Pinsent Masons, 2019). Ultimately, it should be the responsibility of Legal Counsel to develop a plan for GDPR-related litigation and fines.

4.1.2   Processes and procedures

Most respondents stressed that things called operational privacy processes and procedures should be "givens", like maintaining a ROPA, conducting DPIAs, regularly updating policies and processes relevant to data protection, and implementing a PbD&D programme that allows early engagement with the business to safeguard the processing of personal data. Respondents noted the importance of always bearing in mind the data subject, who can be employees, customers, and third parties.

Some respondents had reported breaches or had been investigated by DPSAs. They stressed the importance of having a data protection-centric incident plan (not just an IT recovery plan) which concentrates on meeting the 72-hour deadline for reporting to the DPSA and mitigating the damage of the breach in order to demonstrate to the regulator that the organisation is equipped to pro-actively manage incidents. This data breach procedure should be rehearsed regularly and inculcated into affected stakeholders.

When reporting a breach to the DPSA, data controllers must be open and transparent, and provide prompt, regular, accurate and clearly articulated updates as the investigation unfolds. Each incident should be treated as a high risk, as it could lead to reputational damage and potentially even sanctions; therefore, management attention, the highest prioritisation, and appropriate resource allocation is needed. To demonstrate the commitment of organisations to deal with breaches efficiently, some respondents recommended involving external legal and technical specialists. Most importantly, remediation or mitigation steps should be taken after a breach to avoid repetition of similar incidents in future.

4.1.3   Technology

All respondents agreed that a robust IT infrastructure is essential. Encryption of laptops and external storage devices should be a given; for example, stolen laptops would not result in a reportable data breach if any personal data is encrypted. There is a never-ending risk of cyberattacks using new methods; therefore, organisations must maintain a regularly tested incident response plan and team.

4.1.4   DPSA response to data breaches

Respondents' expectations of DPSAs investigating breaches was that they should reward transparency of data controllers by showing leniency with fines, especially where controllers can demonstrate commitment to compliance. Respondents also believe the current functionality of online reporting in many countries, using one form to self-report multiple incidents should be re-evaluated, especially as investigations often bring more facts to light after the 72-hour reporting deadline, and no mechanism is in place to report updates electronically to the case worker. They also recommended that self-assessment should be built into the online reporting process, which would reduce the number of reports the DPSAs receive, while self-selecting reports and initiating investigations into the breaches that matter most. Respondents opined that more frequent audits by DPSAs could reduce data breach risk, due to the educational effect: sharpening the awareness of controllers that they are exposed to regulatory audit even before data is breached.

To help especially SMEs, respondents suggested more transparency in how the "effective, proportionate and dissuasive" purposes of sanctions is achieved (Article 83(1)), as by noting common themes in repeated complaints about certain industries and reacting with sector-specific guidance. DPSAs should share "war stories" from everyday data incidents and successful mitigation controls, to help proactively promote security and privacy. Guidance and best practices should be shared across EEA DPSAs, contributing to a more consistent overall approach to what constitutes an incident and serious breach. This needs to involve regulatory collaboration, as respondents believe a disconnect exists between protecting consumer rights *versus* individual rights, for example.

4.2   Insights obtained from authors' participant observation of privacy events

The author participated in numerous privacy events with legal and technical professionals to better understand what practical measures organisations could take to comply with GDPR. In brief, when asked by the author how to optimise compliance to minimise the risk of administrative fines for data breaches, practitioners provided a wide range of answers. Like the survey results, these were categorised in the three domains: governance and policy, processes and procedures, and technology.

4.2.1   Governance and policy

Judit Fontova, Privacy Associate at law firm Kemp Little, says the organisational set-up matters. To assure its independence, she recommends the DPO should be separated from Legal Counsel and not attend legal proceedings (Fontova, 2020). To help organisations enforce this independence, Kemp Little offers to outsource DPO functions (Bapat, 2020). Bridget Treacy, from law firm Hunton Andrews Kurth, adds that accountability and demonstrating compliance are crucial (Treacy, 2020). Law firms like Sidley Austin recommend external legal advice and warn of the risk of class actions and consumer claims following administrative fines, which may be consequential (Sidley Austin, 2020). Evidencing this concern, the British Airways Data Breach Action (website at https://www.bagroupaction.com/) is representing claimants in a "class action" against BA.

Paul Jordan, Managing Director (Europe) of the International Association of Privacy Professionals, said the EDPB recommends that organisations not only demonstrate accountability but also set up training plans to address the "human errors" that account for most breaches (Jordan, 2020).

4.2.2 Processes and procedures

As part of breach-preparedness, Treacy recommends designing and implementing an incident response plan, which should include procedures to manage breach notifications; and developing a regulatory response strategy (Treacy, 2020). Paul Breitbarth, from software firm Nymity, puts stock in assessing one's risk profile, and reporting to board level (Breitbarth, 2020). Doug Boykin, of OneTrust software firm, averred that ROPAs and DPIAs remain the primary "accountability" tools to demonstrate compliance in the event of regulatory inquiries. He stressed that this should include third party processes and systems, and due diligence when onboarding new vendors (Boykin, 2020).

4.2.3 Technology

Privacy software vendors like OneTrust strongly recommend a risk assessment to determine the nature, likelihood, and severity of breaches (OneTrust, 2020b), and ongoing security and privacy programmes like installing updated technology and a privacy platform (OneTrust, 2020a). The importance of technology is highlighted by Microsoft: their Enterprise Office 365 comes with a Compliance Portal, a Data Loss Prevention programme to create customised policies, and Information Protection functionality to enable encryption and marking of sensitive documents (Microsoft, 2020).

4.3 Implement appropriate technical and organisational security measures

The *regulator's perspective* provides lessons learned from recent data breaches (Section 3.5, conclusions), and identifies good practices and expected measures for complying with the GDPR's information security and breach containment obligations. The first case study presented organisational measures to reduce the likelihood and impact of physical breaches; the second case study made recommendation on technical controls to deal with the risk of cyberattacks; and the third case study provided an approach to reducing organisational liability for acts of rogue employees. All three cases pose risks that business faces daily, and therefore need to be addressed.

The *organisational perspective* provides insights obtained from respondents to the survey (Section 4.1). The author's participant observation (Section 4.2) also revealed practical and appropriate measures to comply with the law. Comparing the regulator's expectations with organisational measures taken shows a clear synergy between what is demanded and what organisations are aiming for (avoiding liability).

After comparing the *legal perspective* with the two perspectives above, the conclusion is that both the data controller and data processor are obligated to implement technical and organisational measures which must be demonstrably embodied in policies, processes and procedures that safeguard personal data. This includes but is not limited to:

- privacy policy, and privacy and fair processing notices (transparency of processing in Recital 39, 58 and 78);

- retention schedules and retention policies to keep personal data no longer than necessary ("storage limitation" in Article 5(1)(e));

- information security policies, pseudonymisation/anonymisation and encryption, data backups and business recovery, data breach policy, identity access management to safeguard personal data ("integrity and confidentiality" in Article 5(1)(f) and security of processing in Article 32(1)); and

- risk assessments (DPIAs) before implementing new processes that bear high risks to natural persons, and consideration of privacy in each phase of processing (PbD&D in Article 25) (Kemp Little, 2020; Know your compliance, 2020; Smedinghoff, 2015:15-17).

The question is how best to design and implement the long list of recommendations made in this Blue Paper. As explained in Section 2.4, organisations often use existing [IT] governance frameworks and standards. In the absence of any specific framework addressing the data breach requirements in the GDPR, this Blue Paper offers the DBAF in its final chapter to provide organisations a structured approach to designing and implementing appropriate measures to meet these obligations and thereby limit liability.

4.4 Demonstrate compliance: Independent assurance and approved certifications

The GDPR makes controllers and processors responsible for demonstrating compliance, and recommends adopting an approved code of conduct (Article 40, Recital 98 and 99) or using an approved certification mechanism (Article 42, Recital 77 and 81).

Codes of conduct setting standards for the industry are expected to be developed by industry associations in collaboration with DPSAs (Article 40(5)). This allows organisations to influence these standards through membership of industry associations. Ian Walden has noted that, in recent years, standards which were once set by monopolistic state-owned enterprises are increasingly being set by any number of participants, with industry associations playing an expanding role that challenges the dominance of inter-governmental organisations (Walden, 2018:792).

Certifications may be obtained through a DPSA-accredited body (Article 43(1)(b)), which implies independent assurances from an experienced and vetted provider (Rodrigues et al., 2016). While currently the UK's ICO like most DPSAs does not operate an approved GDPR certification scheme (ICO – certification scheme), it is expected that GDPR certifications like ISO, PCI-DSS and other accreditations will be obtainable in the near future through external GDPR certification bodies. The DBAF presented in Chapter Five can help organisations focus on such certification.

4.5   Synthesis for practitioners

The validated insights from multiple sources and from all the foregoing contributors have helped the author develop a *new model* for organisations endeavouring to comply with the GDPR. Firstly, the regulators clarified what their priorities are by the pattern of their sanctioning of organisations. Secondly, the professional survey respondents reported their main challenges in complying to the GDPR. Thirdly, the author's participant observation cemented his conceptualisation of what exactly companies most urgently need to do. These are the creators of the DBAF set forth in the next and final Chapter.

PART III

A new compliance model: The Data Breach Accountability Framework

When it comes to privacy and accountability,
people always demand the former for themselves
and the latter for everyone else.

– David Brin
(Scientist and author)

Chapter 5

CONCLUSIONS:
HOW ORGANISATIONS CAN IMPROVE
THEIR COMPLIANCE MATURITY

This chapter gives a summary assessment of the data breach sanctions of the national DPSAs and of the oversight provided at European level, all of which are responsible for making the GDPR work. Next, the *Data Breach Accountability Framework* is presented, a model recommendation for practitioners framed through synthesising the triple-perspective of the lawyers, regulators, and organisations deployed above for triangulation purposes. This new model will help organisations build a legally defensible compliance position to better manage the risk of being sanctioned for GDPR infringements in general, and data breaches in particular.

5.1 GDPR enforcement by national DPSAs and oversight at European level

National DPSAs

The data from multiple sources revealed a significant discrepancy between enforcement cases, the total value of fines, and the risks to data subjects caused by breaches. A few of the national DPSA fines are statistical outliers; *viz.*, British Airways, Marriott International and Google, but still, some national DPSAs are stricter than others. This raises the issue of organisations with establishments in multiple Member States exploiting the one-stop-shop mechanism by appointing a Lead Supervisory Authority (Articles 60-62) in the least-strict jurisdiction. This implies a *race to the bottom* (Olney, 2013; The Economist, 2013), should certain Member States weaken their enforcement standards in order to attract or retain fees-paying, job-creating businesses in their jurisdiction. The data collected in this research project supports this possibility. Ireland may be already hosting the HQs of many American tech giants partly because of a lighter *tax* regime than other Member States, and its regulatory regime seems equally light. Ireland was recently criticized by Ulrich Kelber, Germany's Federal Commissioner for Data Protection, for its "unbearable" delays. Kelber called on the EU to replace the one-stop-shop mechanism with an all-EU data protection authority (Neuerer, 2020). This proposal is supported by privacy groups and by other regulatory authorities, including the Hamburg Data Protection Commissioner, Prof. Johannes Caspar (Scott, 2020), all of whom have openly talked about the failure of national DPSAs to collaborate toward harmonisation. The German and Irish regulators have not been able to find a *modus vivendi*, hence the German DPSA calls for a pan-European solution.

The EDPB

At European level, the EDPB is tasked with contributing "to the consistent application" of the GDPR (Article 63, Recital 139). However, the research done for this Blue Paper shows that a range of inconsistencies persists in the teeth of the consistency mechanism (Article 63), which is built into the GDPR, and the guidance issued. A disconnect between the intent of the legislator and the design of the regulation encumbers its actual implementation by national DPSAs and by data controllers aiming to comply.

The DPSAs' own lack of transparency – their untimely announcement of decisions, anonymisation of offenders, sometimes insufficient case detail – suggests setting up a *Sanctions Register* similar in format to that offered in the *Sanctions Directory* appended hereto. This policy recommendation would contribute to regulatory transparency and consistency across EEA nations and by national DPSAs. But it also would be useful to data controllers, to educate them on the implications of infringing the GDPR and what actions to avoid.

5.2 Building a legally defensible compliance position: *The Data Breach Accountability Framework*

This Blue Paper takes an organisational standpoint serving the goal of preventing, detecting, reducing, and mitigating (non-reportable) security incidents and (reportable) data breaches, in order to avoid or minimise the cost of administrative fines. The conclusions brought together in the DBAF are based on analysis of the law, a review of scholarly literature, my own empirical research which includes my participant observation at legal and compliance events, the feedback from a survey of privacy professionals, and three case studies, plus a substantive review of all the sanctions in the two years of GDPR's existence.

The DBAF is structured around the 9 domains typically used by organisations when establishing privacy compliance frameworks. It is intended as an aid to developing an accountability framework for data protection security and thereby building a defensible compliance position. This is achieved by linking the principles and provisions of the GDPR with standard technical and organisational controls. It should be noted that data breaches usually lead to wider investigations into root causes, which is why organisations need to consider measures that help to prevent and mitigate the effects of non-compliance with Articles 32 and 5(1)(f). The DBAF, which is presented in the Executive Summary, brings these strands of argument to bear on practical GDPR-compliance implementation by data controllers and -processors. It is based on the following domains:

1. *Privacy Governance – DPO function and reporting*:

   A robust privacy governance structure enables the DPO to report data breaches to senior management and clearly defines data controller and processor responsibilities.

2. *Policies and Processes for PbD&D*:

   Policies, processes, procedures and guidance safeguard the processing of personal data and cover the entire data lifespan from collection to destruction. The risks of processing have been assessed in Data Protection Impact Assessments; processing activity has been recorded in a Register of Processing Activities; and a Data Retention Policy and Retention Schedule defines for how long personal data should be retained.

3. *Individual Rights*:

   When responding to Data Access Requests, the requested information ought to be provided without compromising its integrity and confidentiality.

4. *Security for Privacy and Data Breach identification & notification*:

   The design and implementation of appropriate technical and organisational controls safeguards personal data from accidental or unlawful destruction, loss, alteration and disclosure. This may be achieved by encryption, pseudonymisation or anonymisation, data management, and incident and breach management response plans. Codes of conduct and formal certifications by third parties attest that the actions taken meet legal requirements.

5. *Procurement and Third-Party Management*:

   Complete data protection due diligence when on-boarding new suppliers to assure that they will safeguard personal data as required. Robust legal instruments, such as supplier contracts and data processing agreements must include clear instructions concerning data transfers to third countries, as well as responsibilities and reporting timelines for data breaches, while laying out the liabilities.

6. *Approach to Consent and Direct Marketing*:

   Appropriate security when using personal data for marketing purposes prevents its unintended disclosure. Examples include protection of spreadsheets and centralised records-keeping where possible.

7. *Training, awareness, and communications*:

   To provide regular privacy and information security training means to keep an attendance record and to follow-up absentees. It also means to offer specialised training for functions that process volumes of personal data or special data categories.

8. *International Data Transfer:*

Implementing technical and organisational measures safeguards data transfers. This includes data processing agreements, inter-group agreements, model clauses, and other mechanisms that prioritise data subjects' rights in case of breach.

9. *Monitoring compliance:*

Conducting regular internal and external information security and privacy audits, maintaining an incident and breach register, and including incidents and breaches in a metrics / Key Performance Indicators scheme are *de rigueur*. Reporting this to senior management enables them to make informed decisions to provide the required budget and other resources to mitigate information security risks.

Finally, the question remains whether organisations that develop defensible compliance positions based on the DBAF still face the risk of sanctions under Article 5(1)(f) and Article 32. There are a number of reasons why organisations may still fail to comply with the GDPR. The GDPR is clear that "the state of the art, the costs [...], the nature, scope and purpose of processing as well the risks of varying likelihood and severity [...] posed by the processing" (Article 25(1)) must all be taken into account. Organisations may come to different risk assessments than the DPSA after investigation, or their budgets may not allow them to fully implement all technical and organisational measures. Furthermore, the organisation may lack sufficient interdisciplinary teams to advise on all of the legal, technical, and organisational requirements.

This Blue Paper herein has shown some discrepancy between national DPSAs in how they enforce the GDPR. The Spanish regulator, for example, has sanctioned an organisation for accidentally emailing personal data to the wrong customer, while other regulators like Ireland's drag out investigations of multinational behemoths. Threats by insiders and cyberattacks are bound to continue, and if their own technology is not "state of the art", organisations may suffer compliance breaches. However, those that design and implement the controls identified in the DBAF will be in a much stronger position to prevent breaches and to demonstrate to the regulator that they have followed the law in case a breach happens anyway.

BIBLIOGRAPHY

BIBLIOGRAPHY

Abogados, Ramón y Cajal (09 October 2019) "Fines imposed since the entry in force of the GDPR". Available at https://www.ramonycajalabogados.com/en/fines-imposed-entry-force-gdpr (accessed April 2020).

AEPD (Agencia Española de Protección de Datos) (4 May 2020) "Memoria AEPD 2019", Annual Report. Available at https://www.aepd.es/sites/default/files/2020-05/memoria-AEPD-2019.pdf (accessed July 2020).

Agarwal, Ritu; Tanniru, Mohan (September 1990) "Systems development life-cycle for expert systems", in Knowledge-Based Systems, Volume 3, Issue 3, 170-180. Available at https://www.researchgate.net/publication/222740326_Systems_development_life-cycle_for_expert_systems (accessed July 2020).

AICPA/CICA (2007) "Generally Accepted Privacy Principles (GAPP)", Privacy Framework developed by the American Institute of Certified Public Accountants and Canadian Institute of Chartered Accountants.

Article 29 WP (6 February 2018) "Guidelines on Personal data breach notification under Regulation 2016/679", wp250rev.01, as last revised and adopted on 6 February 2018.

Article 29 WP (4 October 2017a) "Guidelines on Data Protection Impact Assessment (DPIA) and determining whether processing is 'likely to result in a high risk' for the purpose of Regulation 2016/679", wp248rev.01, as last revised and adopted on 4 October 2017.

Article 29 WP (5 April 2017b) "Guidelines on Data Protection Officers ('DPOs')", wp243rev0.1, as last revised and adopted on 5 April 2017.

Article 29 WP (25 March 2014) "Opinion 03/2014 on Personal Data Breach Notification", wp213.

Baker McKenzie – "GDPR Enforcement Tracker". Available at https://globaltmt.bakermckenzie.com/gdpr-enforcement-tracker/ (accessed October 2020).

Bapat, Anita (25 September 2019) "DPO Service Offering" at Kemp Little "DPO Round Table: DPO Challenges" hosted by Anita Bapat (Head of Data Protection & Privacy) and Marta Dunphy-Moriel (Data Protection & Privacy Partner), London.

Becker, Howard S. (December 1958), "Problems of inference and proof in participant observation", American Sociological Review, Volume 23, Issue 6, 652-660.

Bird & Bird – "GDPR Tracker". Available at https://www.twobirds.com/en/in-focus/general-data-protection-regulation/gdpr-tracker/ and at https://www.twobirds.com/en/in-focus/general-data-protection-regulation/gdpr-tracker/penalties (accessed May 2020).

Blair, Keily; Lloyd, James and Brady, Lewis (2 April 2020) "Class actions for security breaches in the UK are here to stay", Cyber, Privacy & Data Innovation, Orrick Blog – Trust Anchor. Available at https://blogs.orrick.com/trustanchor/2020/04/02/class-actions-for-security-breaches-are-here-to-stay (accessed June 2020).

Boykin, Doug (9 June 2020) "Two years on: What changed and what you need to know", Data Protection World Forum and One Trust webinar.

Breitbarth, Paul (4 February 2020) "Reporting to the board on privacy compliance", Director at TrustArc, EU Policy and Strategy, presentation at PrivSec 2020: Privacy, Security, Governance, Queen Elizabeth II Centre, London.

Burgess, Robert (1984) In the Field: An Introduction to Field Research (Allen & Unwin: London).

Burton, Cédric (2020) Article 33: "Notification of a personal data breach to the supervisory authority", in Kuner, Christopher; Bygrave, Lee; Docksey, Christopher and Drechsler, Laura (2020) The EU General Data Protection Regulation (GDPR): A Commentary (Oxford: Oxford University Press), 640-653.

California Senate Bill No. 1368 (25 September 2002) "Personal information: privacy", Chapter 915, 1001-02 Leg, Reg Sess., codified at CAL. Civil Code §§ 1798.29 and 1798.80-84 (2009). Available at https://leginfo.legislature.ca.gov/faces/billTextClient.xhtml?bill_id=200120020SB1386 (accessed June 2020).

Cavoukian, Ann (September 2013) "Privacy by Design", Second Edition, published by the Information and Privacy Commissioner of Ontario (Ontario, Canada).

Cavoukian, Ann (June 2012) "Privacy by Design: From rhetoric to reality", Information and Privacy Commissioner of Ontario / Canada. Available at https://www.ipc.on.ca/wp-content/uploads/Resources/PbDBook-From-Rhetoric-to-Reality.pdf (accessed April 2020).

Cavoukian, Ann (August 2011a) "Privacy by Design in Law, Policy and Practice: A White Paper for regulators, decision-makers and policy-makers", Information and Privacy Commissioner of Ontario. Available at https://collections.ola.org/mon/25008/312239.pdf (accessed April 2020).

Cavoukian, Ann (January 2011b) "Privacy by Design: The 7 Foundational Principles – Implementation and mapping of fair information practices", Information and Privacy

Commissioner of Ontario. Available at
https://iapp.org/media/pdf/resource_center/pbd_implement_7found_principles.pd
f (accessed April 2020).

Cazalilla, Alberto López and Martín, Ruth Benito (6 July 2020) "Spain: Data Protection Laws
and Regulations 2020", ICLG website – Compare & Research the Law. Available at
https://iclg.com/practice-areas/data-protection-laws-and-regulations/spain (accessed
July 2020).

Cellerini, Elena Jelmini and Lang, Christian (July 2018) "Cyber Liability: Data Breach in
Europe", Volume 85, Issue 3, Defense Counsel Journal.

Chartered Institute of Internal Auditors (7 October 2019) "Governance of risk: Thee lines of
defence". Available at https://www.iia.org.uk/resources/audit-
committees/governance-of-risk-three-lines-of-defence/ (accessed June 2020).

Cohen, Louis; Manion, Lawrence and Morrison, Keith (1986) "Research Methods in
Education", Fifth Edition (London: Routledge).

Companies House website – Doorstep Dispensaree LTD. Available at
https://beta.companieshouse.gov.uk/company/09634666 (accessed June 2020).

Claridge, Agatha (17 June 2020) "Klick DPO webinar: Implementing new technology",
Kemp Little webinar.

Cordery Legal Compliance, London (2 January 2020) "First UK GDPR fine". Available at
https://www.corderycompliance.com/first-uk-gdpr-fine/ (accessed June 2020).

Crendon Insurance Brokers Ltd. – Data Protection. Available at
https://www.crendoninsurance.co.uk/insurance-products-services/data-protection-
insurance/ (accessed June 2018).

Data Protection Commissioner v Facebook Ireland Limited and Maximillian Schrems (Case
C-311/18).

Delbridge, Rick; Kirkpatrick, Ian (1994) "Theory and Practice of Participant Observation",
in Wass, V. J.; Wells, Peter E. (eds.) Principles and Practice in Business and
Management Research (Aldershot, UK: Dartmouth Publishing), 35-61.

Dittel, Alexander and Dunphy-Moriel, Marta (November 2020) "Enforcement guidance:
ICO says it will not shoot to kill", Privacy Laws & Business newsletter, issue 112, pp.
5-7.

Dittle, Alex (17 June 2020) "Klick DPO webinar: Cybersecurity – A more defined playfield"
webinar.

DLA Piper (2020) "DLA Piper GDPR data breach survey: January 2020", a report by DLA
Piper's Cybersecurity and Data Protection team.

DLA website – "Newsroom". Available at
https://www.dlapiper.com/en/us/news/2020/01/114-million-in-fines-have-been-
imposed-by-european-authorities-under-gdpr/ (accessed January 2020).

EDPB (13 November 2019) "Guidelines 4/2019 on Article 25 Data Protection by Design and by Default", Ref. 4/2019.

EDPB website – "GDPR: Guidelines, Recommendations, Best Practices". Available at https://edpb.europa.eu/our-work-tools/general-guidance/gdpr-guidelines-recommendations-best-practices_en (accessed May 2020).

EDPB website – "National News". Available at https://edpb.europa.eu/news/national-news/2018, https://edpb.europa.eu/news/national-news/2019 and at https://edpb.europa.eu/news/national-news/2020 (accessed May 2020).

ENISA, European Union Agency for Cybersecurity (December 2014) "Privacy and Data Protection by Design – from policy to engineering" [previously European Network and Information Security Agency].

EU Agency for Cybersecurity – NIS Directive website. Available at https://www.enisa.europa.eu/topics/nis-directive (accessed April 2020).

European Commission (24 June 2020) COM(2020)264final Communication on "Data protection as a pillar of citizens' empowerment and the EU's approach to the digital transition – two years of application of the General Data Protection Regulation", SWD(2020)115final, Brussels.

European Commission Directive (EU) 2016/1148 (6 July 2016) concerning "measures for a high common level of security of network and information systems across the Union" (NIS Directive).

European Commission Directive 2002/58/EC (12 July 2002) concerning "the processing of personal data and the protection of privacy in the electronic communications sector" (Directive on privacy and electronic communications).

European Commission Regulation (EU) 2016/679 (27 April 2016) "on the protection of natural persons with regard to the processing of personal data and on the free movement of such data, and repealing Directive 95/46/EC" (General Data Protection Regulation).

Fontova, Judit Garrido (10 August 2020), Privacy and Data Protection Lawyer at Kemp Little LLP, interview.

Fontova, Judit Garrido (27 February 2020) "Legal Team vs DPO", presentation at Kemp Little "DPO Round Table" hosted by Marta Dunphy-Moriel (Privacy Partner) and Alex Dittle (Senior Associate), London.

Fox, Linda (9 March 2020) "Cathay Pacific fined £500,000 after 'brute force' data breach", PhocusWire. Available at https://www.phocuswire.com/Cathay-Pacific-data-breach-fine (accessed May 2020).

FRA (European Union Agency for Fundamental Rights) (2020) "Your Rights Matter: Data Protection and Privacy", Survey of Fundamental Rights annual report.

FRA, COE and EDPB (2018) "Handbook on European Data Protection law", edited by the

European Union Agency for Fundamental Rights, European Court of Human Right, the Council of Europe and the European Data Protection Supervisor (Luxembourg: Publications of the European Union).

GDPR Enforcement Tracker. Available at https://www.enforcementtracker.com/. Tracked by CMS, law and tax firms – website at https://cms.law/en/int/insight/gdpr (accessed May 2020).

Hart, Lucy (21 February 2020) "UK Data Privacy Compliance: Lessons from the ICO's first fine", Baker McKenzie. Available at website https://www.bakermckenzie.com/en/insight/publications/2019/02/uk-data-privacy-compliance-lessons (accessed May 2020).

IAPP and EY (2019) "IAPP-EY Annual Privacy Report 2019". Available at https://iapp.org/resources/article/iapp-ey-annual-governance-report-2019/ (accessed April 2019).

ICO website – Accountability and governance. Available at https://ico.org.uk/for-organisations/guide-to-data-protection/guide-to-the-general-data-protection-regulation-gdpr/accountability-and-governance/ (accessed June 2020).

ICO website – PbD&D [Data Protection by design and default]. Available at https://ico.org.uk/for-organisations/guide-to-data-protection/guide-to-the-general-data-protection-regulation-gdpr/accountability-and-governance/data-protection-by-design-and-default/ (accessed in March 2019).

ICO website –certification scheme. Available at https://ico.org.uk/for-organisations/guide-to-data-protection/guide-to-the-general-data-protection-regulation-gdpr/certification-schemes-detailed-guidance/register-of-certification-scheme-criteria/ (accessed July 2020).

ICO website – The principles. Available at https://ico.org.uk/for-organisations/guide-to-data-protection/guide-to-the-general-data-protection-regulation-gdpr/principles/ (accessed May 2020).

ICO website – What is NIS. Available at https://ico.org.uk/for-organisations/the-guide-to-nis/what-is-nis/ (accessed May 2020).

ICO website – "Doorstep Dispensaree Ltd (20 December 2019)". Available at https://ico.org.uk/action-weve-taken/enforcement/doorstep-dispensaree-ltd-en/ (accessed April 2020).

ICO (30 October 2020a) "Penalty Notice: Marriott International Inc", fine under Section 155, Data Protection Act 2018, case ref: COM0804337. Available at https://ico.org.uk/media/action-weve-taken/mpns/2618524/marriott-international-inc-mpn-20201030.pdf and https://ico.org.uk/action-weve-taken/enforcement/marriott-international-inc/ (accessed December 2020).

ICO (30 October 2020b) "ICO fines Marriott International Inc £18.4million for failing to keep customers' personal data secure". Available at https://ico.org.uk/about-the-ico/news-and-events/news-and-blogs/2020/10/ico-fines-marriott-international-inc-184million-for-failing-to-keep-customers-personal-data-secure/ (accessed December 2020).

ICO (30 October 2020) "Penalty Notice: Marriott International Inc", fine under Section 155, Data Protection Act 2018, case ref: COM0804337.

ICO (16 October 2020a) "Penalty Notice: British Airways plc", fine under Section 155, Data Protection Act 2018, case ref: COM0783542. Available at https://ico.org.uk/media/action-weve-taken/mpns/2618421/ba-penalty-20201016.pdf and https://ico.org.uk/action-weve-taken/enforcement/british-airways/ (accessed in January 2021).

ICO (16 October 2020b) – "ICO fines British Airways £20m for data breach affecting more than 400,000 customers"; available at https://ico.org.uk/about-the-ico/news-and-events/news-and-blogs/2020/10/ico-fines-british-airways-20m-for-data-breach-affecting-more-than-400-000-customers/ (accessed in January 2021).

ICO (10 February 2020) "Monetary Penalty Notice to Cathay Pacific Airways Limited". Available at https://ico.org.uk/media/action-weve-taken/mpns/2617314/cathay-pacific-mpn-20200210.pdf (accessed June 2020).

ICO (20 December 2019c) "London pharmacy fined after 'careless' storage of patient data", press release. Available at https://ico.org.uk/about-the-ico/news-and-events/news-and-blogs/2019/12/london-pharmacy-fined-after-careless-storage-of-patient-data/ (accessed May 2020).

ICO (17 December 2019a) "Enforcement Notice against Doorstep Dispensaree Ltd. (under Data Protection Act 2018 (Part6, Section 149)", enforcement notice. Available at https://ico.org.uk/media/action-weve-taken/enforcement-notices/2616741/doorstop-en-20191217.pdf (accessed May 2019).

ICO (17 December 2019b) "Enforcement Powers of the Information Commissioner: Doorstep Dispensaree Ltd", penalty notice.

ICOa (25 June 2019d) "Notice of Intent for Doorstep Dispensaree Ltd".

ICOb (25 June 2019e) "Preliminary Enforcement Notice for Doorstep Dispensaree Ltd". Available at https://www.legislation.gov.uk/ukpga/2006/46/contents (accessed May 2020).

International Association of Privacy Professionals (IAPP). Available at https://iapp.org/news (accessed May 2020).

ISACA website – COBIT. Available at https://www.isaca.org/resources/cobit (accessed April 2020).

ISACA (2019), "Control Objectives for Information and Related Technologies 5.0" (short COBIT framework), (Rolling Meadows, IL: Information Systems Audit and Control

Association).

ISO - PD ISO/ IEC TS 19608 "Guidance for developing security and privacy functional requirements based on ISO/IEC 15408".

ISO/IEC 27701:2019 "Security techniques — Extension to ISO/IEC 27001 and ISO/IEC 27002 for privacy information management — Requirements and guidelines".

ISO/IEC 20000-1:2018 "Information technology — Service management".

ISO/IEC TS 19608:2018 "Guidance for developing security and privacy functional requirements".

ISO/ICE 27001:2017 "Information technology – Security techniques – Information security management systems – Requirements".

ISO/IEC 38500:2008 for "Corporate governance of information technology", published jointly by the International Organization for Standardization (ISO) and the International Electrotechnical Commission (IEC).

ISO (International Organization for Standardization) website. Available at https://www.iso.org/home.html (accessed May 2020).

ITGP Privacy Team (2017) "EU General Data Protection Regulation (GDPR): An implementation and compliance guide", Second Edition, IT Governance Publishing.

IT Governance Institute of the Information Systems Audit and Control Association (ISACA). Available at https://www.itgovernance.co.uk/it_governance (accessed May 2020).

Jones Day Lawyers (November 2018) "GDPR's Potential Fines and Other Exposures Raise Cyber Insurance Coverage Questions" commentaries. Available at https://www.jonesday.com/en/insights/2018/11/gdprs-potential-fines-and-other-exposures-raise-cy (accessed June 2019).

Jordan, Paul (4 June 2020) "BCR in 2020 and Beyond", Ankura and McDermott Will & Emery presentations and panel discussion, webinar with panel.

Jorgensen, Danny L (1989) "The methodology of participant observation" (Thousand Oaks, CA: Sage Publications).

Kapoor, Keshav; Renaud, Karen and Archibald, Jacqueline (5 April 2018) "Preparing for GDPR: Helping EU SMEs to manage Data Breaches", in Symposium on digital behaviour interventions for cyber-security, 2018 Convention of the Society for the Study of Artificial Intelligence and Simulation of Behaviour, 13-20.

Kemp Little (May 2020) "Demystify Data Protection".

Know your compliance (17 June 2020) "GDPR Appropriate Technical and Organisational Measures". Available at https://www.knowyourcompliance.com/gdpr-technical-organisational-measures/ (accessed June 2020).

Leese, Matthias (2015) "Privacy and Security – On the evolution of a European Conflict", in Gutwirth, Serge et al. Reforming European Data Protection Law. Law, Governance and Technology Series, Volume 20, 271-287.

Lexis Nexis website – "Sanctions and enforcement under the GDPR". Available at https://www.lexisnexis.co.uk/legal/guidance/sanctions-and-enforcement-under-the-gdpr (accessed May 2020).

López-Lapuente, Leticia and Bosch, Reyes Bermejo (October 2019) "Spain: The Privacy, Data Protection and Cybersecurity Law Review", Sixth Edition. Available at https://thelawreviews.co.uk/edition/the-privacy-data-protection-and-cybersecurity-law-review-edition-6/1210070/spain (accessed August 2020).

Lynskey, Orla (2019) "The Foundations of EU Data Protection Law" (Oxford: Oxford University Press).

McLean, Jo (3 November 2020) "Lessons learnt from recent ICO fines", webinar, Addleshaw Goddard, London.

Microsoft (25 March 2020) "Office 365 and Data Protection: Data Loss Prevention and Compliance Manager" webinar with Pooja Patel (Microsoft) and Leon Butler (MS Security & Compliance Specialist).

NCSL (National Conference of State Legislatures) – Security Breach Notification Laws. Available at https://www.ncsl.org/research/telecommunications-and-information-technology/security-breach-notification-laws.aspx (accessed June 2020).

Neuerer, Dietmar (28 January 2020) "Datenschützer Kelber bringt neue EU-Behörde gegen Facebook & Co. ins Spiel", Handelsblatt. Available at https://www.handelsblatt.com/politik/deutschland/datenschutz-verstoesse-datenschuetzer-kelber-bringt-neue-eu-behoerde-gegen-facebook-und-co-ins-spiel/25479302.html?ticket=ST-3835548-TEIpagICcva7QsSsMzGa-ap6 (accessed June 2019).

Notos Xperts "Fines list - Infringements in numbers". Available at https://notos-xperts.de/en/tools/fines-list/ (accessed May 2020).

O'Donoghue, T. and Punch, K. (2003) Qualitative Educational Research in Action: Doing and Reflecting (Routledge: London).

Olney, William (August 2013) "A race to the bottom? Employment protection and foreign direct investment", Journal of International Economics, Volume 91, Issue 2, 191-203.

OneTrust (28 May 2020a) "GDPR 2 Years On: What changed and what need to know" webinar with panel.

OneTrust (22 April 2020b) "Privacy Connect: Privacy in the community" webex seminar.

One Trust Data Guidance website – Regulatory Research Software. Available at https://www.dataguidance.com/; and "Cross-Border Charts". Available at https://platform.dataguidance.com/premium?type=portal_advisory (accessed April 2020).

Pinsent Masons (25 January 2019) "Insurers seek clarity on coverage for GDPR fines".

Available at https://www.pinsentmasons.com/out-law/news/insurers-seek-clarity-on-coverage-for-gdpr-fines (accessed June 2019).

PrivSec (2 May 2019) "The implications of the Morrisons data leak for organisations in the GDPR era". Available at https://gdpr.report/news/2019/05/02/how-the-morrisons-data-leak-has-impacted-victims-in-the-gdpr-era/ (accessed June 2020).

PwC "UK Privacy and Security Enforcement Tracker: Exploring the actions taken by the UK privacy regulator for infringements of privacy laws during 2018". Available at https://www.pwc.co.uk/issues/data-protection/insights/privacy-and-security-enforcement-tracker.html (accessed May 2020).

Rodrigues, Rowena; Barnard-Wills, David; De Hert, Paul; Papakonstantinou, Vagelis (June 2016) "The future of privacy certification in Europe: an exploration of options under article 42 of the GDPR", International Review of Law, Computers & Technology, Volume 30, Issue 3, 248-270.

Rogowski, Walter (August 2013) "The right approach to data loss prevention", Computer Fraud & Security, Issue 8, 5-7.

Ronco, Emmanuel; Farmer, Natalie and Hassard, Chloe (30 January 2020) "UK ICO finally issues GDPR fine", in Cleary Gottlieb's Cleary Cybersecurity and Privacy Watch. Available at https://www.clearycyberwatch.com/2020/01/uk-ico-finally-issues-gdpr-fine/ (accessed May 2020).

Romanian National Supervisory Authority for Personal Data Processing – "enforcement actions". Available at https://www.dataprotection.ro/?page=masuri_corective_iunie_sept_2019&lang=en (accessed May 2020).

Romano, Andrea (9 August 2020), privacy lawyer at the European Union Intellectual Property Office (EUIPO) in Alicante/ Spain, interview.

Rubinstein, Ira; Good, Nathaniel (August 2012) "Privacy by Design: A counterfactual analysis of Google and Facebook Privacy Incidents", New York University Public Law and Legal Theory Working Papers, New York University School of Law.

Schrems, Max and Guilloit, Vickie (30 July 2020) "An in-depth interview with Max Schrems", Last Thursday in Privacy webcast, PrivSec and Data Protection World Forum.

Scott, Mark (25 May 2020) "Hamburg privacy boss calls for overhaul of EU privacy rules: Johannes Caspar said the failure of EU agencies to cooperate had undermined GDPR", Politico. Available at https://www.politico.eu/article/johnannes-caspar-gdpr-data-protection-privacy/ (accessed June 2020).

Sheldon, Laura (May 2016) "Implementing Information Security Architecture and Governance: A Big Framework for Small Businesses", Syracuse University School of Information Studies. Available at https://www.researchgate.net/publication/308522451_Implementing_Information_S ecurity_Architecture_and_Governance_A_Big_Framework_for_Small_Business (accessed June 2020).

Sidley Austin (27 February 2020) "Privacy Network event" hosted by William Long (Partner, European Privacy Practice), London.

Smedinghoff, Thomas J. (10 October 2015) "An Overview of Data Security Legal Requirements for All Business Sectors". Available at https://papers.ssrn.com/sol3/papers.cfm?abstract_id=2671323 (accessed June 2020).

The Economist (27 November 2013) "Racing to the bottom: Countries skimp enforcement of decent working conditions to get FDI", The Economist. Available at https://www.economist.com/free-exchange/2013/11/27/racing-to-the-bottom (accessed June 2020).

The GDPR Network website – Checklist of GDPR fines. Available at https://www.thegdpr.net/2019/09/03/open-checklist-of-gdpr-fines-to-this-level/ (accessed May 2020).

The Supreme Court of the United Kingdom (1 April 2020a) "Press Summary: WM Morrison Supermarkets plc (Appellant) v Various Claimants (Respondents)", [2020] UKSC 12.

The Supreme Court of the United Kingdom (1 April 2020b) WM Morrisons Supermarkets Plc (Appellant) v Various Claimants (Respondent), [2020] UKSC 12. Available at https://www.supremecourt.uk/cases/uksc-2018-0213.html (accessed June 2020).

Treacy, Bridget (4 February 2020) "Privacy compliance challenges in 2020", UK Privacy and Cybersecurity practice at Hunton Andrews Kurth, presentation at PrivSec 2020: Privacy, Security, Governance, Queen Elizabeth II Centre, London.

Williams, Paul (19 September 2006) "A helping hand with governance", Computer Weekly.

Winn, Jane K. (8 June 2009a) "Are 'better' security breach notification laws possible", University of Washington School of Law, Berkeley Technology Law Journal, Volume 24. Available at https://papers.ssrn.com/sol3/papers.cfm?abstract_id=1416222 (accessed May 2020).

Winn, Jane K. and Wright, Benjamin (2009b) "The Law of Electronic Commerce", Aspen Law & Business, Fourth Edition.

Walden, Ian (2018) "Telecommunications Law and Regulation", Fifth Edition (Oxford: Oxford University Press).

TOOLKITS
Resources for Professionals

TABLE OF TOOLKITS
– Resources for Professionals –

Toolkit 1

TABLES ANALYSING THE RESULTS OF THE DATA BREACH SURVEY

These are the results of the survey of privacy professionals about sanctions and data breaches under the GDPR. Out of the 32 survey responses received back, 17 came from the UK and 15 from the EEA. The answers were assigned numerical values as per this Coding values table.

Coding values table

classification	Numerical value
very unlikely / strongly disagree	1
unlikely / disagree	2
neither / unsure	3
likely / agree	4
very likely / strongly agree	5

Figure 8: Infringements for which regulators are most likely to impose sanctions (Q2)

Ref.	Answer	Average value
A.	Purpose limitation (Art. 5(1)(b))	3.8
B.	Data minimisation (Art. 5(1)(c))	3.6
C.	Legitimate interest (Art. 6)	3.6
D.	Consent (Art. 7)	4.3
E.	Fulfilment of individual rights, incl. access, erasure, processing restriction (Arts. 12-21)	4.1
F.	Insufficient cooperation with DPSA (Art. 31)	3.2
G.	Data breaches (Art. 32)	4.7
H.	Breach notification to DPSA (Art. 33)	4.0

Ref.	Answer	Average value
I.	Breach notification to data subjects (Art. 34)	3.8
J.	Failure to appoint a DPO (Art. 37)	3.4
K.	Other	N/A

Figure 9: Views on GDPR enforcement (Q3)

Ref.	Answer	Average value
A.	Since the GDPR regulation came into force in May 2018, has the Regulator become stricter in penalising data breaches?	3.6
B.	Since the GDPR regulation came into force in May 2018, are the penalties for breach appropriate as helping to enforce compliance?	3.4

Figure 10: Consistency of sanctioning of breaches across the EEA (Q4)

Ref.	Question	Answer	
A.	Do you believe that the sanctioning of breaches is consistently enforced across the EU?	Inconsistent	21
		Consistent	2
		Don't know	9
B.	If you believe it is inconsistently enforced, which countries' DPSAs are the strictest? (multiple answers possible)	Germany	13
		France	11
		UK	3
		Spain	3
		Belgium	2
		Austria	1
		Bulgaria	1
		Hungary	1
		Italy	1
		Netherlands	1

Figure 11: Most likely triggers of enforcement actions following a data breach (Q5)

Ref.	Answer	Average value
A.	Self-reporting to DPSA	3.0
B.	Investigation by DPSA	4.1
C.	Enforcement by courts and the CJEU	4.3
D.	Customer complaint to DPSA	3.9
E.	Employee complaint to DPSA	3.9
F.	Consumer legal action against company	3.8
G.	Other	N/A

Toolkit 2

SURVEY QUESTIONNAIRE

Survey on GDPR sanctions for data breaches

The aim of this survey is to gain valuable insight into your views on the Data Protection Supervisory Authority's (DPSA) Regulatory enforcement for data breaches and your company's responses. I want to assure you that your survey answers will be **kept strictly in confidence** and the **results anonymised**. Many thanks for your participation.

1.   Please provide a few circumstantial details about yourself.

What is your current job title/ role?	
In which industry sector is your organisation?	

2.   Based on your experience, for which infringements is the regulator most likely to impose sanctions?

GDPR article/ principle	very unlikely	unlikely	neither	likely	very likely
A. Purpose limitation (Art. 5(1)(b))	☐	☐	☐	☐	☐
B. Data minimisation (Art. 5(1)(c))	☐	☐	☐	☐	☐
C. Legitimate interest (Art. 6)	☐	☐	☐	☐	☐
D. Consent (Art. 7)	☐	☐	☐	☐	☐
E. Fulfilment of individual rights, incl. access, erasure, processing restriction (Arts. 12-21)	☐	☐	☐	☐	☐
F. Insufficient cooperation with DPSA (Art. 31)	☐	☐	☐	☐	☐

G.	Data breaches (Art. 32)	☐	☐	☐	☐	☐
H.	Breach notification to DPSA (Art. 33)	☐	☐	☐	☐	☐
I.	Breach notification to data subjects (Art. 34)	☐	☐	☐	☐	☐
J.	Failure to appoint a DPO (Art. 37)	☐	☐	☐	☐	☐
K.	Other					

3. Since the GDPR regulation came into force in May 2018, …

	strongly disagree	lisagree	unsure	agree	strongly agree
has the Regulator become stricter in penalising data breaches?	☐	☐	☐	☐	☐
are the penalties for breach appropriate as helping to enforce compliance?	☐	☐	☐	☐	☐

4. Do you believe that the sanctioning of breaches is consistently enforced across the EU?

	Yes	No	Don't know
Please answer here.	☐	☐	☐
If you believe it is inconsistently enforced, why do you think this is so?			
If you believe it is inconsistently enforced, which countries' DPSAs are the strictest? (*multiple answers possible*)			

5. **Please rank what you believe is most likely to trigger enforcement actions following a data breach?**

		strongly disagree	disagree	unsure	agree	strongly agree
A.	Self-reporting to DPSA	☐	☐	☐	☐	☐
B.	Investigation by DPSA	☐	☐	☐	☐	☐
C.	Enforcement by courts and the CJEU	☐	☐	☐	☐	☐
D.	Customer complaints to DPSA	☐	☐	☐	☐	☐
E.	Employee complaints to DPSA	☐	☐	☐	☐	☐
F.	Consumer legal actions against company	☐	☐	☐	☐	☐
G.	Other					

6. **What advice would you give others about how to avoid enforcement actions for data breaches (assuming your organisation is doing its best to comply)?**

7. **"If I were the head of my national DPSA, enforcing compliance with Data Protection laws and specifically data breaches, I would do the following:"**

Please return the completed survey by email as per the instructions.
Many thanks.

Toolkit 3

TABLES AND DIAGRAMS ANALYSING THE RESULTS OF THE GDPR ENFORCEMENT AND SANCTIONS REVIEW

Figure 12: Total cases of sanctions by provision establishing liability

GDPR Article	Legal basis classification and provision details	Total cases
Article 5	General data protection processing principles.	287 cases of Art 5 [Art. 5(1)(a)-(f) and Art. 5(2))]
• Art. 5(1)(a)	Violation of principle "Lawfulness, fairness and transparency".	74
• Art. 5(1)(b)	Violation of principle "Purpose limitation".	30
• Art. 5(1)(c)	Violation of principle "Data minimisation".	73
• Art. 5(1)(d)	Violation of principle "Data accuracy".	13
• Art. 5(1)(e)	Violation of principle "Storage limitation".	14
• Art. 5(1)(f)	Violation of principle "Integrity and confidentiality".	70
• Art. 5(1)	Violation of "General data processing principles".	274 (sum from above)
• Art. 5(2)	Violation of accountability principle.	18
Article 6	Insufficient legal basis for data processing (Lawfulness of processing). *Lawfulness: adequate legal basis for processing personal data, including obligations to obtain specific consent or to perform a contract.*	202

GDPR Article	Legal basis classification and provision details	Total cases
Article 7	Insufficient legal basis (consent). *Insufficient or not freely given consent to process personal data, including using clear and plain language when obtaining consent.*	26
Article 9	Insufficient legal basis (processing of special data categories). *Insufficient legal basis for special data processing.*	23
Article 12	Insufficient fulfilment of data subject rights (general). *Individual rights: use of clear and plain language when informing data subjects about their individual rights.*	36
Article 13	Insufficient fulfilment of data subject rights (information to be provided [to data subject]). *Individual rights: inadequate privacy notification at the time of data collection.*	53
Article 14	Insufficient legal basis (data collection). *Individual rights: inform data subject when obtaining data from a 3rd party.*	20
Article 15	Insufficient fulfilment of data subject rights (right of access). *Individual rights: data subject's access rights (DSAR) and the right to be informed of the appropriate safeguards taken by third parties.*	40
Article 17	Insufficient fulfilment of data subject rights (right of erasure). *Individual rights: erasure without undue delay.*	20
Article 18	Insufficient fulfilment of data subject rights (right to restrict processing). *Individual rights: risk of inaccuracy, unlawful, no purpose or objection by the data subject.*	3
Article 21	Insufficient fulfilment of data subject rights (right to object). *Individual rights: right to object to the processing, including profiling, unless*	23

GDPR Article	Legal basis classification and provision details	Total cases
	legitimate grounds can be demonstrated.	
Article 25	Inappropriate technical and organisational measures for data protection and privacy by design and by default. *Implement appropriate technical and organisational measures (e.g. pseudonymisation) to safeguard privacy.*	19
Article 28	Insufficient data processing agreement. *Third party processor responsibilities and sub-processor authorisation.*	9
Article 31	Insufficient cooperation with DPSA. *Cooperation of the controller and processor with the Data Protection Supervisory Authority.*	12
Article 32	Insufficient technical and organisational measures to secure data processing. *Security for data protection: implementing and testing the effectiveness of appropriate technical and organisational security measures.*	113
Article 33	Insufficient breach notification to DPSA. *Security for data protection: notification to the DPSA no later than 72 hours after becoming aware of the breach.*	20
Article 34	Insufficient breach notification to data subject. *Security for data protection: communication in clear and plain language to data subject (if the breach is likely to result in high risks).*	6
Article 35	Insufficient legal basis (DPIA). *DPIA for automated processing and special data categories.*	5
Article 36	Insufficient legal basis (prior DPSA consultation). *Prior consultation with DPSA to processing where the DPIA assessment under Article 35 indicates that the processing would result in*	1

GDPR Article	Legal basis classification and provision details	Total cases
	high risk in absence of mitigating measures by the controller.	
Article 37	Failure to designate a DPO. *Failure or neglect to designate organisational DPO.*	5
Article 58	Insufficient cooperation with DPSA (investigative powers). *Investigative, corrective, and advisory powers of the DPSA need cooperation.*	23

Figure 13: Fines by country: total value, total cases, and average value of fines

Country	Total value of fines	Total cases	Average value of fines
Austria	€ 18,075,100	10	€ 1,807,595
Belgium	€ 343,000	17	€ 20,176
Bulgaria	€ 5,826,417	23	€ 253,322
Croatia	unknown[12]	1	unknown
Republic of Cyprus	€ 173,600	18	€ 9,756
Czech Republic	€ 19,070	11	€ 1,734
Denmark	€ 417,426	8	€ 52,178
Estonia	€ 56	1	€ 56
Finland	€ 207,500	5	€ 41,500
France	€ 54,400,000	8	€ 6,800,000
Germany	€ 62,860,291	33	€ 1,904,857
Greece	€ 769,000	12	€ 64,083
Hungary	€ 658,792	34	€ 19,376

---

[12]   IAPP and other sources have reported the administrative fine in this case to be €20m, mistaking the legal limit in any case for the fine in this case, which is unreported. Croatian law requires reporting the final amount is above a threshold of 100,000 Croatian Kuna (or approximately €13,150). This implies that the amount in this case was less than the threshold.

Country	Total value of fines	Total cases	Average value of fines
Iceland (EEA country)	€ 29,588	2	€ 14,794
Ireland	€ 180,000	3	€ 60,000
Isle of Man (not EEA)	€ 13,500	1	€ 13,500
Italy	€ 69,651,897	35	€ 1,990,054
Latvia	€ 157,000	2	€ 78,500
Liechtenstein (EEA country)	none	none	none
Lithuania	€ 76,500	2	€ 38,250
Luxembourg	none	none	none
Malta	€ 5,000	1	€ 5,000
Netherlands	€ 3,950,000	7	€ 564,286
Norway (EEA country)	€ 1,351,500	13	€ 103,962
Poland	€ 1,585,988	13	€ 121,999
Portugal	€ 824,330	5	€ 164,800
Romania	€ 581,780	46	€ 12,647
Slovakia	€ 90,000 (unknown fines for 4 cases)	6	€ 15,000
Slovenia	none	none	none
Spain	€ 4,965,728	175	€ 28,375
Sweden	€ 7,479,430	7	€ 1,068,490
United Kingdom	€ 44,221,000	4	€ 11,055,250
Total	€ 298,916,013	503	€ 594,266

Figure 14: Fines by sectors – total value, total cases, and average value of fines

Economic sector	Total value of fines	Total cases	Art. 32 cases	Average value of fines
Automotive industry, cars, and motorbikes	€40,600	9	3	€4,511

Economic sector	Total value of fines	Total cases	Art. 32 cases	Average value of fines
Commercial engineering	€25,717	5	1	€5,143
Education, private and public	€440,225	17	6	€25,896
Financial services (insurance, investment, retail banking)	€24,175,125 (one to be confirmed)	43	14	€562,226
Healthcare (hospitals, clinics)	€4,075,910	35	17	€116,455
Hospitality & leisure (restaurants, hotels, sports clubs)	€21,360,510	29	4	€736,569
Information technology & services (tech companies, web-based services)	€58,062,888	13	3	€4,466,376
Media & entertainment	€1,679,182	19	6	€88,378
Private persons, incl. professional contractors	€108,462	30	2	€3,615
Public services & administration (government, political parties, councils, industry associations)	€25,970,425	65	16	€399,545
Real estate & property (agents, property developers, construction firms)	€15,942,550	18	4	€885,697
Retail (grocery, clothing, consumer goods)	€54,876,448	18	5	€1,959,873
Service companies (professional services, accountancy, law firms, IT services, [tele]marketers, content providers)	€613,897	24	3	€25,579
Transport & logistics (airlines, shipping companies)	€22,637,172	20	6	€1,131,858
Utilities, energy suppliers (gas, electricity)	€12,190,173	22	4	€554,123

Economic sector	Total value of fines	Total cases	Art. 32 cases	Average value of fines
Utilities, telecoms operators	€54,953,870	88	19	€624,476
Utilities, water suppliers	€76,000	2	none	€38,000
Unknown	€1,403,468	31	2	€45,273

Toolkit 4

GDPR SANCTIONS DIRECTORY

The following table is a compendium of GDPR enforcement actions across all EEA countries from 25 May 2018, the date on which the GDPR came into force, until 24 May 2020, two full years later. During these 24 months 332 GDPR enforcement actions entailing fines were undertaken by EEA Member State Data Protection Supervisory Authorities (DPSAs). Please note that these decisions are published on national DPSA websites, which means that they are usually only available in that nation's official language. (The EU has 24 official languages, of which three – English, French and German – are the European Commission's "procedural languages".) In Germany each of the 16 Federal States has its own DPSA. The German national DPSA (The Federal Commissioner for Data Protection and Freedom of Information, BfDI) and most of the Federal States' DPSAs publish their decisions only in annual reports; they do not maintain accessible enforcement logs. Note also that some EEA national DPSAs have a policy of not naming the organisations fined in decisions. One explanation for this is that the DPSAs of some nations may not enforce penalties, but only the national courts. Private persons are also not named, although in some cases their professional capacity is mentioned. At European level the European Data Protection Board (EDPB) maintains a log only of what it deems key decisions.

Comprehensive research was exacted to compile the compendium below, involving the perusal of websites of multiple law firms, legal and regulatory research firms, and industry associations. The information had to be validated against the original decision notices on the national DPSA websites or the EDPB website. Despite thorough investigation, the lack of transparency and accessibility, and the inconsistency in announcement and publication by the sundry national DPSAs, meant that research may not have found every case of sanction. All significant fines, however, should be listed in the Directory. A total of 332 GRDP sanctions have been identified and analysed, and this is deemed statistically sufficient for drawing significant conclusions from the data.

The GDPR Sanctions Directory lists the following information:
1. **Date of decision**: The decisions are listed in chronological order, starting with the latest up to 24 May 2020 and going back to 25 May 2018.
2. **Nation**: This is the nation imposing the penalty. Please note that Toolkit 6 lists all

national DPSAs in the EEA.

3.   **Fined entity**:   This is the sanctioned respondent's name along with its industry/public service sector.   Figure 15 exhibits the economic sectors recognised, and breaks down each sector by total cases and the most-breached GDPR articles.

Figure 15: Economic sectors (GDPR Sanctions Directory)

Note: Administrative fines may sanction infringements of several GDPR Articles at once

Economic sector	Total cases	Top two breaches of each Article
Automotive industry, cars, and motorbikes	9	4 cases Art. 5(1) 3 case Art. 32
Commercial engineering	5	2 cases Art. 5(1) 2 case Art. 25(1)
Education, private and public	17	11 cases Art 5(1) 6 cases Art. 9 5 cases Art. 32
Financial services (insurance, investment, retail banking)	43	22 cases Art. 5 14 cases Art. 32
Healthcare (hospitals, clinics)	35	17 cases Art. 32 15 cases Art. 5
Hospitality & leisure (restaurants, hotels, sports clubs)	29	20 cases Art. 5(1) 10 cases Art.6
Information technology & services (tech companies, web-based services)	13	6 cases Art. 6 5 cases Art. 5
Media & entertainment	19	10 cases Art. 5 9 cases Art. 6
Private persons, incl. professional contractors	30	20 cases Art. 5 14 cases Art. 6
Public services & administration (government, political parties, councils, industry associations)	65	39 cases Art. 5 35 cases Art. 6 16 cases Art. 32
Real estate & property (agents, property developers, construction firms)	18	16 cases Art. 5 8 cases Art. 6
Retail (grocery, clothing, consumer goods)	18	14 cases Art. 5 10 cases Art. 6

Economic sector	Total cases	Top two breaches of each Article
Service company (professional services, accountancy, law firms, IT services, [tele]marketers, content providers)	24	12 cases Art. 5 10 cases Art. 6
Transport & logistics (airlines, shipping companies)	20	12 cases Art. 5 7 cases Art. 6 6 cases Art. 32
Utilities, energy suppliers (gas, electricity)	22	10 cases Art. 6 8 cases Art. 5.
Utilities, telecoms operators	88	51 cases Art. 5 32 cases Art. 6 19 cases Art. 32
Utilities, water suppliers	2	1 case Art. 5 1 case Art. 35
Unknown	31	12 cases Art. 6 11 cases Art. 5 8 cases Art. 15

4. **Fines in €**: Please note that not all EEA nations use the euro, and exchange rates applicable on the day of the penalty were availed of. The non-euro nations and their currencies are: Bulgaria (Lev), Croatia (Kuna), Czech Republic (Koruna), Denmark (Krona), Hungary (Forint), Poland (Złoty), Romania (Leu), Sweden (Krona) and the UK (Pound Sterling). Although the UK left the EU on 31 January 2020, the transition period where the UK has a special status will last until 31 December 2020, and UK enforcement actions under the DPA 2018 will be treated equally to the implementation of GDPR in EEA nations. The nations of the European Economic Area are not members of the EU, but yet which do belong to the EFTA or GDPR regime, include (with their currencies) Iceland (Króna), Liechtenstein (Swiss Franc) and Norway (Krone). Switzerland is a member of EFTA, but not a member of the EU or EEA; therefore, the GDPR does not apply.

Figures that break down the number of fines by nation and the value of fines is provided in the core text (see Figure 2 "Total cases by country" and Figure 3 "Total value of fines by country"). More information is available in the Toolkits Section, namely Figure 13 "Fines by country").

5. **Legal basis for fines**: This is usually the "primary violation" (main legal basis) on which the decision is based, together with the principles for processing personal data

as per Article 5(1)(a)-(f) and Article 5(2) GDPR (if mentioned in the decision). Please note that some decisions are based on violations of multiple Articles; however, in most cases the compliance breach stems from one primary violation, which may or may not have led to secondary violations.

The table below summarises the GDPR Articles and the legal basis classification of the penalties.

Figure 16: Classification of legal basis for fines (GDPR Sanctions Directory)

Legal Basis for fine	Legal basis classification
Art. 1	General data protection processing principles violations.
Art. 5(1)(a)	Violation of principle "Lawfulness, fairness and transparency".
Art. 5(1)(b)	Violation of principle "Purpose limitation".
Art. 5(1)(c)	Violation of principle "Data minimisation".
Art. 5(1)(d)	Violation of principle "Data accuracy".
Art. 5(1)(e)	Violation of principle "Storage limitation".
Art. 5(1)(f)	Violation of principle "Integrity and confidentiality".
Art. 5(1) and (2) various	Violation of "General data processing principles".
Art. 6	Insufficient legal basis for data processing ("Lawfulness of processing")
Art. 7	Insufficient legal basis (consent).
Art. 9	Insufficient legal basis (processing of special data categories).
Art. 10	Unlawful processing of personal data relating to criminal convictions and offences.
Art. 12	Insufficient fulfilment of data subject rights (general).
Art. 13	Insufficient fulfilment of data subject rights (information to be provided [to data subjects]).
Art. 14	Insufficient legal basis (data collection).
Art. 15	Insufficient fulfilment of data subject rights (right of access).
Art. 17	Insufficient fulfilment of data subject rights (right of erasure).

Legal Basis for fine	Legal basis classification
Art. 18	Insufficient fulfilment of data subject rights (right to restrict processing).
Art. 21	Insufficient fulfilment of data subject rights (right to object).
Art. 24	Inappropriate technical and organisational measures by controller.
Art. 25	Inappropriate technical and organisational measures for data protection by design and by default.
Art. 28	Insufficient data processing agreement.
Art. 31	Insufficient cooperation with DPSA.
Art. 32	Insufficient technical and organisational measures to secure data processing.
Art. 33	Insufficient breach notification to DPSA.
Art. 34	Insufficient breach notification to data subject.
Art. 35	Insufficient legal basis (DPIA).
Art. 36	Insufficient legal basis (prior DPSA consultation).
Art. 37	Failure to designate a DPO.
Art. 58	Insufficient cooperation with DPSA (investigative powers).

6. **Article(s) quoted**: the main Articles mentioned in the decision of the DPSA, indicating for which violations of the GDPR the respondent is being penalised.

7. **Summary of the DPSA decision and reference**: summarises the events that triggered the sanctioning process. Only in a few cases does the record provide information on whether a DPSA investigation was triggered by self-notification (which can be assumed for most Art. 32 data breaches), or by one or several complaints by data subjects, or was a *sua sponte* initiative of the DPSA. For the reader who wants further information on the decision, a weblink to the DPSA's enforcement notice is referenced, or where unavailable, to a press release or law journal article, if any.

Figure 17: GDPR Sanctions Directory

Note: All Articles in this table refer to the General Data Protection Regulation

Date	Nation	Entity fined	Fines [€]	Main legal basis	GDPR Article
YEAR 2020 (until 24 November 2020)					
2020-11-24	Romania	Dada Creation S.R.L. [Retail]	€5,000	Insufficient measures to secure data processing.	Art. 32, Art. 33
	Summary of DPSA decision The data controller **disclosed the orders, delivery details and personal data of over 1000 customers** via its web store. The data was in a document shielded by insufficient access controls to prevent its being downloaded. The controller then failed to report the security breach to the DPSA.				
2020-11-24	Sweden	City of Stockholm [Public services & administration]	€394,000	Violation of "Integrity and confidentiality" principle. Insufficient measures to secure data processing.	Art. 5(1)(f), Art. 32
	The controller allowed a **breach on a school electronic platform**, which comprised multiple systems, including one for monitoring school attendance, a student administration system, an interface for parents, and an administration interface for teachers. Poor access control let too many staff access information about students anonymously using a protected identity. Another system allowed parents relatively easy access to information about other students, such as marks. Poor internet security permitted Google's search engine to compile links to an administrative interface giving access to information about teachers.				
2020-11-23	Spain	Recambios Villalegre S.L. [Information technology & services]	€12,000	Insufficient legal basis for data processing.	Art. 6, Art. 13
	Controller **posted on Facebook and WhatsApp someone's photos**, obtained from the company's video surveillance system, **then accused them of theft in related posts**. The controller encouraged other users to share the photos and accusatory posts. This resulted in hundreds of humiliating, insulting, and threatening comments. The DPSA fined controller €10,000 for publishing the photos and €2,000 for failure to post any notice to customers informing them of video surveillance of the store.				

Date	Nation	Entity fined	Fines [€]	Main legal basis	GDPR Article
2020-11-23	Romania	Vodafone România SA [Utilities, telecoms operator]	€4,000	Insufficient fulfilment of data subject rights (right of access).	Art. 12, Art. 15, Art. 17
	Controller received complaints alleging that operator **failed to respond to erasure and access requests**. Controller could provide no evidence to refute these complaints.				
2020-11-23	Italy	Burgo Group S.p.A [Retail]	€20,000	Violation of "General data processing principles".	Art. 5, Art. 13
	Company director **forwarded email conversation between data subject and a work colleague containing personal data**, including information relating to physical and mental discomfort in the workplace, to four people in the company.				
2020-11-19	Spain	Vodafone España, S.A.U. [Utilities, telecoms operator]	€36,000	Insufficient legal basis for data processing.	Art. 5, Art. 6, Art. 7, Art. 9
	Controller **sent invoice to a data subject without having a contractual agreement** with the data subject.				
2020-11-18	Spain	Anmavas 61, S.L. [Hospitality & leisure]	€2,000	Insufficient cooperation with DPSA.	Art. 58
	Controller **neglected either to grant or deny right to erasure** to data subject, even after receiving warning from DPSA.				
2020-11-18	France	Carrefour Banque [Financial services]	€800,000	Violation of principle "Lawfulness, fairness and transparency".	Art. 5(1)(a), Art. 12, Art. 13
	Subscribers to Pass card (a credit card attached to a loyalty account) who wanted to join the loyalty program **had to opt in to agreement that their details are shared with Carrefour fidélité**. Yet controller expressly affirmed that no data would be transmitted. Controller failed to process data fairly.				
2020-11-18	France	Carrefour France [Retail]	€2,250,000	Violation of "Storage limitation" principle. Insufficient	Art. 5(1)(e), Art. 12, Art. 13, Art. 15,

Date	Nation	Entity fined	Fines [€]	Main legal basis	GDPR Article
				fulfilment of data subject rights.	Art. 17, Art. 21, Art. 32, Art. 33
	Data controller provided users on carrefour.fr website **insufficient information on loyalty programme**, and provided incomplete information on **transfer of data to countries outside the EU**, on **data retention periods**; and kept **data for too long**: more than 28 million customers who had been inactive for 5-10 years were still being stored in the loyalty programme, including 750,000 who had registered via the carrefour.fr site. Data controller required from customers excessive proof of identity to exercise rights. Controller ignored requests from customers to access their personal data and neglected to fulfil numerous erasure requests. Controller also sent advertising via SMS or e-mail without consent or other legal basis.				
2020-11-17	Italy	Provincial Health Authority of Cosenza [Healthcare]	€30,000	Insufficient legal basis for data processing.	Art. 9
	Controller **disclosed first and last names, addresses and tax IDs on website** of persons who had claims for damages against the Authority.				
2020-11-17	Italy	Comune di Collegno [Public services & administration]	€2,000	Insufficient fulfilment of data subject rights (general).	Art. 12, Art. 13, Art. 14
	Controller failed to **respond to data subject access requests,** refusing data from a camera surveillance system.				
2020-11-16	Spain	Homeowners Association [Real estate & property]	€1,600	Violation of "Data minimisation" principle.	Art. 5 (1)(c)
	Controller used **CCTV camera** systems which also monitored public space.				
2020-11-16	Spain	Vodafone España, S.A.U. [Utilities, telecoms operator]	€42,000	Insufficient legal basis for data processing.	Art. 5, Art. 6
	In 2019 controller agreed to early **termination of contract** with data subject and deletion of personal data. **Data subject continued to receive e-mails from controller.**				
2020-11-13	UK	Ticketmaster UK Limited [Media &	€1,405,000	Violation of "Integrity and	Art. 5 (1)(f),

Date	Nation	Entity fined	Fines [€]	Main legal basis	GDPR Article
		entertainment]		confidentiality" principle. Insufficient measures to secure data processing.	Art. 32
	Data controller suffered a **cyberattack** between February and June 23, 2018 in which **9.4 million European customers were potentially affected**. Insufficiently secured chat-bot hosted by third party on its online payment site gave an attacker access to customers' personal financial data such as names, debit card numbers, Ticketmaster usernames and passwords, expiration dates, and Card Verification Value (CVV) numbers. **Around 60,000 cards belonging to Barclays Bank customers were exposed to fraud**, and several international banks reported fraudulent activity to Ticketmaster.				
2020-11-12	Italy	Vodafone [Utilities, telecoms operator]	€12,251,601	Violation of "General data processing principles".	Art. 5 (1) & (2), Art. 6 1), Art. 7, Art. 15(1), Art. 16, Art. 21, Art. 24, Art. 25(1), Art. 32, Art. 33
	Data controller **unlawfully processed personal data of millions of users for telemarketing purposes**. DPSA had received hundreds of complaints and alerts submitted by users against unsolicited phone calls to promote telephone and Internet services. Unauthorised call centres used telephone numbers that were fake or not registered with Italy's Consolidated Registry of Communication Operators (RCO) to place marketing calls. Other violations included handling of contact lists purchased from external providers and lack of customer resource management security measures.				
2020-11-11	Germany	1&1 Telecom GmbH [Utilities, telecoms operator]	€900,000 [reduced from €9,99m]	Insufficient measures to secure data processing.	Art. 32
	Controller's **defective authentication procedure led to a data breach**. Callers obtained personal customer data from company's customer service department by entering customer's name and date of birth. The fine was reduced because of cooperation with DPSA. On appeal, the Bonn District Court found the fine was unreasonably high, and reduced it from €9,55 million to €900,000, as the				

Date	Nation	Entity fined	Fines [€]	Main legal basis	GDPR Article
		violation was insignificant as unable to cause massive data leakage.			
2020-11-11	Spain	Vodafone España, S.A.U. [Utilities, telecoms operator]	€42,000	Insufficient legal basis for data processing.	Art. 5, Art. 6
		Controller, a telecoms operator, **ported a customer's telephone number without consent**: a signature on the porting contract was missing.			
2020-11-10	Spain	Miguel Ibáñez Bezanilla, S.L. (license plate seller) [Automotive industry]	€3,000	Insufficient measures to secure data processing.	Art. 13, Art. 32
		Controller's website requested personal information such as first and last name, copy of ID card and driver's license, and car's VIN number. The **data was not encrypted** and the data processing **policy was not GDPR compliant**.			
2020-11-06	Spain	Xfera Moviles S.A. [Utilities, telecoms operator]	€20,000	Insufficient cooperation with DPSA.	Art. 31
		Controller **failed to cooperate with the DPSA investigating** privacy violations by neither responding to its request for information nor providing requested documentation.			
2020-11-03	Spain	Telefonica Moviles España, S.A.U. [Utilities, telecoms operator]	€75,000	Insufficient legal basis for data processing.	Art. 5, Art. 6
		Data controller **issued several invoices** to data subject and collected invoice amounts from the bank account of one **who was not a customer**. Data subject's complaints were ignored.			
2020-11-03	Spain	Vodafone España S.A.U. [Utilities, telecoms operator]	€30,000	Insufficient legal basis for data processing.	Art. 5, Art. 6
		Data controller **processed personal data due to incorrect assignment of customer contracts**, resulting in company demanding payment from a data subject due to inaccurate records keeping and mixing up customers.			
2020-20-30 (final	UK	Marriott International Inc [Hospitality &	€20,450,00 0	Insufficient measures to secure data	Art. 32

108

Date	Nation	Entity fined	Fines [€]	Main legal basis	GDPR Article
decision – notice on 2019-07-09)		leisure]	[reduced from €110,390,2 00]	processing.	
	Cyberattack incident was notified to ICO by Marriott in Nov 2018. Personal data of 339 million guests globally were exposed by hackers, of which 7 million were UK residents and 30 million residents of 31 other EEA countries. Vulnerability is believed to have begun when Starwood Group's systems were compromised in 2014. Marriott had acquired Starwood in 2016, but customer data breach was not discovered until 2018. ICO ruled that Marriott did insufficient due diligence when acquiring Starwood and could have done more to secure its systems. Note: Final decision saw a reduction from £99,200,396 to £18.4 million because of Marriott's full cooperation with DPSA plus economic impact of COVID-19 pandemic.				
2020-10-28	Spain	Vodafone España S.A.U. [Utilities, telecoms operator]	€36,000	Insufficient legal basis for data processing.	Art. 5, Art. 6
	Data controller unlawfully processed personal data due to inaccurate records keeping and mixing up customers.				
2020-10-28	Spain	Play Orenes S.L. [Media & entertainment]	€4,000	Violation of "Data minimisation" principle.	Art. 5(1)(c)
	Data controller used CCTV cameras outside its premises, which recorded data in public space.				
2020-10-26	Italy	Università Campus Bio-medico di Roma (Polyclinic) [Education, private and public]	€20,000	Violation of "Lawfulness, fairness and transparency" and "Integrity and confidentiality" principles.	Art. 5(1) (a) & (f), Art. 5(2), Art. 9, Art. 33
	In a data breach notification pursuant to Art. 33 GDPR, DPSA investigation found that patients accessing their own online medical reports via their smartphones could also access personal data of 74 other patients. This was caused by a human error in integrating two IT systems.				
2020-10-26	Spain	Organic Natur 03 S.L. [Retail]	€4,000	Insufficient fulfilment of data subject	Art. 13

Date	Nation	Entity fined	Fines [€]	Main legal basis	GDPR Article
				rights (information to be provided).	
The controller's membership contract contained pre-defined privacy clauses, which prevented effective negotiation and **need for consent**.					
2020-10-26	Spain	Conseguridad SL (private security company) [Service company]	€50,000	Failure to designate a DPO.	Art. 37
The controller **failed to appoint a Data Protection Officer**.					
2020-10-23	Hungary	Deichmann Cipőkereskedelmi Korlátolt Felelősségű Társaságnak [Retail]	€54,800	Insufficient fulfilment of data subject rights (right of access & to restrict processing).	Art. 12, Art. 15, Art. 18(1)(c), Art. 25
Data controller denied data subject **access to CCTV recordings** in a local store, which data subject requested to prove no money was returned after paying in the store. Controller denied access to recordings, arguing this would require an official order, then deleted the video recordings, even though data subject had requested controller to keep a copy of them.					
2020-10-22	Cyprus	Cyprus Police [Public services & administration]	€6,000	Insufficient measures to secure data processing.	Art. 32
Police officer got **unauthorized access to database holding personal data** of vehicle owners and used it for unofficial purposes. Information was passed to a third party. It was found that insufficient prevention of unauthorized access allowed the unauthorised disclosure.					
2020-10-21	Lithuania	Vilnius City Municipality Administration [Public services & administration]	€15,000	Violation of "Data accuracy" and "integrity and confidentiality" principles.	Art. 5(1) (d) & (f)
Personal data of applicant for **adoption of a child was commingled with personal data of the biological parents**. This information subsequently became accessible in the Population Register of the Republic of Lithuania, due to a synchronization error of Population Information System of Municipal					

Date	Nation	Entity fined	Fines [€]	Main legal basis	GDPR Article
		Administration with the databases of the State Centre for Business Registers.			
2020-10-20	Romania	Globus Score SRL [Commercial engineering]	€2,000	Insufficient cooperation with DPSA.	Art. 58(1)(a) & (e)
		Data controller refused **to provide DPSA with requested information**.			
2020-10-20	Cyprus	Grant Ideas Ltd [Unknown]	€1,000	Insufficient legal basis for data processing.	Art. 5, Art. 6
		Data controller **sent emails to data subjects** without sufficient legal basis.			
2020-10-19	Cyprus	Bank of Cyprus Public Company Ltd [Financial services]	€15,000	Violation of "Integrity and confidentiality" principle. Insufficient measures to secure data processing.	Art. 5(1)(f) Art. 5(2), Art. 15, Art. 32, Art. 33
		Data controller was **unable to respond to a data subject access request as subject's insurance contract had been lost**. This infringed individual rights of data subject: − the obligation to protect personal data under Art. 5 (1)(f) and Art. 32. As data subject was not informed about loss of the contract arising from security breach, this also infringed Data Breach Notification Obligations.			
2020-10-19	Austria	Private person	€600	Violation of "Lawfulness, fairness and transparency" principle.	Art. 5(1)(a), Art. 9
		Data controller published **information about patients on his personal Facebook** page between February and June 2020, **including health data** per Art. 4 (15): patient names, medical diagnoses, medication data, hospital admissions and discharges, social security numbers, and the names of treating physicians.			
2020-10-19	Austria	Private person	€150	Violation of "Lawfulness, fairness and transparency" principle.	Art. 5(1)(a), Art. 6
		Private person recorded a woman while she was using one of the WC cabins by placing a smartphone with camera under the WC.			
2020-10-16	UK	British Airways [Transport &	€22,046,00	Violation of "Integrity and	Art. 5(1)(f),

Date	Nation	Entity fined	Fines [€]	Main legal basis	GDPR Article
(final decision – notice on 2019-07-08)		logistics]	0 [reduced from €204,600,000]	confidentiality" principle. Insufficient measures to secure data processing.	Art. 32
	Massive breach of Art. 32, relating to cyberattack notified to the ICO by British Airways in Sept 2018, which involved **user traffic to British Airways website being diverted to** hackers who harvested personal data, starting around June 2018. Data of **500,000 subjects were compromised**. DPSA found that a variety of security arrangements exposed log-in, payment card, and travel booking details as well as names and address. DPSA intended to fine British Airways £183.39 million. Note: **The final decision was to reduce fine from £183.39 million to £20 million due to the economic impact of the COVID-19 pandemic on the airline industry.**				
2020-10-15	Romania	S.C. Marsorom S.R.L. [Automotive industry]	€3,000	Insufficient measures to secure data processing.	Art. 32
	Data controller **disclosed personal data** of customers *via* company's website due to information security issues.				
2020-10-14	Norway	Bergen Municipality [Public services & administration]	€276,000	Violation of "Integrity and confidentiality" principle. Insufficient measures to secure data processing.	Art. 5(1)(f), Art. 32(1)(b)
	Data controller **failed to secure personal information** in Vigilo communication system between school and home, which contains module whereby school and parents can communicate via a portal or app. Before module was put to use, controller failed to establish or communicate the necessary guidelines (a confidential address) to secure the personal data of children and parents.				
2020-10-09	Spain	Café Restaurante B.B.B [Hospitality & leisure]	€900	Violation of "Data minimisation" principle.	Art. 5(1)(c), Art. 6, Art. 7, Art. 9
	Data controller operated **CCTV cameras which captured the public space** outside the premise.				

Date	Nation	Entity fined	Fines [€]	Main legal basis	GDPR Article
2020-10-09	Spain	Private Person	€2,000	Violation of "Data minimisation" principle.	Art. 5(1)(c), Art. 6
	Data controller **operated CCTV camera that also recorded the private space** of a neighbour.				
2020-10-09	Spain	Centro de Investigación y Estudio para la Obesidad, SL [Healthcare]	€50,000	Violation of "Data minimisation" principle. Insufficient measures to secure data processing.	Art. 5(1)(c), Art. 6, Art. 7, Art. 9
	Data controller **transferred data to an insurance company without sufficient legal basis**, as the medical treatment in question had never been carried out.				
2020-10-09	Spain	Caja Rural San José de Nules S. Cooperativa de Crédito [Financial services]	€5,000	Violation of "Integrity and confidentiality" principle.	Art. 5(1)(f)
	Controller published information with names and surnames of its employees which **disclosed their financial situation**.				
2020-10-06	Spain	Lycamobile [Utilities, telecoms operators]	€60,000	Insufficient measures to secure data processing.	Art. 5, Art. 6, Art. 32
	Controller **processed personal data because of incorrect information** about who owned prepaid phone cards, due to mismatch between registered owners in the company's business register and the actual card owners				
2020-10-06	Spain	Callesgarcia, S.L. [Retail]	€4,000	Insufficient legal basis for data processing.	Art. 5, Art. 6(1)
	Controller **used photo of data subjects for commercial purposes** without sufficient legal basis.				
2020-10-03	Spain	Avata Hispania, S.L. [Professional services]	€3,000	Insufficient legal basis for data processing.	Art. 5, Art. 6, Art. 28(3)(g)

Date	Nation	Entity fined	Fines [€]	Main legal basis	GDPR Article
Data controller **continued to process personal data after controller had terminated contractual relationship** with the processor.					
2020-10-01	Germany (DPSA Hamburg)	H&M Hennes & Mauritz Online Shop A.B. & Co. KG [Retail]	€35,258,708	Violation of "Integrity and confidentiality" principle. Insufficient measures to secure data processing.	Art. 5(1)(f), Art. 6, Art. 32
Controller had comprehensively recorded circumstances of employees' private lives since at least 2014, and stored this information on a network drive; e.g., company conducted a "Welcome Back Talk" after employees returned to work after vacation or illness. In this context **personal data was exposed, including information on symptoms of illness and medical diagnoses.** Some managers used informal through-the-grapevine gossip to acquire deep knowledge of employees; e.g., family problems and religious beliefs. **Data stored on the network drive was accessible to up to 50 managers**, and used to evaluate work performance and make employment decisions. After technical configuration error in October 2019, the data stored on network drive was accessible company-wide for hours. Management apologized to employees and offered monetary compensation. Protective measures were introduced per DPSA's recommendations.					
2020-10-01	Romania	Megareduceri TV S.R.L. [Retail]	€3,000	Insufficient cooperation with DPSA.	Art. 31, Art. 58
Controller **failed to comply with a DPSA order.**					
2020-10-01	Romania	Asociația de proprietari Militari R [Public services & administration]	€2,000	Insufficient cooperation with DPSA.	Art. 31, Art. 58
Controller **failed to comply with a DPSA order.**					
2020-09-30	Italy	Azienda Ospedaliera di Rilievo Nazionale 'Antonio Cardarelli' [Healthcare]	€80,000	Violation of "Lawfulness, fairness and transparency" and "Integrity and confidentiality" principles. Insufficient	Art. 5(1)(a) & (f), Art. 6(1)(b) & (c), Art. 13, Art. 28, Art. 32

Date	Nation	Entity fined	Fines [€]	Main legal basis	GDPR Article
				measures to secure data processing.	
*Processor **unlawfully disclosed online the personal data of participants in a public competition.** Due to configuration error, a list of codes assigned to the competitors was temporarily accessible on the platform, which in turn gave access to documents with their personal data. In addition to the security infringement, controller also did not comply with hospital's data processing agreement with data processor, which was also sanctioned (see the entry for "Scanshare" below).*					
2020-09-30	Italy	Scanshare s.r.l. [Public services & administration]	€60,000	Violation of "Lawfulness, fairness and transparency" and "Integrity and confidentiality" principles. Insufficient measures to secure data processing.	Art. 5(1)(a) & (f), Art. 6, Art. 9, Art. 32
*Processor **unlawfully disclosed online the personal data of participants in a public competition.** Configuration error on the platform temporarily gave access to a list of codes assigned to the competitors, which in turn allowed access to documents with their personal data. Scanshare, which was the data processor on behalf of controller "Azienda Ospedaliera di Rilievo Nazionale 'Antonio Cardarelli'", a private hospital, was also sanctioned.*					
2020-09-30	Spain	Venu Sanz Chef, S.L. [Education]	€3,000	Insufficient legal basis for data processing.	Art. 5(1)(b), Art. 6
*Controller **used personal data for advertising** without sufficient legal basis.*					
2020-09-25	Spain	Xfera Moviles S.A. [Utilities, telecoms operators]	€60,000	Insufficient legal basis for data processing.	Art. 5(1)(a), Art. 6
*Controller **failed to remove subject's personal data at the time** of cancellation of telephone services contract and sent a warning to data subject after cancellation, resulting in the processing of personal data without sufficient legal basis.*					

Date	Nation	Entity fined	Fines [€]	Main legal basis	GDPR Article
2020-09-25	Norway	Odin Flissenter AS [Real estate & property]	€13,900	Insufficient legal basis for data processing.	Art. 5, Art. 6(1)(f)
	Controller **performed credit check of sole proprietor who had no customer relationship or any other connection to company.** It processed personal data which identified the proprietor and his personal finances, while credit ratings showed details of his finances.				
2020-09-22	Spain	GLP Instalaciones 86, SL [Utilities, energy suppliers]	€60,000	Insufficient legal basis for data processing.	Art. 5, Art. 6
	Data subject had contacted Energy Group S.A. for assistance installing air conditioning system. Two different companies contacted data subject, one of which was GLP Instalaciones 86, impersonating Energy Group S.A. Energy Group S.A. objected that the company was neither an authorized installers nor employees of Energy Group S.A. . Thus, the imposter had **processed subject's personal data**, – name, surname, telephone number, bank details, and e-mail address, – **without valid legal basis**.				
2020-09-22	Spain	Iweb Internet Learning, SL [Education]	€7,800	Insufficient fulfilment of data subject rights.	Art. 7, Art. 12, Art. 13
	Controller issued **privacy policy lacking clarity and consent was inadequately obtained**, only general consent without listing specific data processing purposes.				
2020-09-22	Norway	Norwegian Public Roads Administration [Public services & administration]	€37,400	Violation of "Data minimisation" principle. Insufficient legal basis for data processing.	Art. 5(1)(c) & (2), Art. 6, Art. 7, Art. 9
	Controller **fixed road cameras to monitor contract parties, employees, subvendors and subvendors' employees**, using them to document breaches of contract several months after incidents took place.				
2020-09-17	Spain	Vodafone España SAU [Utilities, telecoms operator]	€60,000	Insufficient legal basis for data processing.	Art. 5, Art. 6

Date	Nation	Entity fined	Fines [€]	Main legal basis	GDPR Article
Controller sent e-mails containing **electronic bills after data subject had terminated the contract**.					
2020-09-17	Spain	Grupo Carolizan [Hospitality & leisure]	€3,000	Violation of "Data minimisation" principle.	Art. 5(1)(c)
Controller installed **CCTV camera system** in arcade area of an establishment, without a reasonable cause capturing **images of pedestrians** in public space.					
2020-09-16	Spain	Property owners' community [Real estate & property]	€10,000	Violation of "General data processing principles".	Art. 5
Controller on a community notice billboard **disclosed a document containing personal data,** including information about data subject's identity as well as debts.					
2020-09-11	Spain	Political party [Public services & administration]	€1,500	Insufficient legal basis for data processing.	Art. 5, Art. 6
Political party **sent an e-mail to a former party member who had resigned**, to ask him to act as an election representative.					
2020-09-11	Greece	Private person	€8,000	Violation of "General data processing principles".	Art. 5(1)
Controller operated **CCTV camera that monitored public space** outside the premises.					
2020-09-08	Poland	Warsaw University of Life Sciences [Education]	€11,200	Insufficient measures to secure data processing.	Art. 32
Theft of a private notebook from university employee who used the device for business purposes led to breach of personal data related to recruitment activities.					
2020-09-08	Romania	Sanatatea Press Group S.R.L. [Media & entertainment]	€2,000	Violation of "Integrity and confidentiality" principle. Insufficient measures to	Art. 5(1)(f), Art. 32

Date	Nation	Entity fined	Fines [€]	Main legal basis	GDPR Article
				secure data processing.	
Controller sent **personal data collected for registration for an online course to other participants** due to a technical failure.					
2020-09-07	Spain	Barcelona Airport Security Guard Association ('AVSAB') [Transport & logistics]	€3,000	Violation of "Integrity and confidentiality" principle.	Art. 5(1)(f)
Employee infringed the integrity and confidentiality of personal data owned by data controller. Employee was a member of the security committee and **used WhatsApp to send messages containing personal information** about employees to private phone numbers.					
2020-09-07	Italy	Istituto Comprensivo Statale Crucoli Torretta [Education]	€2,000	Violation of "Integrity and confidentiality" principle. Insufficient measures to ensure information security.	Art. 5(1)(f), Art. 32
Controller **published personal data of students on Istituto website** with notes about health and progress in school. The breach happened due to technical error.					
2020-09-07	Belgium	Former mayor of a commune [Public services & administration]	€5,000	Violation of "Integrity and confidentiality" principle. Insufficient measures to secure data processing.	Art. 5(1)(b) & (f), Art. 6(4), Art. 32
Controller sent **election advertising messages to citizens** without sufficient legal basis.					
2020-09-03	Norway	Bergen Municipality [Public services & administration]	€276,000	Violation of "Integrity and confidentiality" principle. Insufficient measures to	Art. 5(1)(f), Art. 32

Date	Nation	Entity fined	Fines [€]	Main legal basis	GDPR Article
				secure data processing.	
DPSA learned from Municipality of Bergen about **breach of Municipality's communication tool between a school and home users.** The tool, insufficiently secured against data threats, allowed the school and parents to access personal data other than their own via a portal or app.					
2020-09-03	Italy	Comune di Casaloldo [Public services & administration]	€2,000	Violation of "Lawful, fairness and transparency" and "Data minimisation" principles. Insufficient legal basis for data processing.	Art. 5(1)(a) & (c), Art. 6
Controller **published personal data on Comune's website.**					
2020-09-02	Poland	Unknown (reprimand for the processing of students' personal data)	Warning only	Violation of "Lawfulness, fairness and transparency" and "purpose limitation" principles.	Art. 5(1)(a) & (b), Art. 6(1)(c)
Controller processed data without legal basis of survey carried out by a school in year 2019/2020. **Titled "Diagnosis of student's home and school situation", it probed students' personal situations.** Controller processed personal data of minors: names; class attendance; legal guardians (parents); family status (single parent, intact family); death of a legal guardian (parent) or separation of legal guardians (parents), their education and professional situation; number of persons in household; financial situation, health condition and addictions of legal guardians (parents), housing situation; and information on social benefits.					
2020-09-01	Spain	Telefónica Móviles España SAU [Utilities, telecoms operator]	€75,000	Insufficient legal basis for data processing.	Art. 5, Art. 6
Controller processed personal data such that **data subject received hundreds of unsolicited calls and SMS messages.**					

Date	Nation	Entity fined	Fines [€]	Main legal basis	GDPR Article
2020-09-01	Romania	Apartment building owners' association [Real estate & property]	€500	Insufficient measures to secure data processing.	Art. 5, Art. 6(1), Art. 12, Art. 13, Art. 25, Art. 32
	Controller exported a still image from **video surveillance system and posted it on building's billboard.** Insufficient notification of CCTV was provided.				
2020-08-31	Poland	Surveyor General of Poland ('GKK') [Real estate & property]	€22,700	Insufficient legal basis for data processing.	Art. 5(1)(a), Art. 6(1), Art. 58(1)
	Controller without sufficient legal basis **processed personal data on GEOPORTAL2 platform (www.geoportal.gov.pl)**, which is required for the land and mortgage registers. This included names, surnames, and other personal data.				
2020-08-28	Spain	Bankia S.A. [Financial services]	€50,000	Violation of "Purpose limitation" principle.	Art. 5(1)(b)
	Controller **kept personal data for several years, even after data subject was no longer a customer.** During this time, data was accessible to bank employees.				
2020-08-28	Spain	Basketball Federation of Castilla and Leon [Hospitality & leisure]	€5,000	Violation of "Integrity and confidentiality" principle. Insufficient legal basis for data processing.	Art. 5(1)(f), Art. 6
	Controller **transmitted personal data to third parties**, which was then **published on Internet without consent** of data subjects. And personal data was disclosed without consent to a newspaper.				
2020-08-20	Belgium	Proximus [Utilities, telecoms operators]	€20,000	Violation of "General data processing principles".	Art. 5(2), Art. 6, Art. 7, Art. 24
	Controller caused multiple data protection infringements during processing of personal data for the purpose of **publishing public telephone directories.**				

Date	Nation	Entity fined	Fines [€]	Main legal basis	GDPR Article
2020-08-18	Spain	Vodafone España SAU [Utilities, telecoms operator]	€75,000	Violation of "General data processing principles".	Art. 5, Art. 6(1), Art. 7, Art. 9
	Controller processed data subject's telephone number for marketing purposes after he had **requested right to erasure** in 2015; despite which, data subject was sent advertising SMS's. Controller stated that subject's number had been used as a "dummy number" by its employees.				
2020-08-18	Spain	Unknown company	€1,200	Insufficient fulfilment of data subject rights (right to object).	Art. 21
	Controller phoned data subject offering a deal on hotels, after data subject **opted for the advertisement exclusion system**. Joining this system **exercised data subject's right to object to processing for marketing purposes**.				
2020-08-18	Ireland	Cork University Maternity Hospital (CUMH) [Healthcare]	€65,000	Insufficient measures to secure data processing.	Art. 5, Art. 32
	Controller **disposed of personal data of 78 patients in a public recycling centre** including documents containing the special category personal data of six patients. The breach involved sensitive health data such as medical history and future care programmes.				
2020-08-17	Spain	Party of the Socialists of Catalonia [Public services & administration]	€5,000	Violation of "Purpose limitation" principle.	Art. 5(1)(b)
	Controller provided personal data to a medical doctor who sent letter to data subject's kin asking for political support. This constituted **different purpose from original purpose of data collection**.				
2020-08-17	Estonia	Private person (Police officer and health worker)	€48 / €56	Insufficient legal basis for data processing.	Art. 5, Art. 6
	Police officer used his access to personal data in a police database for **private research activities**.				
2020-08-10	Italy	Cavauto S.R.L. [Automotive industry]	€10,000	Violation of "Lawfulness, fairness and	Art. 5(1)(a), Art. 6,

Date	Nation	Entity fined	Fines [€]	Main legal basis	GDPR Article
				transparency" principle. Insufficient legal basis for data processing.	Art. 7
Controller **failed to erase former employee's personal data.** On controller's work computer, access to personal data containing employee's browsing history was kept after he had left the company.					
2020-08-10	Italy	Commune of Baronissi [Public services & administration]	€10,000	Violation of "Lawfulness, fairness and transparency" and "Data minimisation" principles. Insufficient legal basis for data processing.	Art. 5(1)(a) & (c), Art. 6
Controller **published on its website personal data** of data subjects, including names, birth dates, place of birth, place of residence, *etc.*					
2020-08-06	Spain	Grow Beats SL [Retail]	€3,000	Insufficient fulfilment of data subject rights.	Art. 12, Art. 13, Art. 14
Controller published a cookie policy on its website, which contained **no information about the purpose of cookies** and no information about type of installed cookies and the length of time they would remain active on user's device.					
2020-08-06	Italy	GTL S.R.L. [Automotive industry]	€3,000	Insufficient fulfilment of data subject rights (general).	Art. 12, Art. 15
Controller **failed to respond to a data subject's access request.**					
2020-08-06	Spain	Just Landed S.L. [Service companies]	€3,000	Insufficient fulfilment of data subject rights.	Art. 13
Controller provided **insufficient cookie information and insufficiently fulfilled**					

Date	Nation	Entity fined	Fines [€]	Main legal basis	GDPR Article
		its information obligations by publishing privacy policy in English only			
2020-08-05	France	Spartoo [Retail]	€250,000	Violation of "Data minimisation" principle.	Art. 5(1)(c), Art. 13, Art. 14
		Retailer with headquarters in France but supplying large number of European countries **recorded all telephone hotline calls**, during which personal data like **addresses and bank details of orders were recorded** as well. Bank details were only partially encrypted and controller's data protection **notice was partly incorrect**.			
2020-08-05	Finland	Acc Consulting Varsinais-Suomi (Independent Consulting Oy) [Service companies]	€7,000	Violation of "General data processing principles". Insufficient legal basis for data processing.	Art. 5, Art. 6
		Controller exploited personal data for **unsolicited marketing SMS's without prior consent**. Controller did not respond to or execute data subject requests, and could not demonstrate it had processed personal data lawfully.			
2020-08-05	Spain	Restaurant [Hospitality & leisure]	€3,000	Violation of "Data minimisation" principle.	Art. 5(1)(c), Art. 12, Art. 13
		Controller operated **CCTV surveillance cameras that also monitored public space** without sufficient information notice.			
2020-08-05	Austria	Bank [Financial services]	€100	Insufficient measures to secure data processing.	Art. 5, Art. 6
		Bank employee made **copy of identity card of a client who exchanged €100 for foreign currency**. Though justified under Anti-Money Laundering regulation, identity checks only apply if €10,000 or more.			
2020-08-05	Italy	School [Education]	€2,000	Violation of "Lawfulness, fairness and transparency" and "Data minimisation" principles. Insufficient	Art. 5(a) & (c), Art. 6

Date	Nation	Entity fined	Fines [€]	Main legal basis	GDPR Article
				legal basis for data processing.	
	Controller placed personal **data of pupils on public notice board**.				
2020-08-04	Denmark	PrivatBo A.M.B.A. [Real estate & property]	€20,100	Insufficient measures to secure data processing.	Art. 5, Art. 32
	Controller distributed 424 USB sticks to tenants advertising real estate sale, which contained, besides real estate information, **personal data of lease agreements and other documents with confidential personal data**.				
2020-08-04	Spain	Vodafone España SAU [Utilities, telecoms operator]	€60,000	Insufficient legal basis for data processing.	Art. 5, Art. 6
	Controller informed data subject about a phone number porting which the **data subject had never commissioned**.				
2020-08-04	Italy	Mapei S.p.A. [Commercial engineering]	€15,000	Violation of "Lawfulness, fairness and transparency" and "Data minimisation" principles. Insufficient legal basis for data processing.	Art. 5(1)(a) & (c), Art. 6, Art. 12, Art. 13, Art. 15, Art. 17
	Controller **left e-mail account of an employee active even after termination of employment** to automatically forward incoming e-mails. Company provided data subject with insufficient information about this. In addition, company did not respond to requests for access and erasure.				
2020-08-04	Italy	National Institute for Social Security – Department of the Province of Brescia [Public services & administration]	€5,000	Insufficient fulfilment of data subject rights (right of access).	Art. 15
	Controller **failed to grant access to personal health data of a data subject**.				

Date	Nation	Entity fined	Fines [€]	Main legal basis	GDPR Article
2020-08-04	Italy	Supermarket [Retail]	€1,000	Violation of "Lawfulness, fairness and transparency" and "Data minimisation" principles. Insufficient legal basis for data processing.	Art. 5(1)(a) & (c), Art. 6
	Controller **displayed letter of dismissal to the personnel manager on supermarket's publicly visible notice board**.				
2020-08-03	Greece	Private Person (Candidate for parliamentary election)	€3,000	Insufficient fulfilment of data subject rights (right of access).	Art. 15
	Data subject received **telephone calls regarding candidacy for parliamentary election**. When data subject requested right to access his personal information, he was informed that he could not receive such information.				
2020-07-31	Spain	Vodafone España SAU [Utilities, telecoms operator]	€45,000	Insufficient legal basis for data processing.	Art. 5, Art. 6
	Controller **unlawfully processed a telephone number for marketing purposes** even after the data subject had exercised its right to erasure.				
2020-07-31	Spain	Tour & People Max S.L. [Hospitality & leisure]	€1,500	Insufficient fulfilment of data subject rights (right to object).	Art. 21
	Controller made **unsolicited marketing calls**, even though data subjects had expressed objections. As well as GDPR, this was seen as a violation of Article 48(1)(b) of Spanish General Data Protection Law 9/2014.				
2020-07-30	Romania	SC Viva Credit IFN SA [Financial services]	€2,000	Insufficient fulfilment of data subject rights (right of erasure).	Art. 17
	Controller did not inform data subject within one month, nor sought an				

Date	Nation	Entity fined	Fines [€]	Main legal basis	GDPR Article
		extension by providing reasons for the **delay of up to three months for a request for data erasure.**			
2020-07-30	Romania	Romanian National Post [Public services & administration]	€2,000	Insufficient measures to secure data processing.	Art. 32
		Controller processed personal data **(telephone numbers and e-mail addresses) of 81 data subjects, which were exposed.** No appropriate technical or organisational measures, such as pseudonymisation, had been put in place.			
2020-07-30	Italy	Commune of Manduria [Public services & administration]	€2,000	Violation of "Lawfulness, fairness and transparency" and "Data minimisation" principles. Insufficient legal basis for data processing.	Art. 5(1)(a) ^ (c), Art. 6
		Controller provided **personal data of a Commune employee to the press** without sufficient legal basis.			
2020-07-29	Italy	Commune of San Giorgio Jonico [Public services & administration]	€3,000	Violation of "Lawfulness, fairness and transparency" and "Data minimisation" principles. Insufficient legal basis for data processing.	Art. 5(1)(a) & (c), Art. 6
		Controller **published personal data on the municipal website** with regard to legal proceedings			
2020-07-29	Italy	Region of Campania [Public services & administration]	€4,000	Violation of "Lawfulness, fairness and transparency" and "Data minimisation" principles. Insufficient	Art. 5(1)(a) & (c), Art. 6

Date	Nation	Entity fined	Fines [€]	Main legal basis	GDPR Article
				legal basis for data processing.	
	Controller **published an enforcement order regarding civil proceedings on the Region's website.** The document listed the parties' names and places of residence, and even the amount of the claim for damages.				
2020-07-28	Denmark	Arp-Hansen Hotel Group A/S [Hospitality & leisure]	€147,800	Violation of "Storage limitation" principle.	Art. 5 (1)(e)
	DPSA inspected a number of IT systems to find out if the data controller had sufficient procedures in place to ensure that **personal data is retained only as long as necessary for the purposes of collection.** DPSA found that one of the reservation systems contained a large amount of personal data past the expiry dates in the Retention Schedule.				
2020-07-28	Belgium	Communal political association [Public services & administration]	€3,000	Insufficient legal basis for data processing.	Art. 5(1), Art. 6, Art. 14
	Controller posted election flyers to local residents during the elections in 2018. For this purpose, the association **used the electoral roll of 2012 and compared it with that of 2018** without a sufficient legal basis and appropriate notice to data subjects.				
2020-07-27	Romania	SC CNTAR TAROM SA [Transport & logistics]	€5,000	Insufficient measures to secure data processing.	Art. 32
	Controller with inadequate technical and organisational measures for secure data processing **disclosed data of five passengers.** The company was required to take corrective action, including training its employees and conducting risk assessment procedures.				
2020-07-23	Spain	El Periódico de Catalunya, S.L.U. [Media & entertainment]	€10,000	Insufficient legal basis for data processing.	Art. 5, Art. 6
	Controller **failed to execute erasure request.** *Periodico* sent another newsletter to data subject after he submitted the erasure request, which the controller claimed to have fulfilled.				
2020-07-23	Spain	Telefónica Móviles España	€55,000	Insufficient legal basis for	Art. 5, Art. 6

Date	Nation	Entity fined	Fines [€]	Main legal basis	GDPR Article
		SAU [Utilities, telecoms operator]		data processing.	
	Controller processed personal data including first and last names and bank details, to activate **three telephone lines that were never requested**.				
2020-07-23	Spain	Telefónica Móviles España, SAU [Utilities, telecoms operator]	€70,000	Insufficient legal basis for data processing.	Art. 5, Art. 6
	Controller **debited data subject's account for two telephone lines that were never ordered or approved**, constituting unlawful processing of personal data, as subject's data was stored in the invoicing system of controller without a legal basis.				
2020-07-23	Spain	Telefónica Móviles España SAU [Utilities, telecoms operator]	€75,000	Insufficient legal basis for data processing ("Lawfulness of processing").	Art. 5, Art. 6
	Controller ported data subject's **phone number from the current company without consent**. Personal data was transferred from the other telephone company to Telefónica Móviles España to change ownership of the line without sufficient legal basis.				
2020-07-23	Spain	Xfera Moviles S.A. [Utilities, telecoms operator]	€5,000	Insufficient cooperation with DPSA.	Art. 58
	Controller **failed to provide within the time limit certain information and documents to DPSA**, who had requested it following a data subject's complaint.				
2020-07-23	Spain	El Real Sporting de Gijón S.A.D. [Hospitality & leisure]	€5,000	Insufficient legal basis for data processing.	Art. 6, Art. 7
	Controller was fined for **communicating for direct marketing purposes without sufficient consent**. The forms submitted to club members contained default opt-in which violated GDPR's opt-out consent.				
2020-07-24	Hungary	Forbes Hungary [Media & entertainment]	€560	Violation of "General data processing principles". Insufficient	Art. 5(1)(a), (b), (c), (d) & (e), Art. 6

Date	Nation	Entity fined	Fines [€]	Main legal basis	GDPR Article
				legal basis for data processing.	
	Controller neglected to change an employee's address to his new address. It also failed to delete the old address and insufficiently enabled the subject to exercise his rights.				
2020-07-24	Hungary	Private Person (Employer)	€1,700	Insufficient fulfilment of data subject rights (right of access & erasure).	Art. 5 (1)(d), Art. 6, Art. 12, Art. 15, Art. 17
	Controller published a list of the 50 wealthiest Hungarians and a list of the largest family businesses **without a sufficient balance of interests** to justify legitimate interest as the legal basis.				
2020-07-20	Spain	Banco Bilbao Vizcaya Argentaria, SA (BBVA) [Financial services]	€24,000	Insufficient legal basis for data processing.	Art. 5, Art. 6
	Controller **processed solvency and credit information files without a prior contractual relationship** with data subject.				
2020-07-20	Spain	Iberia Lae SA Operadora Unipersonal [Transport & logistics]	€40,000	Insufficient cooperation with DPSA.	Art. 58
	Controller **did not respond to data subject's request for access to telephone records.** Controller ignored request despite the prior order of DPSA.				
2020-07-20	Spain	Comercial Vigo Brandy S.L. [Retail]	€1,500	Insufficient fulfilment of data subject rights (information to be provided).	Art. 12, Art. 13, Art. 14
	Controller installed **CCTV surveillance without adequate information on notice signage**.				
2020-07-20	Spain	Orange Espagne S.A.U. [Utilities, telecoms operator]	€80,000	Insufficient legal basis for data processing.	Art. 5, Art. 6

Date	Nation	Entity fined	Fines [€]	Main legal basis	GDPR Article
		Controller **unlawfully activated several telephone line contracts** using subject's personal data, constituting a processing infringement, as the data was entered into the firm's database and processed there without a legitimate legal basis.			
2020-07-20	Spain	Xfera Moviles S.A. [Utilities, telecoms operator]	€70,000	Violation of "Integrity and confidentiality" principle.	Art. 5(1)(f)
		Data subject received a call from another Xfera Móviles customer informing him that the firm had **charged his bank account**, disclosing personal details of the other data subject (name, surname, ID card number, and phone number). It was an error of the controller.			
2020-07-16	Hungary	Google Ireland Ltd. [Information technology & services]	€28	Insufficient fulfilment of data subject rights (right of access).	Art. 12, Art. 15
		Controller **failed to respond in due time to data subject's request for access** to information about data processed in the context of Google AdWords.			
2020-07-15	Poland	Office for Geodesy and Cartography [Public services & administration]	€22,300	Insufficient cooperation with DPSA.	Art. 31, Art. 58
		Controller **refused to DPSA access to the premises** in the course of an audit.			
2020-07-14	Belgium	Google Belgium SA [Information technology & services]	€600,000	Insufficient legal basis for data processing. Insufficient fulfilment of data subject rights.	Art. 5, Art. 6, Art. 17 (1)(a), Art. 12
		Controller infringed Belgian citizen's right to be forgotten **by not dereferencing outdated articles that data subject had considered damaging** to reputation, and for **lack of transparency** on Google's application form for delisting. DPSA found that articles relating to unfounded harassment complaints may have grave consequences for data subject; natural persons are entitled to have articles dereferenced. This even applies to political office holders, though their public status makes them generally entitled to be less protected; thus, articles relating to political persons may be stored for a longer period of time. Google's rejection of application for dereferencing breached Article 17 and it was sanctioned with a €500,000 fine. An additional €100,000 fine was imposed for			

Date	Nation	Entity fined	Fines [€]	Main legal basis	GDPR Article
		breach of the principle of transparency, as Google did not sufficiently justify to data subject its rejection of the application.			
2020-07-14	Belgium	Operator of CCTV for a residential building [Real estate & property]	€5,000	Insufficient legal basis for data processing.	Art. 6, Art. 7
		Controller of **video cameras on a residential property** installed cameras to monitor the shared area of two blocks of flats. Controller claimed the owners had given consent by signing the notarised purchase contracts, but DPSA rejected this after reviewing contracts.			
2020-07-13	Italy	Merlini s.r.l. [Retail]	€200,000	Insufficient legal basis for data processing.	Art. 5(1) & (2), Art. 6, Art. 7, Art. 28, Art. 29
		Controller carried out **telemarketing activities** on behalf of Wind Tre S.p.A. through a third party data processor without sufficient legal basis for data processing (under Arts. 5-7) and without sufficient contractual agreements (under Arts. 28, 29) with the third-party provider.			
2020-07-13	Italy	Wind Tre SpA [Utilities, telecoms operators]	€16,700,000	Insufficient legal basis for data processing.	Art. 5(1) & (2), Art. 6, Art. 12, Art. 24, Art. 25
		Controller engaged in **unlawful direct marketing data processing activities; hundreds of data subjects received unsolicited communications by SMS, e-mail, telephone calls and automated calls without consent**. They were unable to exercise their right to withdraw consent and object to processing for direct marketing purposes because the Data Protection Policy lacked complete contact details. DPSA stated that the data of the subjects were published on public telephone lists despite their objections. Several company apps were also set up such that the user had to give consent to various processing activities each time he accessed them, with the possibility of withdrawing consent allowed only after 24 hours.			
2020-07-13	Italy	Iliad Italia S.p.A. [Utilities, telecoms operators]	€800,000	Violation of "Integrity and confidentiality" principle.	Art. 5(1)(a) & (f), Art. 25
		Controller **activated SIM cards and recorded payment data in a manner which**			

Date	Nation	Entity fined	Fines [€]	Main legal basis	GDPR Article
	was unlawful. DPSA also stated that firm had not the necessary legal basis for **direct marketing** and violated the security requirements for the storage of customer data in the personal area of its website.				
2020-07-10	Poland	East Power Sp. z o.o. [Service companies]	€3,400	Insufficient cooperation with DPSA.	Art. 31, Art. 58
	After three subpoenas to the controller, which failed to provide sufficient explanations upon a direct marketing complaint, DPSA found that **controller had deliberately obstructed the proceeding** and failed to comply with its obligations to cooperate with DPSA.				
2020-07-10	Norway	Municipality of Rælingen [Public services & administration]	€47,500	Insufficient measures to secure data processing.	Art. 32, Art. 35
	Controller **processed 15 children's health data unlawfully in connection with disability** through the digital learning platform "Showbie". Municipality had failed to carry out a DPIA before starting the processing, and had not taken adequate technical and organisational measures, risking unauthorised access to personal data.				
2020-07-10	Spain	Auto Desguaces Iglesias S.L. [Automotive industry]	€1,500	Violation of "Data minimisation" principle.	Art. 5(1)(c)
	Controller **installed surveillance cameras that had recorded a public road**.				
2020-07-10	Spain	Centro Internacional De Crecimiento Laboral Y Profesional S.L. [Public services & administration]	€1,000	Insufficient legal basis for data processing.	Art. 5, Art. 6
	Data subject was sent **marketing messages without consent or possibility to object**.				
2020-07-10	Spain	Vodafone España SAU [Utilities, telecoms operator]	€12,000	Violation of "Data accuracy" principle.	Art. 5(1)(d)
	Controller **changed customer's master data to the name of a third party**, which was customer's ex-spouse.				
2020-07-10	Spain	Global Business Travel Spain SL	€5,000	Insufficient measures to	Art. 32(2) &

Date	Nation	Entity fined	Fines [€]	Main legal basis	GDPR Article
		[Hospitality & leisure]		secure data processing.	(4)
		Controller **processed an employee's health data without taking appropriate security measures.** DPSA found that controller failed to take adequate technical and organisational measures to protect data from unauthorised disclosure.			
2020-07-10	Spain	School Fitness Holiday & Franchising SL [Hospitality & leisure]	€5,000	Violation of "Lawfulness, fairness and transparency" principle.	Art. 5(1)(a)
		Controller **breached the transparency principle.** (No further information has been made public.)			
2020-07-10	Spain	Xfera Moviles S.A. [Utilities, telecoms operator]	€55,000	Violation of "Integrity and confidentiality" principle. Insufficient measures to secure data processing.	Art. 5(1)(f), Art. 32
		Controller changed a mobile phone connection contract to another customer, **making accessible subject's personal data** (address and telephone numbers) without authorisation.			
2020-07-09	Romania	Proleasing Motors SRL [Automotive industry]	€15,000	Insufficient measures to secure data processing.	Art. 32
		Controller **published on Facebook a document containing a password for access to personal data of 436 customers.**			
2020-07-06	The Netherlands	Bureau Krediet Registration ('BKR') (National Credit Register) [Financial services]	€830,000	Insufficient fulfilment of data subject rights (right of access).	Art. 12, Art. 15
		Controller required **a fee for data access requests and only provided access to their data once a year free of charge.** And controller set up a prohibitively complex process for data subjects wishing to receive a copy of their data by post. BKR created too many obstacles for people wishing to access their data.			

Date	Nation	Entity fined	Fines [€]	Main legal basis	GDPR Article
2020-07-02	Spain	Iberdrola Clientes [Utilities, energy suppliers]	€24,000	Violation of "Integrity and confidentiality" principle.	Art. 5(1)(f)
	Controller **provided to third person another customer's electricity bill with personal details** such as name, address, and bank account. The fine of €40,000 was reduced to €24,000 for voluntary payment and not contesting the fine.				
2020-07-02	Spain	De Vere Spain S.L. [Financial services]	€4,000	Insufficient fulfilment of data subject rights (right to object).	Art. 21
	Controller **did not respond to request to stop processing personal data**, so that data subject continued to receive marketing calls.				
2020-07-02	Norway	Odin Flissenter AS [Real estate & property]	€28,000	Insufficient legal basis for data processing.	Art. 5, Art. 6
	Controller performed due diligence on owner of a firm, and so **processed personal data relating to a natural person without having a sufficient legal basis**.				
2020-07-02	Spain	Saunier-Tec Mantenimientos de Calor y Frio, SL. [Utilities, energy suppliers]	€3,600	Insufficient breach notification to DPSA.	Art. 33
	Controller had taken steps to remedy a data breach but did **not inform DPSA sufficiently**. DPSA's fine of €4,800 was reduced to €3,600 for voluntary payment and not contesting the fine.				
2020-07-02	Spain	Xfera Moviles S.A. [Utilities, telecoms operators]	€5,000	Insufficient cooperation with DPSA.	Art. 31, Art. 58
	Controller **did not cooperate sufficiently with DPSA**.				
2020-07-02	Italy	Mapei S.p.A. [Real estate & property]	€15,000	Insufficient fulfilment of data subject rights (right of access).	Art. 5, Art. 12, Art. 13, Art. 15
	Controller **failed to respond to a data subject's access request**. Also, it had **left**				

Date	Nation	Entity fined	Fines [€]	Main legal basis	GDPR Article
		the e-mail account of the person concerned active even after termination of the contract.			
2020-06-30	Germany (Baden-Wuerttemberg)	Allgemeine Ortskrankenkasse ("AOK") (insurance company) [Healthcare]	€1,240,000	Violation of "Lawfulness, fairness and transparency" and "Data minimisation" principles. Insufficient measures to secure data processing.	Art. 5(1)(a) & (c), Art. 6, Art. 32
	Controller organised several competitions and collected personal data of the participants, including contact details and health insurance affiliation, from 2015 to 2019. It also wanted to use the data for marketing if the participants consented. Using technical and organizational measures, including internal guidelines and data protection training, controller tried to select only data subjects for marketing who consented, but the measures failed the legal standard. **Personal data of more than 500 lottery participants were used for marketing without consent.**					
2020-06-30	Denmark	Lejre Municipality Child and Youth Centre [Public services & administration]	€6,700	Violation of "General data processing principles".	Art. 5, Art. 6, Art. 33, Art. 34
	Controller regularly **uploaded minutes of meetings with sensitive personal data** to its Personnel Portal, including data of minors, which was accessible to employees of the community centre, including those not working on these cases.					
2020-06-30	Ireland	Tusla Child and Family Agency [Public services & administration]	€40,000	Insufficient breach notification to DPSA.	Art. 33
	Controller sent letter with abuse allegations to **third party who uploaded it to social networks.**					
2020-06-29	Greece	New York College S.A. [Education]	€5,000	Violation of "General data processing principles".	Art. 5(1) & (2)
	Controller contacted the complainant directly by telephone with regard to an educational programme and **processed personal data in a non-transparent**					

Date	Nation	Entity fined	Fines [€]	Main legal basis	GDPR Article
		manner.			
2020-06-25	Isle of Man	Department of Home Affairs [Public services & administration]	€13,500	Insufficient fulfilment of data subject rights (right of access).	Art. 12, Art. 15
	Controller **failed to yield right of access to personal data**. The Isle of Man adopted the GDPR, even though it is neither an EU nor EEA country. The Isle of Man Information Commissioner (https://www.inforights.im/) and https://www.inforights.im/individuals/data-protection/					
2020-06-23	Spain	Miraclia [Utilities, telecoms operator]	€7,500	Violation of "General data processing principles". Insufficient legal basis for data processing.	Art. 5, Art. 6
	Controller recorded telephone jokes via an app, which constitutes processing of personal data under GDPR, according to DPSA's decision. Voices of individuals may be personal data if associated with other information, such as telephone number. **The consent notice of users** at the end of the conversation **was insufficient**.					
2020-06-22	Spain	Unknown	€2,000	Violation of "General data processing principles".	Art. 5, Art. 6, Art. 13, Art. 14
	Controller **set up CCTV cameras which covered public space and recorded passing pedestrians**, and the public notice of CCTVs recording was insufficient.					
2020-06-22	Norway	Østfold HF Hospital [Healthcare]	€112,000	Insufficient measures to secure data processing.	Art. 32
	Controller **stored patient data**, including sensitive data like reason for hospitalisation, from 2013 to 2019. **Access to the folders was unprotected**. DPSA decided that this was not just a GDPR, but also a Norwegian Patient Records Act breach.					
2020-06-19	Belgium	Unknown	€10,000	Insufficient fulfilment of data subject rights (right of	Art. 5, Art. 6, Art. 12, Art. 15

Date	Nation	Entity fined	Fines [€]	Main legal basis	GDPR Article
				access).	
Controller sent **direct marketing message without consent**. When data subject requested information, controller did not respond.					
2020-06-19	Norway	Aquateknikk AS [Financial services]	€28,000	Insufficient legal basis for data processing.	Art. 5, Art. 6
Controller **requested personal data without legal basis**.					
2020-06-19	Spain	National Police Brigade [Public services & administration]	€6,000	Insufficient legal basis for data processing.	Art. 5, Art. 6
Investigating a firm, controller **made copies of business records, which contained data of third parties**.					
2020-06-18	Romania	Enel Energie [Utilities, energy suppliers]	€4,000	Insufficient measures to secure data processing.	Art. 32
Controller took inadequate measures to prevent **unauthorised disclosure of personal data**. Data subject complained to another customer by email, which triggered this investigation.					
2020-06-16	Spain	Café Bar [Hospitality & leisure]	€2,000	Violation of "Data minimisation" principle.	Art. 5(1)(c), Art. 6, Art. 13, Art. 14
Controller used **CCTV cameras to record third parties without providing sufficiently informational notice**.					
2020-06-16	Sweden	Housing Association [Real estate & property]	€1,900	Violation of "General data processing principles". Insufficient legal basis for data processing.	Art. 5(1) & (2), Art. 6, Art. 13
Controller **used surveillance cameras recording video and sound 24 hours, 7 days a week**. DPSA decided this has additional privacy implications, especially in a residential building, and that in this case there was no justification for sound recording. DPSA ordered housing association to stop the **cameras recording staircases and entrances**, to stop sound recording, and to give more					

Date	Nation	Entity fined	Fines [€]	Main legal basis	GDPR Article
		information on camera surveillance in public notice.			
2020-06-16	Belgium	Unknown	€1,000	Insufficient fulfilment of data subject rights (right to object).	Art. 6(1), Art. 17(1)(c), Art. 21, Art. 31
		Controller **sent the data subject marketing emails, even after subject objected** to the processing of his personal data and requested erasure. Controller did insufficiently cooperate with the DPSA and did not respond to inquiries.			
2020-06-15	Spain	Xfera Moviles S.A. [Utilities, telecoms operators]	€75,000	Insufficient legal basis for data processing.	Art.6
		Controller sent data subject a notice via a debt collection agency **demanding payment, even though data subject had been no customer** of the firm since September 2017. DPSA decided that the processing of plaintiff's personal data took place without consent.			
2020-06-12	Hungary	Digi Távközlési Szolgáltató Kft. ("Digi") [Information technology & services]	€288,000	Insufficient measures to secure data processing.	Art. 5(1)(b) & (e), Art. 32 (1) & (2)
		Controller's database contained **large amount of customer data no longer relevant to actual purpose of collection**, and for which **no retention period had been set**. DPSA ruled that controller had not taken appropriate measures to reduce risks in data management and data security, and had not used encryption mechanisms.			
2020-06-11	Romania	Telekom Romania [Utilities, telecoms operator]	€3,000	Insufficient measures to secure data processing.	Art.32
		Controller's inadequate security measures led to unlawful processing of personal data without verifying accuracy, leading to both **unauthorised disclosure and processing of personal data**.			
2020-06-09	Spain	Consulting de Seguridad e Investigacion Mira Dp Madrid S.L. [Service company]	€5,000	Insufficient legal basis for data processing.	Art. 5, Art. 6

Date	Nation	Entity fined	Fines [€]	Main legal basis	GDPR Article
Controller **sent data subject marketing messages without having obtained prior consent**.					
2020-06-09	Spain	Chenming Ye (Bazar Real) [Retail]	€540	Insufficient legal basis (data collection).	Art. 13, Art. 14
Controller used **CCTV camera in a shop without providing sufficient information in notice**.					
2020-06-09	Spain	Private person (property owner)	€1,000	Violation of "Data minimisation" principle.	Art. 5(1)(c)
Controller ran **CCTV camera which also captured public roads**.					
2020-06-09	Spain	Equifax Iberica, S.L. [Financial services]	€75,000	Insufficient fulfilment of data subject rights (right of access).	Art. 15
Controller received request for erasure of personal data from National Association of Financial Credit Institutions ("ASNEF"). Controller, a credit rating agency, responded that exercise of data subject's access right was excessive due to an earlier request, therefore deletion would not be carried out. DPSA decided this was **breach of right to erasure under GDPR and national data protection laws**.					
2020-06-09	Spain	Xfera Moviles S.A. [Utilities, telecoms operators]	€39,000	Violation of "Integrity and confidentiality" principle.	Art. 5(1)(f)
Controller **sent SMS to plaintiff about non-payment, followed by suspension of service** in relation to another data subject.					
2020-06-09	Spain	Glovoapp23 [Information technology & services]	€25,000	Failure to designate a DPO.	Art. 37
Controller **did not appoint a Data Protection Officer** to process individual rights requests, and firm's website did not contain contact information to whom requests were to be sent.					
2020-06-09	Spain	Telefonica Moviles España, S.A.U. [Utilities,	€40,000	Insufficient legal basis for data	Art. 6

Date	Nation	Entity fined	Fines [€]	Main legal basis	GDPR Article
		telecoms operator]		processing.	
Controller's sales representative **failed to check identity of a client carefully enough** when ordering connection for four telephone lines in his name.					
2020-06-09	Spain	Salad Market SL [Hospitality & leisure]	€3,000	Insufficient legal basis (data collection).	Art. 13, Art. 14
Controller operated **video surveillance on business premises** without sufficient notice. The controller also provided insufficient information on notice about its website's **use of cookies**.					
2020-06-09	Spain	Private person (Attorney)	€2,000	Insufficient measures to secure data processing.	Art. 32
Attorney submitted **documents in the course of legal proceedings which contained personal data of third parties**.					
2020-06-09	Spain	Private person (Property owner)	€2,000	Violation of "Data minimisation" principle.	Art. 5(1)(c)
Controller used **CCTV camera which also captured public roads**.					
2020-06-08	Belgium	Municipal employee [Public services & administration]	€5,000	Insufficient legal basis for data processing.	Art. 5(1)(a) & (b), Art. 6(1)
Controller sent election flyers to a group of employees of same municipal administration **using a list of contact data to which it should have had no access**.					
2020-06-04	Spain	Iberdrola Clientes [Utilities, energy suppliers]	€4,000	Insufficient cooperation with DPSA.	Art. 58
Controller was asked to provide specific information to DPSA about a complaint; however, **controller did not reply within the required time frame**.					
220-06-03	Poland	Private Person (Entrepreneur running a non-public nursery and pre-school)	€1,168	Insufficient cooperation with DPSA.	Art. 31, Art. 58(1)(e)

Date	Nation	Entity fined	Fines [€]	Main legal basis	GDPR Article
	Controller did **not answer requests for further information by DPSA in due time** following a data breach.				
2020-05-29	Belgium	Non-profit organisation [Public services & administration]	€1,000	Insufficient fulfilment of data subject rights (right to object).	Art. 6, Art. 21
	Controller **sent direct marketing messages despite data subjects' objections and requests for erasure.** Controller claimed to rely on "legitimate interest" as legal basis, not on data subjects' express consent. DPSA rejected all claims of legitimate interest outweighing GDPR rights.				
2020-05-29	Finland	Taksi Helsinki Oy [Public services & administration]	€72,000	Violation of "General data processing principles".	Art. 5, Art. 6, Art. 35
	Controller had **not assessed the risks and consequences of processing personal data before introducing surveillance system** that recorded audio and video in its taxis. It **failed to complete a DPIA of processing activities**, too, including processing of camera surveillance data, of location data, of automated decision making, and of profiling as part of a loyalty program.				
2020-05-22	Finland	Posti Group Oyj (postal service) [Public services & administration]	€100,000	Insufficient fulfilment of data subject rights (general).	Art. 12, Art. 13, Art. 14, Art. 15
	Controller sent direct marketing adverts to data subjects who had **requested that their postal data is deleted.** Controller had not informed data subjects of their rights, including right to object to disclosure of data. Data processing also was not transparent. The investigation was conducted by Finnish DPSA on receiving customer complaints.				
2020-05-22	Finland	Kymen Vesi Oy [Utilities, water supplier]	€16,000	Insufficient legal basis (DPIA).	Art. 35
	Controller **failed to carry out DPIA of processing of location data** of employees in a vehicle information system, which led to unlawful processing of personal location data. Data was used for monitoring working hours.				
2020-05-22	Finland	Unnamed company [Unknown]	€12,500	Insufficient legal basis for data processing.	Art. 5, Art. 6
	Firm **demanded of job applicants' and employees' personal data including**				

141

Date	Nation	Entity fined	Fines [€]	Main legal basis	GDPR Article
		religious beliefs, state of health, pregnancy, and family status. This exceeded needs for employment relationship, hence collection of personal data had no valid legal basis. DPSA ordered controller to delete unnecessary data and reprimanded it for deficiencies in documentation.			
2020-05-17	Ireland	Tusla Child and Family Agency [Public services & administration]	€75,000	Insufficient legal basis for data processing.	Art. 5, Art. 6
		In three cases the agency **wrongly disclosed information about children to unauthorised parties.** In one case, contact and location data of mother and child were disclosed to alleged offender, and in other two, data of children in foster care were improperly disclosed to blood relatives/ kin, including to a father in prison. Two other inquiries continue into data breaches involving the same agency. This was the Irish DPA's first fine under GDPR.			
2020-05-15	Denmark	JobTeam A/S DKK [Service company]	€6,700	Insufficient fulfilment of data subject rights (right of access).	Art. 15
		Data controller deleted personal data without legal basis after receiving access request. Data subject complained to DPSA following this incident.			
2020-05-12	Sweden	Health and Medical Board in Region Örebro County [Healthcare]	€11,200	Insufficient legal basis for data processing.	Art. 5, Art. 6, Art. 9, Art. 32(4), Art. 58
		Data controller **mistakenly published on regional website sensitive personal** data about patient admitted to forensic psychiatric clinic. Investigation was conducted by national DPSA following complaint by data subject.			
2020-05-05	Romania	Banca Comercială Română SA [Financial Services]	€5,000	Insufficient measures to secure data processing.	Art. 32
		Bank failed to take adequate technical/organisational measures to **adequately secure information.** Organisation collected and transmitted customers' identification documents via WhatsApp. Investigation was conducted by national DPSA following complaint by data subject.			
2020-04-30	Netherlands	Unknown [Unknown]	€725,000	Insufficient legal basis (processing of special data	Art. 5, Art. 9

Date	Nation	Entity fined	Fines [€]	Main legal basis	GDPR Article
				categories).	
	Organisation requested all staff to scan their fingerprints to create a record of attendance, but proved unable to rely on exceptions to **processing of special category of personal data**, and unable to provide evidence that employees had given their consent to this data processing.				
2020-04-28	Sweden	National Government Service Centre (NGSC) [Public services & administration]	€18,700	Insufficient breach notification to DPSA. Insufficient breach notification to data subject. Insufficient cooperation with DPSA (investigative powers of the DPSA).	Art. 28, Art. 33, Art. 34, Art. 58
	Data controller **failed to notify data subjects of data breach for almost five months** and failed to notify DPSA of data breach for almost three months. Breach was caused by lack of security of IT systems.				
2020-04-28	Belgium	Proximus SA [Utilities, telecoms operator]	€50,000	Failure to designate a DPO.	Art. 31, Art. 37, Art 38(6), Art. 58
	Telecoms operator appointed its head of compliance, audit and risk to be its Data Protection Officer (DPO). Fusion of roles created **conflict of interest** constituting an infringement of Article 38(6). Organisation lacked policy to prevent conflict of interest, so data breach investigations and other incidents could not be handled independently.				
2020-04-03	Poland	Vis Consulting Sp. z o.o. [Service company]	€4,400	Insufficient cooperation with DPSA (investigative powers of the DPSA).	Art. 31, Art. 58(1) (e) & (f)
	Company from telemarketing industry, **made it impossible to conduct inspection**. After prior notification on planned inspection, inspectors found no one at address indicated in National Court Register (KRS), only company leasing office space to data controller (so-called "virtual office"). Company's owner is				

Date	Nation	Entity fined	Fines [€]	Main legal basis	GDPR Article
		subject to criminal liability for this.			
2020-03-25	Romania	SOS Infertility Association [Healthcare]	€2,000	Insufficient cooperation with DPSA (Investigative powers of the DPSA).	Art. 58(1)
		Data controller failed to **provide the DPSA with requested information** within 5 working days, and had processed personal data without sufficient legal basis.			
2020-03-25	Romania	Operatorul Enel Energie Muntenia SA [Utilities, energy supplier]	€3,000	Insufficient measures to secure data processing.	Art. 32
		Company **sent email to client that contained personal data** of a third-party data subject. Company failed to take measures to adequately secure information.			
2020-03-25	Romania	Vodafone Romania SA [Utilities, telecoms operator]	€4,150	Insufficient measures to secure data processing.	Art. 3(1)-(3) & (6), Art. 32
		Company **sent email to customer that contained personal data** of third-party data subject. Company failed to take measures to adequately secure information.			
2020-03-25	Romania	Dante International SA [Service company]	€3,000	Insufficient legal basis for data processing.	Art. 6, Art. 21(3)
		Company sent marketing emails to client who previously **unsubscribed from commercial communications**.			
2020-03-25	Spain	Xfera Moviles SA (Yoigo) [Utilities, telecoms operator]	€5,000	Insufficient cooperation with DPSA (investigative powers of the DPSA).	Art. 58(1)
		Company failed to **provide DPSA with timely requested information** within 5 days. DPSA had requested information about data subject who requested access to personal data.			
2020-03-24	Germany	Company	€50,000	General data protection	Art. 1(28),

Date	Nation	Entity fined	Fines [€]	Main legal basis	GDPR Article
	(Brandenburg)	[Unknown]		processing principles violations. Insufficient data processing agreement.	Art. 9, Art. 12(1), Art. 28(9)
	Lack of transparency for **lack of data processing agreement**.				
2020-03-24	Germany (Brandenburg)	Swimming pool operator [Hospitality & leisure]	€12,000	Insufficient legal basis for data processing.	Art 6(1), Art. 28(9)
	Unlawful **video surveillance of employees and visitors**, and data was processed without data protection officer, or data processing agreement with partner service provider for maintenance of the cameras.				
2020-03-20	Greece	Speech and Special Education Centre – Míchou Dímitra Language and Pedagogical Centre [Education]	€8,000	Insufficient fulfilment of data subject rights.	Art. 15(1) & (3), Art. 58
	The data subject complained that the **requested access to his child's data and to tax information was rejected** by data controller; and data controller violated DPSA order on access to data. A €3000 fine for failure to grant access to the data and a €5000 fine for violating DPSA orders were imposed.				
2020-03-19	Spain	Oliveros Ustrell, S.L. [Services company]	€6,000	Insufficient legal basis for data processing. Violation of "General data processing principles".	Art. 5, Art. 6(1)
	Company forwarded unsigned contract to operator Vodafone. When asked for the contact, data **controller was unable to provide evidence of the contact**. Consequently, personal data of subject was processed with insufficient legal basis. The fine was reduced from €10,000 to €6,000 because of prompt payment.				
2020-03-18	Spain	Telefónica España, S.A.U. [Utilities, telecoms	€30,000	Insufficient cooperation with DPSA (investigative	Art. 58(2)(c)

Date	Nation	Entity fined	Fines [€]	Main legal basis	GDPR Article
		operator]		powers of the DPSA).	
Data controller failed to comply with DPSA decision [TD/00127/2019] to **reply to data subjects' access and erasure requests**.					
2020-03-18	Romania	Vodafone Romania SA [Utilities, telecoms operator]	€3,000	Violation of principles "Data accuracy" and "Integrity and confidentiality".	Art. 5(1)(d), (f) & (2)
Data controller sent reply to **notification to wrong email** address. A fine for insufficient measures to secure data processing was imposed.					
2020-03-18	Greece	Public Power Corporation S.A. [Utilities, energy supplier]	€5,000	Insufficient fulfilment of data subject rights (right of access).	Art. 15(3)
Failure to respond to **data subject's request** for copy of its data within the statutory deadline.					
2020-03-16	Spain	Centro De Estudio Dirigidos Delta, S.L. [Service company]	€5,000	Violation of principle "Integrity and confidentiality".	Art. 5(1)(f)
Organisation **sent message containing personal data (names, ID numbers) to third party** via WhatsApp without data subjects' consent. This is an "integrity and confidentiality" violation.					
2020-03-16	Spain	Private person	€4,000	Insufficient legal basis for data processing. Violation of principle "Data minimisation".	Art. 5(1)(c), Art. 6(1)
A private person **secretly photographed** female bathers. The incident was reported to the DPSA by the local police.					
2020-03-16	Spain	Amalfi Servicios de Restauracion S.L. [Hospitality & leisure]	€6,000	Violation of principle "Data minimisation". Insufficient	Art. 5(1)(c), Art. 13, Art. 14

Date	Nation	Entity fined	Fines [€]	Main legal basis	GDPR Article
				fulfilment of data subject rights (information to be provided). Insufficient legal basis (data collection).	
	Organisation **video-surveilled public space,** committing a "data minimisation" violation as well as insufficient fulfilment of data subject rights, and acting with insufficient legal basis for data collection.				
2020-03-14	Germany (Nordrhein-Westfalen)	Private person (truck driver) (YouTube Channel)	€229	Insufficient legal basis for data processing. Violation of principle "Integrity and confidentiality".	Art. 5(1)(f), Art. 5, Art. 12
	Driver operated **dashcam to record public road traffic** while driving his truck and **uploaded the footage to his YouTube channel.**				
2020-03-13	Croatia	Credit institution established in Zagreb (unnamed) [Financial services]	Unknown (est. below €13,150)	Insufficient fulfilment of data subject rights (right of access).	Art. 15(1) & (3)
	Bank **failed to give customers copies of credit documents** (*e.g.* repayment plan, loan agreement annex, interest rates changes review *etc.*) from May 2018 to April 2019. Bank claimed documents concerned repaid loans and so are not liable to data subjects' right of access. During subjects' complaint proceedings, DPSA ordered bank to fulfil right of access to requested documents. In gauging the fine, DPSA took account esp. of bank's non-compliance with DPSA's order in continuing for a year to violate right of access of over 2,500 customers.				
2020-03-12	Spain	Homeowners Association [Real estate & property]	€2,000	Violation of principle "Data minimisation". Insufficient legal basis (data collection).	Art. 5(1)(c), Art. 13, Art. 14

Date	Nation	Entity fined	Fines [€]	Main legal basis	GDPR Article
		Organisation **video-surveilled public spaces,** violating data minimisation principle. Organisation provided insufficient information to subjects (*e.g.* in data protection notices) about surveillance.			
2020-03-12	Bulgaria	Utility company [Utilities, energy supplier]	€5,113	Unlawful processing of personal data relating to criminal convictions and offences.	Art. 10(1)
		Unlawful data transfer of debt collection data of an alleged debtor.			
2020-03-12	Bulgaria	TOKMET-TE EOOD [Healthcare]	€2,557	Inappropriate technical and organisational measures for data protection by design and by default.	Art 25(1)
		Insufficient measures to implement the principle of **privacy by design**.			
2020-03-12	Bulgaria	LE SOLEI EOOD [Commercial engineering]	€2,557	Inappropriate technical and organisational measures for data protection by design and by default.	Art 25(1)
		Insufficient measures to implement the principle of **privacy by design**.			
2020-03-11	Sweden	Google LLC [Information technology and services]	€7,000,000	Insufficient fulfilment (right of erasure). Violation of principles "Lawfulness, fairness and transparency" and "Purpose limitation".	Art. 5(1)(a) and (b), Art. 6, Art 9, Art. 10. Art. 17
		Organisation **failed to comply with rights of data subjects to have their search results removed** from results list in organisation's search engine. DPSA completed audit in 2017 and instructed organisation to remove search result listings without undue delay. Reviewing organisation again in 2018 after			

Date	Nation	Entity fined	Fines [€]	Main legal basis	GDPR Article
		receiving complaints that some interdicted results were still not removed, DPSA found organisation **non-compliant with legal basis requirement**, as Google had allowed site-owners to re-publish the webpage in question on another web address then displayed in a Google search. This was possible because of Google's practice of informing website owners which search results, specifically which links, have been removed at the request of whom.			
2020-03-10	Denmark	Hørsholm Municipality [Public services & administration]	€6,692	Insufficient measures to secure data processing. Violation of principle "Integrity and confidentiality".	Art. 5(1)(f), Art. 32
		City government employee had his work **computer stolen, which contained personal data of 1,600 city government employees**, including sensitive information and information about social security numbers. DPSA ruled that **hard disk had not been sufficiently protected.**			
2020-03-10	Denmark	Gladsaxe Municipality [Public services & administration]	€13,384	Insufficient measures to secure data processing. Violation of principle "Integrity and confidentiality".	Art. 5(1)(f), Art. 32
		Stolen unencrypted computer contained personal data, incl. sensitive information and personal ID numbers of 20,620 city residents. DPSA ruled that **hard disk had not been sufficiently protected.**			
2020-03-10	Iceland	National Center of Addiction Medicine ('SAA') [Healthcare]	€20,643	Insufficient measures to secure data processing. Violation of principle "Integrity and confidentiality".	Art. 5(1)(f), Art. 32
		DPSA ruled that ex-employee of data controller had received boxes supposed to contain his left personal belongings, but actually contained **patient data, incl. health records of 252 former patients and documents with names of 3,000**			

Date	Nation	Entity fined	Fines [€]	Main legal basis	GDPR Article
		people who had been in rehabilitation for alcohol and drug abuse.			
2020-03-10	Iceland	Breiðholt Upper Secondary School [Education]	€8,945	Insufficient measures to secure data processing. Violation of principle "Integrity and confidentiality".	Art. 5(1)(f), Art. 32
		Teacher **sent email to all students and their parents/guardians (57 people in total)** with attachment **containing data on their well-being, academic performance, and social conditions.** In one instance, the data had to do with an intervention by child protection services.			
2020-03-10	Spain	Gesthotel Activos Balagares [Hospitality & leisure]	€15,000	Violation of principle "Integrity and confidentiality".	Art. 5(1)(f)
		Data subject sent private letter to hotel management and union delegates **containing information about harassment he suffered**, which described his medical condition. Hotel management and union delegates then shared the letter's contents in a meeting with other employees.			
2020-03-09	Poland	Vis Consulting Sp. z o.o. [Service company]	€4,000	Insufficient cooperation with DPSA (investigative powers).	Art. 31, Art. 58(1)(e) and (f)
		Company **prevented DPSA inspection.** On the date the DPSA inspectors were to conduct the inspection, management decided to liquidate the entity.			
2020-03-06	Italy	Liceo Artistico Statale di Napoli (State school of art Naples) [Education]	€4,000	Insufficient legal basis for data processing. Violation of principles "Lawfulness, fairness and transparency" and "Data minimisation".	Art. 5(1)(a) & (c), Art. 6, Art. 9
		High school **unlawfully published health data and other information** on			

Date	Nation	Entity fined	Fines [€]	Main legal basis	GDPR Article
		teachers' performance on Institute website.			
2020-03-06	Italy	Liceo Scientifico Nobel di Torre del Greco (high school) [Education]	€4,000	Insufficient legal basis for data processing. Violation of principles "Lawfulness, fairness and transparency" and "Data minimisation".	Art. 5(1)(a) & (c), Art. 6, Art. 9
		High school **published health data and other information** on over 2000 teachers in teacher-performance rankings published on Institute website.			
2020-03-06	Spain	Private person	€4,000	Violation of principle "Data minimisation".	Art. 5(1)(c)
		Data controller operated hidden **video surveillance cameras that also monitored public spaces.** No data protection notices were provided to the public.			
2020-03-06	Spain	A.A.A Bazar Susana [Retail]	€3,200	Insufficient fulfilment of data subject rights (information to be provided). Violation of principle "Integrity and confidentiality".	Art. 5(1)(f), Art. 13, Art. 14
		Data controller's **privacy notice of video surveillance was insufficient.** The company was also **unable to disclose** the recorded images on request to the data subjects.			
2020-03-05	Poland	School in Gdansk (Danzig) (fine imposed against town of Gdansk) [Education]	€4,650	Insufficient legal basis for data processing. Violation of principle "Data minimisation".	Art. 5(1)(c), Art. 9
		School used **biometric fingerprint scanners to authenticate students** for			

Date	Nation	Entity fined	Fines [€]	Main legal basis	GDPR Article
	payment in the school canteen. Parents gave written consent to data processing, yet DPSA deemed it unlawful, as consent was coerced and not given freely and without a legal basis. 680 children were involved.				
2020-03-04	UK (Note: administrative fine under the DPA 1998. See case study 2.)	Cathay Pacific Ltd. [Transport & logistics]	€590,000 (Note: fine not included in statistics)	Insufficient measures to secure data processing.	DPA 1998: Schedule 1 Part I No 7 DPA, Schedule 1 Part II No 9 DPA, Section 4(4) DPA
	Airline fined £500,000 for failure to secure customers' personal data, leading to exposure of personal details of 9.4 million customers globally, of whom 233,234 were from the EEA and **111,578 from the UK**, when **airline's systems were hacked** via a server connected to internet and malware was installed to harvest data. After receiving 12,000 complaints worldwide, airline hired cybersecurity firm, which reported violation to ICO. Note: The time of the unauthorized access means that ICO must proceed against violation under UK data protection legislation prior to GDPR. Under GDPR the airline would have faced a substantially larger fine.				
2020-03-04	Spain	Vodafone España, S.A.U. [Utilities, telecoms operator]	€60,000	Insufficient legal basis for data processing. Violation of "General data processing principles".	Art. 5, Art. 6(1), Art. 7, Art. 9
	Data subject received **SMS messages from third party indicating activation of a new contract**, because data controller (Vodafone) employee actuated contractual third-party operator on behalf of data subject. Data controller could not demonstrate consent or legitimate interests for this processing of personal data.				
2020-03-04	Hungary	Local government representative [Public services & administration]	€286	Insufficient legal basis for data processing. Violation of principle "Lawfulness,	Art. 5(1)(a)-(c), Art. 6(1), Art. 12, Art. 15,

Date	Nation	Entity fined	Fines [€]	Main legal basis	GDPR Article
				fairness and transparency", "Purpose limitation" and "Data minimisation".	Art. 17
	Local govt representative photographed director of state-owned company tearing off an opposition election poster while accompanied by his child. Local govt representative **uploaded photo to his Facebook page**. Child's image was blurred out, yet the posting hinted she was his daughter. Director had told local representative at the scene that he did not consent to be photographed.				
2020-03-03	The Netherlands	Royal Dutch Tennis Association (Koninklijke Nederlandse Lawn Tennis Bond, "KNLTB") [Hospitality & leisure]	€525,000	Insufficient legal basis for data processing. Violation of principle "Lawfulness, fairness and transparency".	Art. 5(1)(a), Art. 6(1)
	DPSA fined data controller for **selling personal data of over 350,000 of its members**, incl. name, gender and address, to third parties without data subjects' consent. DPSA rejected data controller's claim of legitimate interest in sale of the data even to sponsors of the company.				
2020-03-03	Spain	Solo Embrague (clutch manufacturer) [Automotive industry]	€1,800	Insufficient fulfilment of data subject rights (information to be provided).	Art. 13
	Corporate website **did not provide data protection notice or cookie warning banner** on the website.				
2020-03-03	Spain	Vodafone España, S.A.U. [Utilities, telecoms operator]	€42,000	Insufficient measures to secure data processing. Violation of principle "Integrity and confidentiality".	Art. 5(1)(f), Art. 32
	Company could not evidence measures in place adequate to provide				

Date	Nation	Entity fined	Fines [€]	Main legal basis	GDPR Article
				information security, leading to **unauthorized access to personal data of client**.	
2020-03-03	Spain	Vodafone España, S.A.U. [Utilities, telecoms operator]	€40,000	Insufficient legal basis for data processing. Violation of principle "Lawfulness, fairness and transparency".	Art. 5(1)(a), Art. 6
				Company **sent SMS message to customer's mobile number** confirming a telephone contract with that number, even though data subject **was not a Vodafone customer**. Thus, company processed personal data without data subject's consent or legitimate interests.	
2020-03-03	Spain	Vodafone España, S.A.U. [Utilities, telecoms operator]	€24,000	Insufficient legal basis for data processing. Violation of principle "Purpose limitation".	Art. 5(1)(b), Art. 6
				Company **sent two SMS messages to client's mobile number** informing of a rate change and confirming purchase of new mobile phone, **resulting in the processing personal data without data subject's consent** or legitimate interests.	
2020-03-03	Spain	Vodafone España, S.A.U. [Utilities, telecoms operator]	€48,000	Insufficient measures to secure data processing.	Art. 32
				DPSA identified several deficiencies in information security. One deficiency was that **two people were given the same security access key**.	
2020-02-28	Spain	AEMA Hispánica [Commercial engineering]	€3,600	Violation of principle "Integrity and confidentiality".	Art. 5(1)(f)
				Company **sent one employee's payroll data to another one**, disclosing personal data to a third party without data subject's consent or legitimate interests.	
2020-02-28	Norway	Coop Finnmark SA [Retail]	€36,800	Insufficient legal basis for data	Art. 5(2), Art. 6

Date	Nation	Entity fined	Fines [€]	Main legal basis	GDPR Article
				processing. Violation of accountability principles.	
	Company **distributed video surveillance footage of children under 16** who were allegedly shoplifting, yet no sufficient legal basis this data processing was deemed to exist.				
2020-02-27	Spain	Vodafone España, S.A.U. [Utilities, telecoms operator]	€120,000	Insufficient legal basis for data processing. Violation of principle "Lawfulness, fairness and transparency".	Art. 5(1)(a), Art. 6
	Company could not evidence that the data subject had **given consent to the processing of personal data** for the provision of a telephone contract. DPSA emphasised that the company also unlawfully disclosed the personal data of the data subject to various credit agencies.				
2020-02-26	Spain	XFERA MÓVILES, S.A. [Utilities, telecoms operator]	€36,000	Insufficient legal basis for data processing. Violation of principle "Lawfulness, fairness and transparency".	Art. 5(1)(a), Art. 6
	Company **failed to show legal basis for processing data** for provision of a telecommunications service.				
2020-02-26	Norway	Rælingen Municipality [Public services & administration]	€73,600	Insufficient measures to secure data processing. Violation of principle "Integrity and confidentiality".	Art. 5(1)(f), Art. 32
	Health data of 15 children with physical and mental disabilities was processed in the Showbie digital learning platform, which enables transfer of personal health data between schools and homes. DPSA ruled that no necessary risk				

Date	Nation	Entity fined	Fines [€]	Main legal basis	GDPR Article
		assessments, privacy impact assessments, or tests had been carried out before application was used. Lack of security controls at log-on allowed access to data of other students.			
2020-02-25	Spain	HM Hospitales [Healthcare]	€48,000	Insufficient legal basis for data processing. Violation of principle "Lawfulness, fairness and transparency".	Art. 5(1)(a), Art. 6(1)(a)
		Data subject complained admission to hospital depended on filling in a form containing a checkbox indicating that not ticking it would give consent to the transfer of his data to third parties. DPSA ruled this **opt-out form provided by data controller violated GDPR provisions for obtaining consent.**			
2020-02-25	Spain	Casa Gracio Operation [Hospitality & leisure]	€6,000	Violation of principle "Data minimisation".	Art. 5(1)(c)
		Company used video **cameras on premises of hotel which captured the public roads** outside the hotel without notice to public.			
2020-02-21	Greece	Public Power Corporation S.A. [Utilities, energy supplier]	€5,000	Insufficient fulfilment of data subject rights (right of access).	Art. 15
		Data subjects were given insufficient rights of access to their personal data during processing, not even a copy of which personal data was being processed, on the grounds the data subjects had stated no sufficient reason for their request. DPSA clarified that no reasons need to be given.			
2020-02-21	Spain	Private person	€1,500	Violation of principle "Data minimisation".	Art. 5(1)(c)
		Data controller **illegally surveilled public roads and private property** by video camera.			
2020-02-20	Spain	Electric Renting Group SL [Automotive industry]	€2,500	Violation of principle "Integrity and confidentiality".	Art 5(1)(f)

Date	Nation	Entity fined	Fines [€]	Main legal basis	GDPR Article
Data controller **sent marketing emails to open distribution list where individual emails were disclosed.**					
2020-02-20	Spain	Hotel (no name) [Hospitality & leisure]	€3,600	Violation of principle "Purpose limitation".	Art. 5(1)(b)
Data controller conducted video **surveillance in hotel without providing privacy notice.**					
2020-02-20	Bulgaria	TOKMET-TK EOOD [Healthcare]	€2,560	Insufficient measures to secure data processing.	Art. 25(1), Art. 32
Company processed personal data of subject but failed to adopt technical/organizational measures to secure data. Data controller unlawfully processed personal data nine times in just five months, which caused subject damages.					
2020-02-20	Bulgaria	LE SOLEIL EOOD [Commercial engineering]	€2,560	Insufficient measures to secure data processing.	Art. 25(1), Art. 32, Art. 6
Company **processed personal data without consent and without valid contractual relationship** with data subject. Company processed the data seven times in just 3 months but failed to adopt technical/organizational measures to secure data. DPSA announced regular inspections of data controllers' processing activities, mandating the company do risk analysis for customers and employees; conduct periodic training of its employees; and archive and keep documents containing personal data for limited purposes and time.					
2020-02-18	Spain	Mymoviles Europa 2000, S.L. [Telecoms operator]	€1,500	Insufficient fulfilment of data subject rights (information to be provided).	Art. 13
Company **did not publish privacy statement on its website** and its legal notice was insufficient.					
2020-02-13	Germany (Hamburg)	Facebook Germany GmbH [Information technology & services]	€51,000	Failure to designate DPO.	Art. 37(7)
Facebook Ireland **appointed Group DPO for all companies in EU without**					

Date	Nation	Entity fined	Fines [€]	Main legal basis	GDPR Article
		notifying DPSA Hamburg, the competent supervisory authority for Facebook Germany GmbH. DPSA calculated fine based on turnover of German branch (€35 million), and on considerations that Facebook rectified omission to notify and merely acted negligently without violating duty to appoint a DPO itself.			
2020-02-13	Italy	Comune di Urago [Public services & administration]	€4,000	Insufficient legal basis for data processing. Violation of principle ""Lawfulness, fairness and transparency" and "Data minimisation".	Art. 5(1)(a) and (c), Art. 6
		Local council's **website published information** containing personal data, including health information.			
2020-02-11	Romania	Vodafone Romania SA [Utilities, telecoms operator]	€3,000	Insufficient measures to secure data processing. Violation of principle "Integrity and confidentiality".	Art. 5(1)(f), Art. 32
		Data controller **incorrectly processed personal data to process a complaint**, which was then sent to wrong email address. DPSA ruled insufficient security measures were in place to prevent such errors.			
2020-02-11	Spain	Colegio Arenales Carabanchel (School) [Education]	€3,000	Insufficient legal basis for data processing.	Art. 6
		School **transferred pictures and personal data to third parties** who published them without consent of parents.			
2020-02-10	Spain	Vodafone España, S.A.U. [Utilities, telecoms operator]	€42,000	Insufficient measures to secure data processing. Violation of principle "Integrity and	Art. 5(1)(f), Art. 32

Date	Nation	Entity fined	Fines [€]	Main legal basis	GDPR Article
				confidentiality.	
	Complainant obtained **access to third-party data in his personal profile**, which the data subject reported. In calculating fine, DPSA concluded that data controller had acted negligently but unintentionally.				
2020-02-07	Spain	Iberdrola Clientes [Utilities, energy supplier]	€80,000	Insufficient legal basis for data processing. Violation of principle "Lawfulness, fairness and transparency".	Art. 6, Art. 5(1)(a)
	Data controller **terminated data subject's contract without consent** and made three new contracts with data subject, processed his personal data unlawfully, and transferred the personal data to a third party without legal basis. Note: Additional €50,000 fine for breach of prior regulation was imposed (Art. 6.1 LOPD 15/1999).				
2020-02-07	Spain	Xfera Moviles S.A. [Utilities, telecoms operator]	€30,000	Insufficient measures to secure data processing. Violation of principle "Integrity and confidentiality".	Art. 5(1)(f), Art. 32
	Third party had **access to name, telephone number, and address of another customer**.				
2020-02-06	Italy	Reti Televisive Italiane (R.T.I.) s.p.a. [Media & entertainment]	€20,000	Insufficient legal basis for data processing. Violation of principle "Lawfulness, fairness and transparent" violations.	Art. 5(1)(a), Art. 6, Art. 85
	Television station broadcast documentary on prostitution in Switzerland **without sufficiently anonymising** persons interviewed. The journalist did interview in a place where interviewee may be recognised by her voice and				

Date	Nation	Entity fined	Fines [€]	Main legal basis	GDPR Article
		broadcast too many personal details from interview.			
2020-02-06	Spain	Zhang Bordeta 2006, S.L. [Hospitality & leisure]	€6,000	Infringement of provisions leading to administrative fines.	Art. 83.2(a) & (b)
		Data controller was fined for **disproportionate monitoring of public roads via CCTV**. Organisation recorded images of its shop and restaurant with images of public street, which was outside permitted surveillance scope. Public was not sufficiently noticed.			
2020-02-06	Spain	Vodafone España, S.A.U. [Utilities, telecoms operator]	€50,000	Violation of principle "Integrity and confidentiality".	Art. 5(1)(f)
		Data controller **sent invoices revealing personal data to a third party**.			
2020-02-04	Spain	Cafetería Nagasaki [Hospitality & leisure]	€1,500	Insufficient legal basis for data processing. Violation of "General data processing principles".	Art. 5(1)(c), Art. 6
		Company placed its **surveillance cameras such that it monitored public space** outside its premises, capturing the images of passers-by disproportionately.			
2020-02-03	Spain	Xfera Móviles S.A., (telecoms operator of the Group Grupo MásMóvil)	€60,000	Insufficient legal basis for data processing. Violation of "General data processing principles".	Art. 5(1), Art. 6 (1)
		Data controller **unlawfully processed data**, including bank details, addresses, and names of data subjects.			
2020-02-03	Spain	Vodafone España, S.A.U. [Utilities, telecoms operator]	€75,000	Insufficient legal basis for data processing. Violation of principle	Art. 5(1)(a), Art. 6

Date	Nation	Entity fined	Fines [€]	Main legal basis	GDPR Article
				"Lawfulness, fairness and transparency".	
	Company signed a contract for **transfer of a telephone subscription with a third party without the data subject's knowledge or consent.** Data subject received email from the third party for a purchase made by data subject which had no legal basis.				
2020-02-03	Spain	Vodafone España, S.A.U. [Utilities, telecoms operator]	€60,000	Insufficient legal basis for data processing. Violation of "General data processing principles".	Art. 5, Art. 6
	Data subject received email from company **billing him for telephone line the data subject never requested.** This led to his personal data being collected and processed without his consent, incorporating subject's personal data into company information systems without consent. The fine of €100,000 was reduced to €60,000 due to a prompt payment.				
2020-02-03	Spain	Iberia Lineas Aereas de España, S.A. Operadora Unipersonal [Transport & logistics]	€20,000	Insufficient legal basis for data processing. Violation of "General data processing principles".	Art. 5, Art. 6, Art. 21
	Data subject **continued to receive marketing emails despite withdrawal of his consent** and his demand for erasure of personal data. Data subject was told his request had been executed.				
2020-02-03	Spain	Banco Bilbao Vizcaya Argentaria S.L. [Financial services]	€4,800	Insufficient legal basis for data processing. Violation of principle "General data processing principles".	Art. 5, Art. 6, Art. 21
	Data controller **repeatedly sent advertising messages** to data subject over subject's objections to processing of his data.				

Date	Nation	Entity fined	Fines [€]	Main legal basis	GDPR Article
2020-02-03	Spain	Queseria Artesenal Ameco S.L. [Retail]	€5,000	Insufficient legal basis for data processing. Violation of principle "Lawfulness, fairness and transparency".	Art. 5(1)(a), Art. 6(1)
		Company **processed personal data of customers without required consent.**			
2020-02-01	Italy	Tim S.p.A. [Utilities, telecoms operator]	€27,802,496	Insufficient legal basis for data processing. Violation of principles "Lawfulness, fairness and transparency", "Purpose limitation" and "Storage limitation".	Art. 5(1)(a), (b) & (e), Art. 6, Art. 17, Art. 21, Art. 32
		DPSA received 100s of complaints of **aggressive promotional campaigns** from January 2017 to start of 2019. Unsolicited commercial communications and "cold calls" were made **without data subjects' consent** despite their registering on the "do not call register". Further complaints pointed to failure to respond to data subjects' request for GDPR rights, esp. access to their data and objection to processing for promotional purposes.			
		The fine was calculated for **lack of consent for marketing activities** (telemarketing and cold calling), invalid consent collected by TIM apps, **lack of sufficient security measures** to protect personal data (including incorrect exchange of blacklists with call centres), **lack of clear data retention periods**. DPSA imposed 20 corrective measures on TIM, prohibiting use of personal data from those who refused promotional calls from call centres.			
2020-01-29	Spain	Grupo Valsor Y Losan, S.L. [Real estate & property]	€2,500	Violation of principle "Integrity and confidentiality".	Art. 5(1)(f)
		Data controller **disclosed personal data to third party** in a property purchase agreement, breaching integrity and confidentiality of personal data.			

Date	Nation	Entity fined	Fines [€]	Main legal basis	GDPR Article
2020-01-27	Cyprus	LGS Handling Ltd, Louis Travel Ltd, and Louis Aviation Ltd (Louis Group of Companies) [Transport & logistics]	€82,000	Insufficient legal basis for data processing.	Art. 6(1)(f), Art. 9
	Company's HR used calculation model (Bradford factor) to measure worker absenteeism, entailing **profiling, classifying and monitoring sick leave of employees**. This was unlawful processing of personal data. Company incurred 3 fines of €70,000, €10,000 and €2,000 were imposed.				
2020-01-24	Spain	Vodafone España, S.A.U. [Utilities, telecoms operator]	€50,000	Violation of principle "Integrity and confidentiality".	Art. 5(1)(f)
	Company **sent invoices to his neighbour** containing data subject's personal data, including name, identity card, and address.				
2020-01-24	Spain	Automoción X.X.X. S.A. [Automotive industry]	€800	Insufficient legal basis for data processing. Violation of principle "Lawfulness, fairness and transparency".	Art. 5(1)(a), Art. 6
	Company owner's relative created **fake profile of a female colleague on erotic web-portal** containing her contact details, a photo and information of sexual nature. Data subject received phone calls from unwanted suitors. After relative was found to have a personality disorder, the fine was reduced from €1000 to €800.				
2020-01-23	Italy	Azienda Ospedaliero Universitaria Integrata di Verona (Hospital) [Healthcare]	€30,000	Insufficient measures to secure data processing. Violation of principle "Integrity and confidentiality".	Art. 5(1)(f), Art. 32

Date	Nation	Entity fined	Fines [€]	Main legal basis	GDPR Article
		Health data was accessed unauthorised by a trainee and a radiologist who viewed colleagues' health data. Technical/organisational measures taken by hospital to secure data were insufficient. Breach was avoidable if hospital simply followed guidelines for health records issued by DPSA in 2015, which stipulate that access is restricted to personnel involved in patient care.			
2020-01-23	Italy	Sapienza Università di Roma [Education]	€30,000	Insufficient measures to secure data processing. Violation of principle "Integrity and confidentiality".	Art. 5(1)(f), Art. 32
		Data controller **published online identifying data of two people who had reported illegal behaviour** to university. Due to lack of adequate technical access control measures within the whistleblowing management system this information had not restricting access to authorized personnel.			
2020-01-17	Italy	Eni Gas e Luce (Egl) [Utilities, energy supplier]	€8,500,000	Insufficient legal basis for data processing. Violation of principles "Lawfulness, fairness and transparency" "Data minimisation" and "Storage limitation".	Art. 5(1)(a), (c) & (e), Art. 6, Art. 17, Art. 21
		Data controller unlawfully processed personal data for **advertising activities and activation of unsolicited contracts.** The first fine of €8.5 million was for **unlawful processing in connection with telemarketing and telesales activities.** Promotional calls were made without consent of contactee and despite refusal to receive promotional calls, which did not trigger special procedures for checking public opt-out register. Company neglected technical/ organisational measures to protect information provided by users; data was **processed beyond data retention limits**; and data on potential customers was collected from list providers who had no consent for disclosure.			
2020-01-17	Italy	Eni Gas e Luce (Egl) [Utilities, energy supplier]	€3,000,000	Insufficient legal basis for data processing.	Art. 5(1)(a), Art. 6

Date	Nation	Entity fined	Fines [€]	Main legal basis	GDPR Article
				Violation of principle "Lawfulness, fairness and transparency".	
Data controller unlawfully processed personal data for advertising activities and activation of unsolicited contracts. This second fine of €3 million was for pushing **unsolicited contracts for the supply of electricity and gas under "market economy" conditions**. Customers complained to DPSA that they did not learn of new contract until receiving termination notice from contract with previous supplier or the first invoices. In some cases, complaints reported false information in the contracts and forged signatures.					
2020-01-16	Hungary	Healthcare institution [Healthcare]	€1,500	Insufficient legal basis for data processing. Violation of principle "Storage limitation".	Art. 6, Art. 5(1)(e)
Data controller failed to **delete private emails of former employees**, continued to process data without legal basis.					
2020-01-15	Italy	Community of Francavilla Fontana [Public services & administration]	€10,000	Insufficient legal basis for data processing. Violation of principle "Data minimisation".	Art. 5(1)(c), Art. 6
Data controller **website published information on court trial**, incl. subject's personal health and banking data. The document stayed on the website for two months.					
2020-01-14	Spain	Zhang Bordeta 2006, S.L. [Hospitality & leisure]	€3,600	Violation of principle "Data minimisation".	Art. 5(1)(c)
Company owner installed **video surveillance system which imaged the footpath,** a public space.					
2020-1-14	Hungary	Collection service provider [Service company]	€4,487	Insufficient legal basis for data processing.	Art. 6(1)(f), Art. 17, Art. 21

Date	Nation	Entity fined	Fines [€]	Main legal basis	GDPR Article
				Insufficient fulfilment of data subject rights (right of erasure and right to object).	
	Data controller **failed to erase personal data** as requested by subject; stored data without legal basis.				
2020-01-14	Greece	Allseas Marine S.A. (maritime services) [Transport & logistics]	€15,000	Violation of principle "Lawfulness, fairness and transparency".	Art. 5(1)(a) & (2), Art. 24(1), Art. 32
	Data controller processed extensive employee data through **workplace video surveillance system**. Introduction of such a system was unlawful and data controller insufficiently informed its employees about it.				
2020-01-13	Cyprus	Cyprus Police [Public services & administration]	€9,000	Insufficient measures to secure data processing.	Art. 32(1)(b)
	Police gave third-party access to personal data and data controller **failed to take adequate measures to secure the data**, despite warnings from DPSA.				
2020-01-13	Cyprus	Social Insurance Services of the Ministry of Labor, Welfare and Social Insurance [Public services & administration]	€9,000	Insufficient measures to secure data processing.	Art. 32
	Data controller gave third-party access to personal data and data controller **failed to take sufficient measures to secure data**, despite warnings from DPSA.				
2020-01-13	Cyprus	eShop for Sports (M.L. PRO.FIT SOLUTIONS LTD) [Retail]	€1,000	Insufficient legal basis for data processing.	Art. 6
	Data controller sent **SMS marketing messages without consent**. No appropriate measures were taken to enable subjects to block messages or opt out				
2020-01-13	Cyprus	AG QUICKSPA Limited	€1,200	Insufficient measures to	Art. 5(1)(f),

Date	Nation	Entity fined	Fines [€]	Main legal basis	GDPR Article
		[Healthcare]		secure data processing. Violation of principle "Integrity and confidentiality".	Art. 32
		Data controller **sent marketing SMSs despite opt-out** by data subject, due to lack of technical/organisational measures.			
2020-01-13	Spain	Vodafone España, S.A.U. [Utilities, telecoms operator]	€75,000	Insufficient legal basis for data processing. Violation of "General data processing principles".	Art. 5, Art. 6
		Data subject continued to **receive invoices without either a current contract** or payment overdue from previous contract. Data controller admitted to incorrect mailings due to technical error.			
2020-01-09	Spain	Vodafone España, S.A.U. and Vodafone Ono, S.A.U. [Utilities, telecoms operator]	€21,000	Insufficient cooperation with DPSA (investigative powers).	Art. 58(1)(a)
		DPSA imposed seven fines on data controller for **failing to provide information to DPSA** by the required deadline.			
2020-01-07	Spain	Vodafone España, S.A.U. [Utilities, telecoms operator]	€44,000	Violation of principle "Integrity and confidentiality".	Art. 5 (1)(f)
		Data controller **sent contract with personal data to wrong recipient**, which included applicant's name, address, and telephone number.			
2020-01-07	Spain	EDP España S.A.U. [Utilities, energy supplier]	€75,000	Insufficient legal basis for data processing.	Art. 6(1)(b)
		Data controller processed personal data (full name, tax number, address, and mobile phone number) **without** data subject's **consent**.			

Date	Nation	Entity fined	Fines [€]	Main legal basis	GDPR Article
2020-01-07	Spain	EDP Comercializadora, S.A. [Utilities, energy supplier]	€75,000	Insufficient legal basis for data processing.	Art. 6
	Data controller processed personal data in a gas **contract without consent of applicant.** Applicant received an invoice for contract he did not sign. Company claimed he was party to contract with a third party which has a supply contract with company. DPSA ruled company must prove applicant agreed to contract with third party as well.				
2020-01-07	Spain	Asociación de Médicos Demócratas [Public services & administration]	€10,000	Insufficient legal basis for data processing.	Art. 6(1)
	Data controller processed personal data of members, despite warning by DPSA that **processing was without** data subjects' **consent.** In the DPSA's decision 17 email communications were cited.				
2020-01-06	Bulgaria	Utility Company [Unknown Utilities company]	€5,110	Insufficient legal basis for data processing.	Art. 6(1)
	Data controller **processed personal data** of data subject without legal basis, then used it to bring enforcement case against subject for unpaid debts. Data subject suffered damages when bailiff seized his salary.				
YEAR 2019					
2019-12-29	Romania	Royal President S.R.L. [Service company]	€2,500	Insufficient fulfilment of data subject rights (right of access). Violation of principle "Integrity and confidentiality".	Art. 15, Art. 6, Art. 32(1)(b), Art. 5(1)(f)
	Data controller **refused request for access to personal data** and **disclosed personal data without consent** of subjects. Company took insufficient technical/organisational measures to **ensure security of data.** The sanctions were applied following a complaint alleging that the data controller refused to handle a request for exercising the right of access, as well as the fact that it disclosed personal data without the consent of the data subject.				

Date	Nation	Entity fined	Fines [€]	Main legal basis	GDPR Article
2019-12-29	Spain	Audax Renovables S.A. [Utilities, energy suppliers]	€24,000	Insufficient legal basis for data processing.	Art. 6
	Data controller **disclosed personal data to third party**.				
2019-12-19	Greece	Aegean Marine Petroleum Network Inc. [Utilities, energy supplier]	€150,000	Insufficient measures to secure data processing. Violation of principle "Lawfulness, fairness and transparency".	Art. 5(1)(a) & (d), Art. 6, Art. 32
	Third parties accessed data controller's servers containing personal data and copied the contents. Data controller failed to take technical measures to **secure the processing of large amounts of data** and to keep relevant software separate from personal data stored on servers, and failed to inform data subjects of the processing of their data.				
2019-12-18	Romania	Telekom Romania Mobile Communications SA [Utilities, telecoms operator]	€2,000	Insufficient measures to secure data processing. Violation of principle "Data accuracy".	Art. 32, Art. 5(1)(d)
	Company failed to ensure accuracy in processing personal data, leading to **disclosure of subject's personal data to third party**. Sanctions resulted from complainant claiming to have received at his home address invoices addressed to third party.				
2019-12-18	Hungary	Employer [Private person]	€1,512	Insufficient legal basis for data processing. Violation of principle "Storage limitation".	Art. 6(1)(b), Art. 88(1), Art. 5(1)(e)
	The employer continued to **store and archive email account of a former employee without legal basis.**				
2019-12-18	Norway	Nursing Home Agency,	€49,300	Insufficient measures to	Art. 32

Date	Nation	Entity fined	Fines [€]	Main legal basis	GDPR Article
		Municipality of Oslo [Healthcare]		secure data processing.	
	Data controller **stored patient data** from city's nursing homes and health centres **outside electronic health record system** from 2007 to November 2018. City of Oslo sent data breach notification to the DPSA in November 2018.				
2019-12-17	UK	Doorstep Dispensaree Ltd. (Pharmacy) [Healthcare]	€320,000	Insufficient measures to secure data processing.	Art. 5(1)(f), Art. 13, Art. 14, Art. 24(1), Art. 32
	Data controller stored 500,000 documents (from Jan 2016 to June 2018) containing names, addresses, birthdates, NHS numbers and **medical and prescription information in unsealed containers** on site and failed to protect data from weather, resulting in water damage to documentation, which was not secure and not marked as confidential waste The ICO launched its investigation after it was alerted to the insecurely stored documents by the Medicines and Healthcare Products Regulatory Agency, which was carrying out its own separate enquiry into the pharmacy.				
2019-12-17	Belgium	Nursing Care Organisation [Healthcare]	€2,000	Insufficient fulfilment of data subject rights (general, rights of access and erasure).	Art. 12, Art. 15, Art. 17
	Company failed to act on requests from data subject to **access his data** and have his **data erased**.				
2019-12-17	Belgium	Website provider of legal news [Service company]	€15,000	Insufficient fulfilment of data subject rights (general and information to be provided).	Art. 6, Art. 12, Art. 13
	Data controller published **privacy statement only in English** although provider also had Dutch- and French-speaking clients. **Privacy statement was not easily accessible** and did not mention the GDPR legal basis for data processing. DPSA ruled, with reference to the CJEU ruling on Planet 49, that consent was required for use of Google Analytics Cookies.				
2019-12-17	Belgium	Nursing organisation	€2,000	Insufficient fulfilment of	Art. 12(2) &

Date	Nation	Entity fined	Fines [€]	Main legal basis	GDPR Article
		[Healthcare]		data subject rights (general, right of access and right of erasure).	(4), Art. 15, Art. 17
		Data controller failed to respond to **data subject's access and erasure requests**.			
2019-12-16	Sweden	Nusvar AB (operator of website Mrkoll.se) [Service company]	€35,000	Insufficient legal basis for data processing. Violation of principle "Data minimisation".	Art. 5(1)(c), Art. 6, Art 10
		Data controller providing credit information on all Swedes over 16 years of age **published extensive, inadequate and irrelevant information** on credit reports from Dec 2018 to April 2019, incl. data on court cases, non-payment records and convictions.			
2019-12-16	Romania	Globus Score SRL (Advertising agency) [Service company]	€2,000	Insufficient cooperation with DPSA (investigative powers).	Art. 58(1)(a) & (e), Art 83(5)
		Company **failed to comply with measures ordered by DPSA**. Corrective measure was imposed on data controller to transmit to DPSA, in writing, all requested information, within 5 working days from communication of the report of the investigation.			
2019-12-16	Romania	SC Enel Energie S.A. (Electricity distributor) [Utilities, energy supplier]	€6,000	Insufficient legal basis for data processing. Violation of principle "Data accuracy".	Art. 5(1)(d) & (2), Art. 6, Art. 7(1), Art. 21(1)
		Data controller unlawfully processed subject's personal data and was unable to prove subject's **consent to send email notifications**. Operator took insufficient measures to prevent transmission of notifications, despite data subject **repeatedly invoking his right to object**. Data controller received two fines, each amounting to 14,334.30 lei, the equivalent of €3,000.			
2019-12-13	Romania	Entirely Shipping & Trading S.R.L. [Transport & logistics]	€5,000	Insufficient legal basis (consent). Infringement of	Art. 5(1)(c), Art. 6, Art. 7

Date	Nation	Entity fined	Fines [€]	Main legal basis	GDPR Article
				principle "data minimisation".	
	Company processed excessive personal data of employees through **video cameras installed in offices and in** changing rooms.				
2019-12-13	Romania	Entirely Shipping & Trading S.R.L. [Transport & logistics]	€5,000	Insufficient legal basis (consent). Violation of principle "Data minimization.	Art. 5 (1)(c), Art. 6, Art. 7, Art. 9
	Data controller **processed biometric data (fingerprints) of employees for access to certain rooms**; when less intrusive means respecting privacy of data subjects were available; a violation of "data minimisation" principle.				
2019-12-11	Hungary	Healthcare institution [Healthcare]	€1,500	Insufficient legal basis for data processing.	Art. 6
	Data controller failed to delete former employee's private emails. It therefore processed personal data without legal basis and **exceeding data retention periods**.				
2019-12-11	Romania	Unknown company	€1,430	Insufficient legal basis for data processing. Violation of "General data processing principles".	Art. 5, Art. 6, Art. 13, Art. 24, Art. 25
	Company **restored mailbox of director who had left company** a year before and found email containing a work-related document. Director had no warning his former inbox would be reactivated and could not copy/delete his personal data (passwords, financial information). DPSA ruled employee or his representative must be present when employee's data is being accessed, even after employment is terminated. Employees may request a copy of or the deletion of their personal data. Employers must record the access with minutes and photos; if employee cannot be present and independent witnesses are needed. Employers must adopt internal policies on archiving and use of IT assets and email accounts, including procedural rules such as inspection step and authorised officers' involvement.				
2019-12-10	Spain	Megastar SL [Transport & logistics]	€1,600	Violation of principle "Data minimisation".	Art. 5(1)(c), Art. 13

Date	Nation	Entity fined	Fines [€]	Main legal basis	GDPR Article
		Data controller operated **video surveillance system** with an observation angle **that covered public traffic area.** No data protection notices was put up.			
2019-12-10	Spain	Shop Macoyn, S.L. (YBL ABOGADOS) [Retail]	€5,000	Insufficient measures to secure data processing. Violation of principle "Integrity and confidentiality".	Art. 5(1)(f), Art. 32
		Data controller sent marketing emails to recipients that displayed **email addresses of some recipients were visible to other recipients,** when recipient addresses were entered as CC and not as BCC.			
2019-12-10	Romania	Hora Credit IFN SA [Financial services]	€14,000	Insufficient measures to secure data processing. Violation of principle "Lawfulness, fairness and transparency".	Art. 5(1)(a), Art. 25, Art. 32, Art. 33
		Data controller **sent documents containing personal data of third party to wrong email address belonging to data subject.** DPSA ruled organisation processed data without sufficient measures **for verifying and validating accuracy of data collected.** Operator took insufficient security measures with personal data to avoid unauthorized access to personal data by third parties. Data controller **failed to notify DPSA of Art. 33 security incident** within 72 hours from the time it became aware of it. The fines were divided between the violations: €3000, €10000 and €1000.			
2019-12-09	Germany (BfDI)	1&1 Telecom GmbH [Utilities, telecoms operator]	€9,550,000	Insufficient measures to secure data processing.	Art. 32
		Company's customer service department allowed callers to obtain extensive personal data on customers simply by entering a customer name and birthdate. DPSA saw in this authentication procedure a violation of Article 32 DSGVO, which obligates companies to take sufficient technical/ organisational measures to protect processing of personal data. Company's cooperation persuaded DPSA to set fines at the lower end of the scale.			
2019-12-09	Germany	Rapidata GmbH	€10,000	Failure to	Art. 37

Date	Nation	Entity fined	Fines [€]	Main legal basis	GDPR Article
	(BfDI)	[Service company]		designate a DPO.	

Company did not comply with its legal obligation to **appoint a data protection officer**, despite repeated requests by the national DPSA (BfDI).

| 2019-12-04 | Romania | SC CNTAR TAROM SA [Transport & logistics] | €20,000 | Insufficient measures to secure data processing. | Art. 32(1), (2) & (4) |

Company failed to take sufficient measures to secure personal data processing to the GDPR standard, allowing employee gain **unauthorized access to booking application** and to photograph personal data of 22 data subjects and **disclose the list on the Internet**.

| 2019-12-03 | Germany (Rheinland-Pfalz) | Hospital [Healthcare] | €105,000 | Violation of "General data processing principles". | Art. 5 |

Company commingled at admission personal data of two patients, resulting in **incorrect invoicing which revealed technical/organisational insufficiency** in hospital's patient management.

| 2019-12-03 | Spain | Cerrajeria Verin S.L. [Retail] | €1,500 | Insufficient fulfilment of data subject rights (information to be provided). | Art. 13 |

Company collected personal data **without a privacy policy** with accurate information on data processing activities.

| 2019-12-03 | Spain | Linea Directa Aseguradora S.A. [Financial services] | €5,000 | Insufficient legal basis for data processing. Insufficient legal basis (consent). | Art. 6(1)(a), Art. 7, Art. 21 |

Company sent advertising emails for its financial services platform **without the required consent**. Note: This case is currently under review.

| 2019-12-03 | Germany (Rheinland-Pfalz) | University Medical Center of Johannes Gutenberg-university Mainz | €105,000 | Insufficient legal basis for data processing. | Art. 6, Art. 9 |

Date	Nation	Entity fined	Fines [€]	Main legal basis	GDPR Article
		[Education]			
DPSA identified **insufficient technical/organisational measures in patient management**, resulting in incorrect invoicing.					
2019-12-02	Romania	Nicola Medical Team 17 SRL [Healthcare]	€2,000	Insufficient cooperation with DPSA (investigative powers).	Art. 58(1)(a) & (e)
Company failed to comply with **measures ordered by DPSA**. The information provided was insufficient and tardy.					
2019-11-28	Belgium	Mayor (unknown town) [Public services & administration]	€5,000	Insufficient legal basis for data processing. Violation of principle "Purpose limitation".	Art. 6, Art. 5(1)(b)
Data controller **sent election mailings without sufficient legal basis**, in that **the** email addresses used were not collected for this specific purpose.					
2019-11-28	Belgium	City Council (Municipal alderman) [Public services & administration]	€5,000	Insufficient legal basis for data processing. Violation of principle "Purpose limitation".	Art. 5(1)(b) Art. 6(4)
Data controller **sent election mailings** without sufficient legal basis, in that the email addresses used were not collected for this specific purpose.					
2019-11-28	Romania	ING Bank N.V. [Financial services]	€80,000	Insufficient measures to secure data processing. Violation of principle "Integrity and confidentiality".	Art. 5(1)(f), Art. 25(1) Art. 32(1)(d)
Company failed to take sufficient **technical/organisational measures** to secure **automated data processing** during settlement process of bankcard transactions. 25,525 data subjects were damaged by double transactions					

Date	Nation	Entity fined	Fines [€]	Main legal basis	GDPR Article
		executed between 8 and 10 October 2018.			
2019-11-28	Spain	Curenergía Comercializador de último recurso [Utilities, energy supplier]	€75,000	Insufficient legal basis for data processing.	Art. 6(1)(a)
		Data controller **entered personal data of former customer** (full name, VAT identification number, address) into an electricity supply contract.			
2019-11-28	Spain	IKEA Ibérica S.A.U. [Retail]	€10,000	Insufficient legal basis for data processing.	Art. 4, Art. 6(1), Art. 7
		Company installed cookies on end users' terminal devices without prior consent of data subjects.			
2019-11-26	Romania	Modern Barber [Retail]	€3,000	Insufficient cooperation with DPSA (investigative powers).	Art. 58(1)(a) & (e)
		Company **failed to comply with measures ordered** by DPSA. Information requested was insufficient and tardy.			
2019-11-26	Hungary	Hungarian military hospital [Healthcare]	€7,450	Insufficient breach notification to DPSA.	Art. 24(a) & (2), Art. 32, Art. 33(1)
		Data controller **failed to meet 72-hour reporting deadline**, a data breach due to insufficient technical/organisational measures.			
2019-11-26	Spain	Corporación de Radio y Television Española SA SME [Media & entertainment]	€60,000	Insufficient measures to secure data processing.	Art. 32
		Data controller **disclosed personal data stored on USB stick** due to insufficient technical/organisational measures.			
2019-11-26	Spain	Xfera Moviles SA [Utilities, telecoms operator]	€60,000	Insufficient measures to secure data processing.	Art. 32

Date	Nation	Entity fined	Fines [€]	Main legal basis	GDPR Article
Data controller set up **insufficient technical/organisational measures** esp. for managing complaints.					
2019-11-26	Spain	Viaqua Xestión Integral Aguas de Galicia [Utilities, water supplier]	€60,000	Insufficient legal basis for data processing.	Art. 6
Company processed personal data of customer for **third party without data subject's consent**.					
2019-11-25	Romania	Courier Service Company [Transport & logistics]	€11,000	Insufficient measures to secure data processing.	Art. 32
Data controller failed to take sufficient technical/ organisational measures, causing loss of and **unauthorised access to personal data** (name, bank card number, CVV code, address, personal identification number, serial and identity card number, bank account number, authorised credit limit) of **1,100 data subjects**.					
2019-11-25	Romania	FAN Courier Express SRL [Transport & logistics]	€11,000	Insufficient measures to secure data processing. Violation of principle "Integrity and confidentiality".	Art. 5(1)(f), Art 32(1) & (2)
Data controller took **insufficient technical/organisational measures to protect customer data,** in particular, by the destruction, loss, modification, unauthorized disclosure or unauthorized access to the personal data transmitted. This led to unauthorized disclosure/access of the personal data of about 1100 subjects.					
2019-11-22	Romania	BNP Paribas Personal Finance S.A. [Financial services]	€2,000	Insufficient fulfilment of data subject rights (right of erasure).	Art. 12(3), Art. 17
Company failed to respond to **request for erasure** within the time limit.					
2019-11-21	France	Futura Internationale [Real estate & property]	€500,000	Insufficient fulfilment of data subject rights	Art. 5(1)(c), Art. 6, Art. 13,

Date	Nation	Entity fined	Fines [€]	Main legal basis	GDPR Article
				(information to be provided and right to object). Insufficient legal basis (data collection). Violation of principle "Data minimisation".	Art. 14, Art. 21
Company made **cold calls despite complaints** and despite having declared directly to the caller and by post that this was not wanted. The DPSA's on-site investigation revealed among other findings that the company had received several letters objecting to cold calling, that it had **stored excessive information about customers and their health** and that the company failed to informed individuals about the processing of their personal data or the **recording of telephone conversations**.					
2019-11-20	Romania	Homeowners Association [Real estate & property]	€500	Insufficient measures to secure data processing.	Art. 13, Art. 32
Data controller used **video surveillance systems** without proper information and sufficient security measures against persons having access to the system.					
2019-11-20	Spain	Telefónica Móviles España, S.A.U. [Utilities, telecoms operator]	€30,000	Violation of principle "Data accuracy".	Art. 5(1)(d)
Data controller **sent invoices that included personal data to wrong customers**.					
2019-11-19	Spain	Corporación de Radio y Televisión Española S.A. [Media & entertainment]	€60,000	Insufficient measures to secure data processing.	Art. 32
Company and trade union reported security breach to DPSA after **six unencrypted USB sticks containing personal data were lost**. The data loss damaged 11,000 data subjects and included identification and employment data, and data about criminal convictions and health.					
2019-11-19	Spain	Xfera Moviles S.A. [Utilities, telecoms	€60,000	Insufficient measures to secure data	Art. 32

Date	Nation	Entity fined	Fines [€]	Main legal basis	GDPR Article
		operator]		processing.	
	Company sent SMS to data subject which was intended for a third party, allowing him to **access account and personal data** of third party online via the telephone number and password sent by SMS.				
2019-11-19	Spain	Maloney´s Sports Bar S.L. Sports Bar [Hospitality & leisure]	€6,000	Violation of principle "Data minimisation".	Art. 5(1)(c)
	Data controller operated **video surveillance system** where observation angle of cameras extended to the public traffic area.				
2018-11-16	Austria	Company in medical sector [Healthcare]	€55,000	Insufficient fulfilment of data subject rights (information to be provided).	Art.7, Art. 13, Art. 14, Art. 35
	Company processing special data categories in medical sector failed to comply with **data subject rights** and by **not designating a DPO**. Moreover, data subjects had not given their consent to a data processing (Art. 7) and despite handling sensitive data, no data protection impact assessment (Art. 35 GDPR) was carried out.				
2019-11-15	Spain	Confederación General del Trabajo [Public services & administration]	€3,000	Violation of principle "Integrity and confidentiality".	Art. 5(1)(f)
	Data controller **unlawfully disclosed personal data** of 400 trade union members.				
2019-11-15	Romania	Vodafone Romania SA [Utilities, telecoms operator]	€2,100	Insufficient fulfilment of data subject rights (information to be provided).	Art. 13(1)(q)
	Data controller continued **sending marketing messages despite objections** of data subject.				
2019-11-14	Spain	Vodafone España, S.A.U. [Utilities, telecoms operator]	€60,000	Violation of principle "Integrity and confidentiality.	Art. 5(1)(f)

Date	Nation	Entity fined	Fines [€]	Main legal basis	GDPR Article
		Data controller **sent invoices to unauthorised third parties.**			
2019-11-14	Italy	ASL n. 2 Savonese [Healthcare]	€8,000	Violation of principles "Lawfulness, fairness and transparency" and "Data minimisation".	Art. 5(1)(a) & (c), Art. 9
		Data controller **transferred health data without consent** of data subjects.			
2019-11-14	Spain	Telefónica SA [Utilities, telecoms operator]	€30,000	Violation of principle "Data accuracy".	Art. 5(1)(d)
		Company charged complainant fees for operation of phone line that complainant never owned, because **complainant's bank account was linked to another customer**, which led to charges being debited from complainant's account. This breached principle of data accuracy.			
2019-11-13	Spain	General Confederation of Labour ('CGT') [Public services & administration]	€3,000	Insufficient legal basis for data processing.	Art. 6
		Data controller erred in **emailing to 400 union members without consent the personal data of complainant** (home address, family relationships, pregnancy status, and date of ongoing verbal abuse and harassment case).			
2019-11-11	Slovakia	Sociálna poisťovňa (Social Insurance Agency) [Financial services]	€50,000	Insufficient measures to secure data processing.	Art. 32
		Slovak citizens had to send applications for social benefits by post to foreign authorities for verification. Some **applications were lost in the post** and the location of personal data could not be verified.			
2019-11-09	Hungary	Hospital [Healthcare]	€90	Insufficient fulfilment of data subject rights (right of access).	Art. 15
		A patient's right to access data was denied and a **copying fee was unlawfully charged**.			

Date	Nation	Entity fined	Fines [€]	Main legal basis	GDPR Article
2019-11-08	Spain	Madrileña Red de Gas [Utilities, gas supplier]	€12,000	Insufficient measures to secure data processing. Violation of principle "Integrity and confidentiality".	Art. 5(1)(f), Art. 32
		Company took **insufficient measures to verify data subject's identity**. Complainant alleged company responded to his request by emailing his data to third party.			
2019-11-08	Spain	Madrileña Red de Gas S.A.U. [Utilities, energy supplier]	€12,000	Violation of principle "Integrity and confidentiality".	Art. 5(1)(f)
		Company violated principle of integrity and confidentiality of customer data. The DPSA found the data controller **did not have the proper measures** in place to **validate a data subject's identity**.			
2019-11-08	Spain	Cerrajero Online [Retail]	€900	Insufficient fulfilment of data subject rights (information to be provided).	Art. 13
		Company collected personal data without giving **accurate information about data collection** in its data protection policy.			
2019-11-07	Spain	TODO TECNICO S24H S.L [Retail]	€900	Insufficient fulfilment of data subject rights (information to be provided).	Art. 13
		The company collected personal data without providing **accurate information about data collection** in its data protection declaration.			
2019-11-07	Spain	Joker Premium Invex S.L. [Media & entertainment]	€6,000	Insufficient legal basis for data processing. Insufficient legal basis	Art. 6(1)(a), Art. 7

Date	Nation	Entity fined	Fines [€]	Main legal basis	GDPR Article
				(consent).	
Data controller **sent advertising to data subjects without their consent**.					
2019-11-07	Italy	Comune di Tivoli (municipality of Tivoli) [Public Sector & Administration]	€6,000	Insufficient legal basis for data processing. Violation against principle "Lawfulness, fairness and transparency" and "Data minimisation".	Art. 5(1)(a) & (c), Art. 6(1)(c), (1) (e) & (3)(b)
Data controller **published personal data on municipality website**.					
2019-11-06	Spain	Vodafone España S.A.U. [Utilities, telecoms operator]	€60,000	Insufficient legal basis for data processing.	Art. 6
Company sent **customer's invoice data to third parties** following customer invoice complaint. The original fine of €75,000 was reduced to €60,000 on condition of immediate payment and no appeal.					
2019-11-XX	Latvia	Unknown	€150,000	Insufficient legal basis for data processing.	Art. 6
Unlawful data processing. The data processor was fined for infringement of Article 6 GDPR. No further information is available.					
2019-10-31	Spain	Jocker Premium Invex S.L. [Media & entertainment]	€6,000	Insufficient legal basis for data processing.	Art. 6
Company **sent to applicant postal advertisements and commercial offers** although data such as first name, surname and postal address were only communicated to the administrator.					
2019-10-31	Netherlands	UWV ("Uitvoerings-instituut Werknemers-verzekeringen" – Dutch employee	€900,000	Insufficient measures to secure data processing.	Art. 32(1)(b)

Date	Nation	Entity fined	Fines [€]	Main legal basis	GDPR Article
		insurance) [Financial services]			
	Data controller **failed to use multi-factor authentication in accessing online employer portal.** Security was inadequate. Employers and health and safety services could collect and display employees' health data.				
2019-10-31	Netherlands	Menzis Group (Health insurance company) [Financial services]	€50,000	Violation of principle "Purpose limitation" violation "Integrity and confidentiality".	Art. 5(1)(b) & (f)
	**Marketing staff had access to patient data.** This violated the purpose limitation principle among other failures.				
2019-10-30	Germany (Berlin)	Deutsche Wohnen SE [Real estate & property]	€14,500,000	Violation of "General data protection principles".	Art. 5, Art. 25(1)
	Company used archiving system storing tenants' personal data **to store and remove data that is no longer required.** Data was stored without checking if **storage is permissible or even necessary.** Data of tenants had been stored for years and no longer served the purpose of its original collection, incl. **personal and financial circumstances** (salary statements, self-disclosure forms, extracts from employment contracts, taxes, social security and health insurance data, as well as bank statements). Berlin DPSA imposed fines of €6,000 to €17,000 in **15 specific cases** for unlawful storage of personal data. See below.				
2019-10-28	Bulgaria	Employer [Private person]	€511	Insufficient fulfilment of data subject rights (general and right of access).	Art. 12(3), Art. 15(1)
	Former employer **refused to grant access to personal data of subject who submitted an application for access** to the personal data his former employer held.				
2019-10-25	Spain	Vodafone España S.A.U. [Utilities, telecoms operator]	€36,000	Insufficient legal basis for data processing.	Art. 5(1)(a) & (b), Art. 6(1)

Date	Nation	Entity fined	Fines [€]	Main legal basis	GDPR Article
				Violation of principle "Lawfulness, fairness and transparency".	
	Company provided personal data to data subject's daughter as authorised by him; however, company then **provided services and sought payment from him** without consent.				
2019-10-24	Hungary	Military Hospital	€7,400	Insufficient breach notification to DPSA.	Art. 32, Art. 33
	Data controller **failed to meet reporting deadline for data breaches**, and took insufficient technical/organisational security measures.				
2019-10-24	Germany (Baden-Württemberg)	Food craft company [Retail]	€100,000	Insufficient measures to secure data processing. Violation or principle "Lawfulness, fairness and transparency".	Art. 5(1)(a), Art. 32
	Company created applicant portal for online submission of job documents, but **failed to encrypt transmission of data**, nor was applicant **data stored in encrypted or password-protected database**. Unsecured applicant data was linked to Google, so anyone searching for applicant names could **retrieve** their job documents **without access restrictions**.				
2019-10-23	Austria	Austrian Post AG (ÖPAG) [Public services & administration]	€18,000,000	Insufficient legal basis for data processing. Violation of principle "Lawfulness, fairness and transparency".	Art. 5(1)(a), Art. 6
	Data controller created **profiles of over 3 million Austrians**, incl. home address, personal preferences and habits, and possibly party affinity. The data were **sold to political parties and companies**. A civil court judgement in same case gave compensation of €800 over administrative fine.				

Date	Nation	Entity fined	Fines [€]	Main legal basis	GDPR Article
2019-10-23	Spain	Vodafone España S.A.U. [Utilities, telecoms operator]	€60,000	Violation of principle "Integrity and confidentiality".	Art. 5(1)(f)
	Company sent invoice history to a subscriber in response to complaint. The invoice history **contained invoice data of an unknown third party**.				
2019-10-22	Romania	Artmark Holding SRL [Media & entertainment]	€2,100	Insufficient fulfilment of data subject rights (information to be provided).	Art. 13(1)(q)
	Company **sent advertising messages to data subjects without consent.**				
2019-10-21	Spain	Iberdrola Clientes [utilities, energy supplier]	€8,000	Insufficient cooperation with DPSA.	Art. 31, Art 83(4)(a)
	Company refused to change customer's electricity supplier claiming that the customer's data would be included in the solvency list. DPSA asked company to provide information about possibly **adding customer's data to the solvency list** to which the company did not respond.				
2019-10-18	Poland	Major of Aleksandrów Kujawski [Public services and administration]	€9,400	Insufficient data processing agreement.	Art. 5(1)(a) & (f), Art. 28(3)
	Company operating servers that contain information of the Public Information Bulletin (BIP) of the Municipal Office in the city of Aleksandrów Kujawski **had no data processing agreement.**				
2019-10-18	Greece	Wind Hellas Telecommunications [Utilities, telecoms operator]	€20,000	Insufficient fulfilment of data subject rights (right to object).	Art. 21(1)
	A key point in this sanction was that the company has **ignored objections raised by affected parties against marketing calls.**				
2019-10-17	Romania	UTTIS INDUSTRIES SRL [Real estate & property]	€2,500	Insufficient fulfilment of data subject rights (general and	Art. 5(1)(c), Art. 6, Art. 12, Art. 13

Date	Nation	Entity fined	Fines [€]	Main legal basis	GDPR Article
				information to be provided). Violation of principle "Data minimisation".	
Data controller could not prove **data subjects had been informed of processing of personal data (images) by video surveillance system** in operation since 2016, nor prove the legality of the processing.					
2019-10-16	Spain	Xfera Móviles S.A. [Utilities, telecoms operator]	€60,000	Insufficient legal basis for data processing.	Art. 6(1)
Company made **marketing calls without prior consent** of data subjects.					
2020-10-02	Spain	Xfera Moviles S.A. [Utilities, telecoms operator]	€60,000	Insufficient legal basis for data processing. Violation of principle "Lawfulness, fairness and transparency".	Art. 5(1)(a), Art. 6 (1)(a)
Company used personal data without legal basis in phone contract, and **continued to process personal data** even after subject requested to discontinue it.					
2019-10-16	Poland	ClickQuickNow Sp. z o.o. [Service company]	€47,120	Insufficient legal basis (consent). Violation of principle "Lawfulness, fairness and transparency" and "Purpose limitation".	Art. 5(1)(a), (b) & 5(2), Art. 7(3), Art. 12
Data controller obstructed exercise of **right of withdrawal from processing of personal data**. Company failed to take sufficient technical/organisational measures for **simple and effective withdrawal of consent** and exercise of **right to request erasure** of personal data.					
2019-10-15	Hungary	Unknown Company	€2,860	Insufficient legal basis for data	Art. 5(1)(a) & (b),

Date	Nation	Entity fined	Fines [€]	Main legal basis	GDPR Article
				processing. Violation of accountability principle.	Art. 5(2), Art. 6, Art. 13, Art. 24, Art. 25
	Employer checked employee's desktop, laptop and emails to ensure that work duties were covered **during sick leave**, then **suspended his account.** Employee received no pre-notification and could not copy/delete personal data (phone numbers, messages). DPSA ruled employers must record access with minutes and photos, and employment contracts must regulate employees' use of work equipment for private purposes. **Privacy notices must contain reasons for employee monitoring**, like business continuity, internal investigation, discipline, and the specific retention period of employee data. Employers **must have "balancing tests" to prove legitimate interest in general and specific monitoring.**				
2019-10-11	Cyprus	Doctor [Healthcare]	€14,000	Insufficient legal basis for data processing. Violation of "General data processing principles".	Art. 5, Art. 6
	Doctor published sensitive personal data of patient on social media platform Instagram **without her consent.**				
2019-10-10	Spain	Vueling Airlines [Transport & logistics]	€30,000	Insufficient legal basis for data processing. Violation of "General data processing principles".	Art. 5, Art. 6
	Company **failed to allow users to decline their cookies** but **forced their acceptance of all cookies if users wanted to browse website.** The €30,000 fine is reducible to €18,000 if paid immediately.				
2019-10-09	Romania	Raiffeisen Bank S.A. [Financial services]	€150,000	Insufficient measures to secure data processing.	Art. 32
	Data controller **scored assessments on basis of personal data of data subjects registered on Vreau Credit platform,** provided by platform's staff via WhatsApp and the results returned to Vreau Credit via WhatsApp. An investigation				

Date	Nation	Entity fined	Fines [€]	Main legal basis	GDPR Article
		followed by the notification of the data controller by filling in the form on the personal data breach to the DPSA.			
2019-10-09	Romania	Vreau Credit SRL [Financial services]	€20,000	Insufficient measures to secure data processing.	Art. 32, Art. 33
		Bank was also sanctioned for **breach of data security**; also because, until investigation into Raiffeisen Bank S.A. ended, it **did not notify DPSA of personal data breach**, although it had been aware of it since December 2018 This incident led to breach of confidentiality of personal data of clients (data subjects) and to unauthorized/illegal processing of personal data.			
2019-10-08	Bulgaria	The Ministry of Interior Affairs [Public services and administration]	€5,112	Insufficient legal basis for data processing. Violation of principle "Lawfulness, fairness and transparency".	Art. 5(1)(a), Art. 6(1)
		Data controller **unlawfully processed personal data of data subject**. Ministry of Interior sent subject's personal data to the Togolese Republic (Togo).			
2019-10-07	Greece	Telecommunication service provider. [Utilities, telecoms operator]	€200,000	Violation of principle "Data minimisation".	Art. 5(1)(c), Art. 21, Art. 25
		Company made **telemarketing calls** to large numbers of customers **who had opted out**. The opt-out was ignored due to technical errors.			
2019-10-07	Greece	Hellenic Telecommunications Agency SA [Utilities, telecoms operator]	€200,000	Insufficient fulfilment of data subject rights (right to object).	Art. 21(3), Art. 25
		8,000 customers were not deleted upon request due to technical issues.			
2019-10-07	Bulgaria	B.M. [Unknown]	€511	Insufficient cooperation with DPSA.	Art. 31
		Data controller failed to provide **access to information the DPSA needed** to			

Date	Nation	Entity fined	Fines [€]	Main legal basis	GDPR Article
	perform its duties and execute a disposition.				
2019-10-03	Cyprus	Eleftherios Demetriou [Transport & logistics]	€2,000	Insufficient legal basis for data processing.	Art. 6(1)(a), Art. 21
	Data controller sent **SMS messages to data subjects without consent or an opt-out mechanism**.				
2019-10-03	Cyprus	DIKO – Democratic Party of Cyprus [Public services & administration]	€3,000	Insufficient legal basis for data processing.	Art. 6(1)(a), Art. 21
	Data controller made telemarketing calls and **ignored objections of data subjects**.				
2019-10-03	Cyprus	Candidate for EU Parliament [Private person]	€2,000	Insufficient legal basis for data processing. Violation of principle "Purpose limitation".	Art. 5(1)(b), Art. 6(1)(a)
	Candidate during electoral campaign **sent marketing material without consent**.				
2019-10-01	Hungary	Town of Kerepes [Public services & administration]	€15,100	Insufficient legal basis for data processing. Violation of principles "Lawfulness, fairness and transparency", "Purpose limitation" and "Data minimisation".	Art. 5(1)(a), (b) & (c), Art. 6(1)(f)
	City based **video surveillance** on legitimate interests, but legitimate interest **shall not apply to processing carried out by public authorities** in the performance of their duties. The processing lacked any other legal basis.				
2019-09-27	Slovakia	Slovak Telekom A.S. [Utilities, telecoms	€40,000	Insufficient measures to secure data	Art. 32

Date	Nation	Entity fined	Fines [€]	Main legal basis	GDPR Article
		operator]		processing.	
	Data controller **failed to take sufficient security measures** when processing personal data, breaching the obligation to protect the data.				
2019-09-26	Romania	Inteligo Media SA [Media & entertainment]	€9,000	Insufficient legal basis (consent). Violation of principle "Lawfulness, fairness and transparency".	Art. 5(1)(a), Art. 6 (1)(a), Art. 7
	Company's registration process on avocatnet.ro required ticking box to opt out of **receiving solicitations via email.** Unless user noticed opt-out, letters were automatically sent without lawful consent. On investigation, controller could not prove it obtained explicit consent (Art. 7) of 4,357 users whose personal data it processed.				
2019-09-19	Germany (Berlin)	Delivery Hero Germany GmbH [Transport & logistics]	€195,407	Insufficient fulfilment of data subject rights (right of access, right of erasure and right to object).	Art. 15, Art. 17, Art. 21
	Data controller failed to **delete accounts of 10 former customers,** who had not been active on company's delivery service platform for years (in one case since 2008). **8 ex-customers complained about unsolicited advertising emails.** Data subject who expressly objected to this use of his data received 15 more emails. In other cases, company did not provide data subjects with required information, or only after DPSA intervened.				
2019-09-17	Belgium	Merchant [Retailer]	€10,000 (challenged in court)	Violation of principle "Data minimisation".	Art. 5(1)(c)
	Data controller tried to use electronic identity card (eID) to create customer card, requiring **access to personal data located on the eID,** incl. photo and barcode which is linked to data subject's ID number. DPSA decision was challenged and overruled in court.				
2019-09-10	Poland	Morele.net [Information technology & services]	€645,000	Insufficient measures to secure data processing.	Art. 5(f) Art. 32
	Company's organisational/technical measures were insufficient, leading to **unauthorised access to the personal data of 2.2 million people.** Data of 35,000				

Date	Nation	Entity fined	Fines [€]	Main legal basis	GDPR Article
		subjects leaked were related to instalment loan applications and involved identity documents (educational background, registered addresses, correspondence addresses, source of income, net income amounts, cost of living of household, marital status, and amount of credit commitments or maintenance obligations.			
2019-09-03	Bulgaria	National Revenue Agency [Public services and administration]	€28,100	Infringement of provisions leading to administrative fines.	Art. 6 (1), Art. 58 (2) (e),
		Data controller **processed personal data of data subject** which **was unlawfully collected** and used to bring against subject an enforcement case for recovery of €86,569. Data subject's bank account data was collected by National Revenue Agency from Bulgarian National Bank register. These data were then **processed by the National Revenue Agency** by sending distraint orders to the banks where subject had accounts.			
2019-09-03	Bulgaria	Telecommunicati on service provider [Utilities, telecoms operator]	€1,022	Insufficient legal basis for data processing.	Art. 6 (1), Art. 25 (1)
		Company and its commercial representative in Bulgaria **unlawfully processed personal data of subject**. Data was used to conclude service contracts **without his knowledge or consent**.			
2019-09-03	Bulgaria	Telecommunicati on service provider (H. K.) [Utilities, telecoms operator]	€5,113	Insufficient legal basis for data processing.	Art. 6(1), Art. 25(1)
		Company and its commercial representative in Bulgaria **unlawfully processed personal data of subject**. Data was used to conclude service contracts **without his knowledge or consent**.			
2019-09-03	Bulgaria	Commercial representative of telecommunicati on service provider [Utilities, telecoms operator]	€11,760	Insufficient legal basis for data processing.	Art. 6(1)

Date	Nation	Entity fined	Fines [€]	Main legal basis	GDPR Article
		Commercial representative of telecommunications service provider **unlawfully processed personal data of subject**. Data was used to **conclude a contract for mobile services and leasing contracts without consent**.			
2019-09-03	Bulgaria	Private enforcement agent [Private person]	€1,121	Insufficient fulfilment of data subject rights (general and right of access).	Art. 12(4), Art. 15
		Data controller processed personal data of subject through **video surveillance but refused to give access to collected data** after data subject requested access to his personal data from data controller, who also failed to give reasons for rejection.			
2019-08-29	Bulgaria	National Revenue Agency [Public services & administration]	€2,600,000	Insufficient measures to secure data processing.	Art. 32
		Data controller leaked personal data in hack attack due to **insufficient technical/organisational measures**. Personal data of **6 million persons were accessed**.			
2019-08-28	Bulgaria	DSK Bank [Financial services]	€511,000	Insufficient measures to secure data processing.	Art. 32
		Data controller leaked personal data due to insufficient technical/organisational security measures. Third parties had **access to over 23,000 credit records relating to over 33,000 customers** incl. personal data (names, citizenship, ID numbers, addresses, identity cards and biometric data.			
2019-08-28	Spain	Vodafone ONO, S.A.U. [Utilities, telecoms operator]	€48,000	Insufficient measures to secure data processing.	Art. 32
		Customers could **access personal data of other customers** in customer area. A €60.000 fine was reduced to €48.000.			
2019-08-26	Latvia	merchant of an online shop [Information technology & services]	€7,000	Insufficient fulfilment of data subject rights (right of erasure).	Art. 17
		Trader through online store **insufficiently fulfilled "right to be forgotten"**. Data subject repeatedly requested deletion of his personal data, esp. mobile phone			

Date	Nation	Entity fined	Fines [€]	Main legal basis	GDPR Article
	number, which the merchant harvested from an order. Merchant continued to send adverts by SMS to the mobile phone.				
2019-08-22	Austria	Private person (soccer coach)	€11,000	Insufficient legal basis for data processing.	Art. 6
	Football coach **secretly filmed** female players naked in the shower cubicle for years.				
2019-08-20	Sweden	School in Skellefteå [Education]	€18,630	Insufficient legal basis for data processing. Violation of principle "Data minimisation".	Art. 5(1)(c), Art. 9, Art. 35, Art. 36
	School trialled **facial recognition technology to monitor the attendance of students**. Data processing to monitoring attendance may be legit, but DPSA ruled it disproportional to goal. DPSA found biometric data was processed without consent so that students and their guardians were not free to decide if they/their children want to be monitored. DPSA ruled school board could not rely on any of the exemptions listed in Art. 9(2). DPSA also found it a case high risk to personal data as new and unknown technology was used to process sensitive personal data of dependent children and camera surveillance was used in the everyday environment. DPSA found school board could not demonstrate compliance with Art. 35 and **failed to consult DPSA** per Art. 36(1).				
2019-08-19	Spain	Brothel operator [Private person]	€9,000	Violation of principle "Data minimisation".	Art. 5(1)(c)
	Video surveillance cameras were not used only to protect property, but to **monitor employees.** No privacy notice was given.				
2019-08-16	Spain	Avon Cosmetics S.A.U. [Retail]	€60,000	Insufficient legal basis for data processing.	Art. 6
	Company did not verify subject's identity when processing personal data, leading to data being **erroneously entered into a solvency/creditworthiness file**. This prevented him from working with his bank, and a third party fraudulently used personal data.				
2019-08-12	Spain	TELEFONICA MOVILES ESPAÑA, S.A.U. [Utilities,	€36,000	Violation of principle "Lawfulness, fairness and	Art. 5(1)(a)

Date	Nation	Entity fined	Fines [€]	Main legal basis	GDPR Article
		telecoms operator]		transparency".	
Data controller charged claimant's bank account by sending **two invoices for services not subscribed** for that revealed personal data and the address of another customer. €60.000 fine was reduced to €36,000 for acknowledgement of responsibility and prompt payment.					
2019-08-08	Hungary	Government Office Managing the Real Estate Register [Public services & administration]	€1,715	Violation of principle "Lawfulness, fairness and transparency" and "Data minimisation".	Art. 5(1) (a) & (c), Art. 14
Government office posted decision changing the person of the lessee (concluding a lease agreement with real estate owners) to other owners of 40 estates contracted by same lessee. This **exposed personal data of all owners who had a lease agreement** with same lessee.					
2019-08-08	Spain	Brothel operator [Private person]	€20,000	Violation of principle "Data minimisation".	Art. 5(1)(c)
Video surveillance cameras were not used only to protect property, but also to **monitor employees**. **No privacy notice** was posted.					
2019-08-02	Hungary	Public area maintenance company [Service company]	€4,290	Insufficient legal basis for data processing. Violation of principle "Lawfulness, fairness and transparency", "Purpose limitation" and "Integrity and confidentiality".	Art. 5(1)(a), (b) & (f), Art. 6, Art. 13
Employer **unlawfully monitored employee's work by CCTV**, claiming that monitoring was necessary to see if employee fulfilled his employment related duties (which was monitoring certain public areas and signalling any unusual event to his colleagues), and that monitoring also kept surveillance system from unlawful access or use. DPSA ruled this an appropriate way to assess work performance yet employer relied on an **inappropriate legal basis** (public interest, official authority). Employer can protected surveillance system by					

Date	Nation	Entity fined	Fines [€]	Main legal basis	GDPR Article
		other means like installing firewalls or other security upgrades. DPSA also ruled CCTV monitoring notice sheet employer placed at entrance of the workstation was insufficient.			
2019-07-31	Spain	Vodafone España, S.A.U. [Utilities, telecoms operator]	€30,000	Insufficient measures to secure data processing. Violation of principle "Integrity and confidentiality".	Art. 5(1)(f), Art. 32
		Customer's **personal data (purchase history) was disclosed via SMS to another customer.** €50.000 fine was reduced to €30.000.			
2019-07-30	Greece	Pricewaterhouse-Coopers (PwC BS) Business Solutions LL and Accounting Service Provider SA [Service company]	€150,000	Insufficient legal basis for data processing. Violation of principles "Lawfulness, fairness and transparency", "Purpose limitation" and "Data minimisation".	Art. 5(1)(a), (b) & (c), and (2), Art. 6(1), Art. 13(1)(c), Art. 14(1)(c)
		DPSA ruled that **consent as legal basis was insufficient** for processing employees' personal data, as it was intentionally **linked to performance of employment contracts**, *i.e.* with a legal obligation to which controller is subject and on which smooth operation of company depends. Company also gave employees the false impression it was processing their personal data on basis of consent, when in reality it was **processing on a different legal basis**, violating **transparency** and **accountability principle**. Company failed to prove it had carried out prior assessment of legal bases for processing employee personal data.			
2019-07-25	France	Active Assurances (car insurer) [Financial services]	€180,000	Insufficient measures to secure data processing.	Art. 32
		Security breach caused many customer accounts, clients' documents (driver's licences, vehicle registration, bank statements, documents attesting if a person had had a licence withdrawn), and other **data to be accessible online.** DPSA			

Date	Nation	Entity fined	Fines [€]	Main legal basis	GDPR Article
		ruled password mismanagement allowed unauthorized access without authentication.			
2019-07-22	Spain	Restaurant SANTI 3000 S.L. [Hospitality & leisure]	€9,600	Insufficient legal basis for data processing. Violation of principle "Lawfulness, fairness and transparency".	Art. 5(1)(a), Art. 6
		Restaurateur imposed disciplinary sanctions on employee using images from a **mobile phone video recorded by other employee for evidence purposes**. €12.000 fine reduced to €9.600 due to prompt payment.			
2019-07-17	Hungary	Budapest Environs Regional Court [Public services & administration]	€8,575	Insufficient legal basis for data processing. Violation of principle "Purpose limitation".	Art. 5(1)(b), Art. 6
		Court deducted from salary of judges membership fees for judges association, using list of data collected from judges' payroll records. DPSA ruled Court may only process such data for purposes of payroll management. DPSA also ruled Court lacked legal basis for data processing when it gave access to data regarding membership in association to third parties.			
2019-07-16	Bulgaria	National Tax Authority [Public services & administration]	€2,607,500	Insufficient measures to secure data processing.	Art. 32
		Insufficient technical/organisational measures led to **leak of personal data of over 5 million people**.			
2019-07-16	Netherlands	Haga Ziekenhuis hospital [Healthcare]	€460,000	Insufficient measures to secure data processing.	Art. 32
		Patient data was leaked due to insufficient security measures.			
2019-07-10	Spain	Amador Recreativos S.L. [Information technology &	€3,600	Violation of principle "Data minimisation".	Art. 5(1)(c)

Date	Nation	Entity fined	Fines [€]	Main legal basis	GDPR Article
		services]			
	Video surveillance cameras were not used only to protect property, but **to monitor employees**, plus cameras pointed to public road. €6,000 fine was reduced to €3,600 due to responsibility recognition and prompt payment.				
2019-07-05	Romania	Legal Company & Tax Hub SRL [Service company]	€3,000	Insufficient measures to secure data processing.	Art. 32(1) & (2)
	Avocatoo.ro website allowed **unauthorized disclosure and access to personal data** of subjects who had transactions with company (full name, mailing address, email, phone, job, details of transactions) from 10 Dec 2018 to 1 Feb 2019.				
2019-07-03	Spain	Vodafone España, S.A.U. [Utilities, telecoms operator]	€40,000	Insufficient legal basis for data processing.	Art. 6(1)(a) & (b)
	Company charged for Netflix service not ordered by claimant, who proved the service was actually used by third party who got access to claimant's bank account and phone number. Company **could not prove claimant consented** to receive the services, hence the fine.				
2019-07-03	Spain	Vodafone España S.A.U. [Utilities, telecoms operator]	€21,000	Insufficient legal basis for data processing.	Art. 6(1)(a) & (b)
	Data controller **processed personal data of claimant**, incl. bank details, full name, and national ID number, years after the contract ended. €35.000 fine was reduced to €21.000 due to acknowledgement of responsibility and prompt payment.				
2019-07-02	Romania	World Trade Centre Bucharest SA [Hospitality & leisure]	€15,000	Insufficient measures to secure data processing.	Art. 32
	Bucharest Centre **breached data security via printed list** to check breakfast customers and personal data of 46 clients staying at hotel. List was copied without authorisation by people outside the company, leading to **online publication of the personal data**. The National Supervisory Authority performed the investigation following the notification of a personal data breach received from the data controller by filling in the online breach notification form.				
2019-06-27	Romania	UniCredit Bank S.A. [Financial	€130,000	Inappropriate technical and	Art. 5(1)(e),

Date	Nation	Entity fined	Fines [€]	Main legal basis	GDPR Article
		services]		organisational measures for data protection by design and by default. Violation of principle "Data minimisation".	Art. 25(1)

Bank failed to implement sufficient measures to assure (1) determination of the processing means/operations, and (2) integration of safeguards. **Breach resulted in online disclosure of IDs and addresses of 337,042 data subjects from 25 May 2018 to 10 Dec 2018.**

| 2019-06-26 | Hungary | Unknown | €2,850 | Insufficient legal basis for data processing. Violation of principle "Purpose limitation" and "Data minimisation". | Art. 5(1)(b) & (c), Art. 5(2), Art. 6, Art. 17 |

Data controller processed data for claim enforcement purposes on the basis of its legitimate interest after data subject requested the deletion of his contact data, incl. his telephone number. DPSA ruled controller had no **legitimate grounds for processing** data subject's telephone number, as address was sufficient for claim enforcement purposes and for communications.

| 2019-06-26 | Hungary | Financial Enterprise [Financial services] | €2,850 | Insufficient legal basis for data processing. Violation of principle "Purpose limitation". | Art. 5(1)(b), Art. 5(2), Art. 6, Art. 21 |

Data controller transferred his data after subject **objected to processing**. Company claimed sale of contract to a third party necessitated transfer of subject's data. DPSA ruled data controller sold contract and transferred data after data subject's non-fulfilment of contract; thus, controller cannot rely on performance of contract with client subject. A relevant legal basis could be controller's legitimate interest, entailing balancing test between interest in transferring contract to third party and data subject rights.

Date	Nation	Entity fined	Fines [€]	Main legal basis	GDPR Article
2019-06-25	Hungary	Unknown	€15,150	Insufficient breach notification to DPSA.	Art. 33
Data controller **failed to report loss of flash memory with personal data on it.**					
2019-06-18	Netherlands	Haga Properly Hospital [Healthcare]	€460,000	Insufficient measures to secure data processing.	Art. 32
Hospital **failed to maintain internal security of patient records**. Dozens of hospital staff were able unnecessarily to check medical records of a high-profile Dutch person. DPSA issued order on pain of a fine and imposed deadline of 2nd of October 2019 to improve security. If the deadline is missed, hospital must pay €100,000 every two weeks, with a maximum of €300,000.					
2019-06-13	France	Uniontrad Company [Services company]	€20,000	Insufficient legal basis for data processing. Violation of principle "Data minimisation".	Art. 5(1)(c), Art. 12, Art. 13, Art. 32
Company CCTV-monitored employees at their workstations from 2013 to 2017. Twice DPSA alerted company to rules for **cameras in workplace**, particularly employees should not be recorded continually. Insufficient measures in place by the deadline set in formal notice, DPSA audited company again in Oct 2018 and confirmed breach of data protection laws. DPSA issued dissuasive but proportionate fine taking into account company's size (9 employees) and financial situation, which was net in the red in 2017.					
2019-06-11	Spain	Professional Football League (Liga Nacional de Fútbol Profesional, LFP) [Hospitality & leisure]	€250,000	Violation of principle "Lawfulness, fairness and transparency" violations.	Art. 5(1)(a), Art. 7(3)
Entity offered mobile app which once per minute accessed microphone and geolocation of users' mobile phones to detect pubs screening football matches without paying the fee, without **informed consent of** users. The app did not allow data subject to withdrawal consent.					
2019-06-11	Spain	Vodafone España S.A.U. [Utilities, telecoms	€250,000	Insufficient legal basis (consent).	Art. 5(1)(a), Art. 7(3)

Date	Nation	Entity fined	Fines [€]	Main legal basis	GDPR Article
		operator]		Violation of principle "Lawfulness, fairness and transparency".	
		Data controller **processed location data of subject and transferred them to operator**, activating mobile phone microphone.			
2019-06-10	Spain	Debt collecting agency (Géstion De Cobros, Yo Cobro, SL (Collection agency) [Financial services]	€60,000	Violation of principle "Integrity and confidentiality".	Art. 5(1)(f)
		Claimant did not repay microcredit to online credit agency, which assigned claim to debt collectors. Later, agency sent **emails not only to email addresses provided by claimant**, but also to the not-provided institutional email address of his workplace, accessible by co-workers.			
2019-06-03	Denmark	IDDesign A / S [Real estate & property]	€200,850	Violation of principle "Storage limitation".	Art. 5(1)(e) & (2)
		Company **processed personal data of 385,000 customers for longer time than necessary for purpose.** Company had documented no retention schedules of data deletion in a new CRM system. Data controller documented its personal data deletion procedures insufficiently. Fine was imposed by courts as Danish law allows administrative fines only in simple case where accused consents.			
2019-06-03	Hungary	Claim management company [Financial services]	€2,850	Insufficient legal basis for data processing. Violation of principle "General data processing principles".	Art. 5(1)(a-c) & (f), Art. 6
		Per credit agreement with bank, **personal data of subjects was transferred and also provided to third party** (data controller). DPSA ruled controller can neither rely on data subjects' consent nor contract performance as legal basis of data processing, as data subjects had contract with bank, not the data controller. Right legal basis could have been legitimate interest of controller.			

Date	Nation	Entity fined	Fines [€]	Main legal basis	GDPR Article
2019-05-31	Hungary	Local bank [Financial services]	€2,000	Insufficient fulfilment of data subject rights (general, right of access and right to restrict processing).	Art. 12(3), (4), (5), Art. 15, Art. 18
	Data subject **requested access to telephone conversation recordings and CCTV footage.** Bank yielded copies of phone conversation recordings and allowed subject to review CCTV footage at their office, but refused copies of CCTV footage, as it contained third parties' personal data. DPSA ruled bank insufficiently fulfilled data subject rights, as it responded after due date and refused footage copy. Controller may **not claim protection of third parties' data as CCTV covered bank's public area**, plus bank could have anonymised third parties.					
2019-05-28	Belgium	Mayor (unknown town) [Public services & administration]	€2,000	Insufficient legal basis for data processing. Violation of principle "Purpose limitation".	Art. 5(1)(b), Art. 6
	Data controller misused **personal data for campaign purposes**.					
2019-05-28	France	Sergic Immobilier [Real estate & property]	€400,000	Insufficient measures to secure data processing. Violation of principle "Storage limitation".	Art. 5(1)(e), Art. 32
	Company committed (1) **Lack of basic security measures** and (2) **excessive data storage.** Tenants uploaded sensitive documents (ID cards, health cards, tax notices, certificates of family allowance fund, divorce judgments, account statements) **accessible online without any authentication procedure in place.** Company knew of vulnerability since March 2018, but did not resolve it until Sept 2018. Also, company **stored tenant documents longer than necessary.** DPSA reckoned-in risks to data subjects of breach, incl. lack of due care in addressing vulnerability and disclosure of personal data revealing very intimate details of data subjects' lives.					

Date	Nation	Entity fined	Fines [€]	Main legal basis	GDPR Article
2019-05-23	Hungary	Organiser of Sziget Kulturális Menedzser Iroda festival and VOLT festival [Hospitality & leisure]	€92,146	Insufficient legal basis for data processing. Violation of principles "Purpose limitation" and "Data minimisation".	Art. 5(1)(b) & (c), Art. 6, Art. 13
		Data controller relied on **wrong legal bases** and **failed to comply with purpose limitation principle**. Information on the data processing was partly withheld from data subjects.			
2019-05-22	Spain	Vodafone ONO, S.A.U. [Utilities, telecoms operator]	€36,000	Violation of principle "Integrity and confidentiality".	Art. 5(1)(f)
		Data controller **sent marketing email to many clients without using blind copy feature**. €60,000 fine reduced to €36,000.			
2019-05-21	Hungary	Directorate of Social and Child Welfare Institutions of the Ferencvaros District of Budapest [Public services & administration]	€286	Insufficient breach notification to DPSA.	Art. 33
		Directorate employee mistakenly **sent 9 letters to wrong recipient, containing personal data of 18 subjects, incl. data on children, criminal records, and private life**. Recipient told data controller by telephone 5 days after posting that certain letters were received mistakenly. Data controller notified DPSA only weeks later.			
2019-05-16	Lithuania	Payment service provider UAB Mister Tango [Financial services]	€61,500	Insufficient breach notification to DPSA. Violation of "General data processing principles".	Art. 5, Art. 32, Art. 33
		Data controller processed more data than necessary to achieve purpose. From			

Date	Nation	Entity fined	Fines [€]	Main legal basis	GDPR Article
	09-10 July 2018 payment data were publicly available on Internet due to insufficient technical/ organisational measures. 9,000 payments with 12 banks from different countries were affected. Data controller **failed to notify DPSA of the data breach.**				
2019-05-09	Germany (Baden-Württemberg)	Police Officer [Public services & administration]	€1,400	Insufficient legal basis for data processing. Violation of "General data processing principles".	Art. 5, Art. 6
	Police officer **used official ID outside official duties to query subject about license plate** that officer could not retrieve from Central Traffic Information System (ZEVIS) of Federal Motor Transport Authority. Using personal data from query, he carried out investigation inquiring not only into personal data of injured parties, but also home and mobile phone numbers obtained in the previous investigation. Using mobile phone number thus obtained, officer phoned injured party – without official reason or consent. Officer processed personal data outside scope of law on his own authority. This violation is not attributable to police department, as he was not acting within official duties, but for private purposes. Prohibition under § 28 LDSG (Landesdatenschutzgesetz, Data Protection law) of punishment of public bodies pursuant to GDPR does not apply, as violation was not attributable to public body nor is officer a separate public body within the meaning of § 2(1) or (2) LDSG.				
2019-05-06	Czech Republic	Unknow company	€194	Insufficient fulfilment of data subject rights (right of access).	Art. 15(1)
	Employer **processed personal data of employees** In Sept 2018, which was provided by email, for **four months before informing the employees.**				
2019-05-06	Cyprus	Breikot Management Ltd [Media & entertainment]	€3,000	Violation of principle "Data minimisation".	Art. 5(1)(c)
	Data controller **kept personal data for too long** violating principle of data minimisation.				
2019-05-06	Cyprus	Sigma Live Ltd [Media & entertainment]	€5,000	Insufficient legal basis for data	Art. 6(1)(a)

Date	Nation	Entity fined	Fines [€]	Main legal basis	GDPR Article
				processing.	
Data controller **disclosed face of witness** without express consent.					
2019-05-06	Cyprus	Altius Insurance Ltd [Financial services]	€4,000	Insufficient legal basis for data processing.	Art. 6(1)(a) & (b)
Company **sent unconsented SMS marketing messages** via random generation of phone numbers.					
2019-05-06	Cyprus	P.TH. Upkeep & Net Services Ltd [Information technology & services]	€3,400	Insufficient legal basis for data processing.	Art. 6(1)(a)
Data controller **dispatched newsletter despite objection** of data subjects to advertising.					
2019-05-06	Spain	ENDESA ENERGÍA XXI, S.L.U. [Utilities, energy supplier]	€60,000	Insufficient legal basis for data processing. Violation of principle "Integrity and confidentiality".	Art. 5(1)(f)
Company charged complainant's bank account, beneficiary of which was third party convicted under criminal law and under two-year restraining order toward claimant, her domicile and work. Instead of amending contract details as requested by claimant, **company deleted her data and filled in data of third party erroneously**. DPSA ruled disclosure of claimant's data to third party was severe violation of confidentiality.					
2019-04-29	Norway	Oslo Municipal Education Department [Education]	€203,000	Insufficient measures to secure data processing.	Art. 32
Data controller neglected security vulnerabilities in mobile messaging app developed for school use to allow parents and students to send messages to school staff. Insufficient security measures meant **unauthorized persons could log in as authorized users and access personal data** of students, legal representatives, and employees.					
2019-04-25	Poland	Dolnośląski Związek Piłki	€12,950	Insufficient legal basis for	Art. 5(1)(f),

Date	Nation	Entity fined	Fines [€]	Main legal basis	GDPR Article
		Nożnej (Lower Silesian Football Association) [Hospitality & leisure]		data processing. Violation of principle "Integrity and confidentiality".	Art. 6, Art. 32(1)(b)
	Data controller published personal data referring to judges granted judicial licenses online, incl. names, addresses, and membership numbers. No legal basis existed to **make wide range of data on judges available online**. Data controller noticed error and notified DPSA, but in calculating fine (PLN 55,750.50 Polish Złoty), DPSA account for gravity of breach: duration of infringement and the many persons (585 judges) affected. Note: Office of Competition and Consumer Protection took part in case, and noted mitigating facts: good cooperation of controller with DPSA and no evidence that damages accrued to data subjects.					
2019-04-17	Italy	Rousseau Association/ Italian political party Movimento 5 Stelle [Public Sector & Administration]	€50,000	Insufficient measures to secure data processing.	Art. 32
	Data processor ran websites affiliated with political party through "Rousseau Platform". Platform was breached. DPSA ordered implementation of security measures and **updating of privacy notice** outlining the data processing activities. Update was fulfilled but worries about **security measures lingered**. Though proceeding was brought before 25 May 2018, date of entry of GDPR into force, DPSA fined processor under GDPR, as it failed to adopt measures required by order issued after 25 May 2018.					
2019-04-17	Hungary	Unknown	€9,400	Insufficient legal basis for data processing. Violation of principle "Lawfulness, fairness and transparency".	Art. 5(1)(a), Art. 6(1)(b)
	Data controller used **wrong legal basis for processing** of personal data for assignment of claims.					
2019-04-12	Germany (Baden-	Company in financial sector	€80,000	Insufficient measures to	Art. 5(1)(f),

Date	Nation	Entity fined	Fines [€]	Main legal basis	GDPR Article
	Württemberg)	[Financial services]		secure data processing. Violation of principle "Integrity and confidentiality".	Art. 32
	Data controller failed to take necessary care of integrity and confidentiality in **disposing of documents with personal data of two customers.** Without anonymisation, papers were tossed into general waste paper recycling system, where neighbour found them.				
2019-04-12	Germany (Baden-Württemberg)	Unknown [Financial services]	€80,000	Insufficient measures to secure data processing. Violation of "General data processing principles".	Art. 32, Art. 5
	Company **disposed personal data** without sufficient technical/organisational security measures.				
2019-04-10	Germany (Berlin)	N26 GmbH – The Mobile Bank [Financial services]	€50,000	Insufficient legal basis for data processing. Violation of "General data processing principles".	Art. 5 Art. 6
	Bank maintained blacklist to prevent money laundering by processing former customers' personal data.				
2019-04-10	Germany (Berlin)	N26 (online bank) [Financial services]	€50,000	Insufficient legal basis for data processing.	Art. 6
	Data controller **processed personal data of all former customers without consent.** Bank acknowledged it had retained former customers' data to maintain blacklist so as to deny new accounts to these persons, claiming it was obligated under German Banking Act to take security steps against customers suspected of money laundering. DPSA ruled this illegal because only actual suspects may be put on blacklist unless other valid reasons exist for denying bank account. DPSA told press fine proceedings were "not yet been legally				

Date	Nation	Entity fined	Fines [€]	Main legal basis	GDPR Article
		concluded".			
2019-04-08	Bulgaria	Medical centers [Healthcare]	€510	Insufficient legal basis for data processing. Violation of principle "Lawfulness, fairness and transparency".	Art. 5(1)(a), Art. 6 (1) Art. 9(1) & (2)
	Medical centre processed personal data of subject in order to change his General Practitioner. Medical centre used software to generate change of registration form that was submitted to Regional Health Insurance Fund, then **sent to third party, which subsequently also unlawfully processed the personal data** of the data subject.				
2019-04-05	Hungary	Hungarian political party [Public services & administration]	€34,375	Insufficient breach notification to DPSA.	Art. 33(1) & (5), Art. 34 (1)
	Political party **failed to notify DPSA or data subjects of data breach**, and failed to document it. 11,000,000 forint fine was based on 4% of the party's annual turnover and 2.65 % of its anticipated turnover for the coming year. Hacker who exposed vulnerability of party's system and database of over 6,000 individuals published the commands used to retrieve information from database.				
2019-04-05	Hungary	Unknown	€1,900	Insufficient fulfilment of data subject rights (right of access).	Art. 15
	Data controller **failed to fulfil data subject's access request**. DPSA ordered fulfilment within eight days of the receipt of its decision.				
2019-03-26	Poland	Bisnode AB [Service company]	€220,000	Insufficient legal basis (data collection).	Art. 14 (1)-(3)
	Company, is one of Europe's largest provider of smart data & data analytics, **processed for commercial purposes the data of over 6 million subjects from publicly available sources** (Central Electronic Register and Information on Economic Activity). DPSA ruled that this violates information obligation to data subjects by natural persons conducting business activity (incl. entrepreneurs				

Date	Nation	Entity fined	Fines [€]	Main legal basis	GDPR Article
		currently conducting such data collection activity or have suspended it, as well as entrepreneurs who did in past). Controller fulfilled privacy notice by providing information required by GDPR only in relation to persons whose email addresses were used, but failed to comply with information obligation to all other data subjects, due to high operational costs. **Notice on data controller website was deemed insufficient.**			
2019-03-26	Bulgaria	A.P. Retail EOOD [Retail]	€5,100	Insufficient legal basis for data processing. Violation of principle "Lawfulness, fairness and transparency".	Art. 5(1)(a), Art. 6
		Data controller **processed personal data of subject and prepared an employment contract while he was in prison.**			
2019-03-25	Denmark	Taxa 4x35 (Transport & logistics)	€160,000	Violation of principle "Storage limitation".	Art. 5(1)(e)
		Company deleted passenger names from all records after two years, but **deletion excluded all other ride records on 8,873,333 taxi trips.** Company retained subject's phone numbers. DPSA reported company to police, recommending fine of 1.2 million Danish kroner for violation of data-minimization principle. Note: Since Danish law does not provide for administrative fines as in the GDPR (unless it is an uncomplicated case and the accused person consented), fines will be imposed by courts.			
2019-03-25	Portugal	Unknown	€2,000	Insufficient fulfilment of data subject rights (information to be provided).	Art. 13
		Data controller did **not provide privacy notice** when operating a CCTV systems.			
2019-03-21	Czech Republic	Unknown	€9,704	Violation of principles "Lawfulness, fairness and transparency", "Data	Art. 5(1)(a), (c) & (e)

Date	Nation	Entity fined	Fines [€]	Main legal basis	GDPR Article
				minimisation" and "Storage limitation".	

Date	Nation	Entity fined	Fines [€]	Main legal basis	GDPR Article
2019-03-21	Hungary	Demokratikus Koalíció (political party) [Public services & administration]	€34,800	Insufficient breach notification to DPSA.	Art. 33(1) & (5), Art. 34(1)

Data controller **processed sensitive personal data not relevant or limited to purpose**. Data was kept in format allowing identification of data subjects, and was **kept for longer than necessary** to purpose.

2019-03-21	Hungary	Demokratikus Koalíció (political party) [Public services & administration]	€34,800	Insufficient breach notification to DPSA.	Art. 33(1) & (5), Art. 34(1)

Political party provided **insufficient information to DPSA about data breach**, including incomplete documentation.

2019-03-19	Portugal	Unknown	€2,000	Insufficient fulfilment of data subject rights (information to be provided).	Art. 13

Data controller **failed to provide privacy notice** when operating CCTV systems.

2019-03-18	Norway	Bergen Municipality [Public services & administration]	€170,000	Insufficient measures to secure data processing. Violation of principle "Integrity and confidentiality".	Art. 5(1)(f), Art. 32

City suffered **data breach of computer files with usernames and passwords of over 35,000 users** of which most were children. User accounts belonged to primary school pupils and city employees. Personal data was openly accessible. Insufficiency of security measures allowed third parties to log in to all of school's information systems, so to access all types of personal data. DPSA and internal whistle-blower warned municipality several times.

2019-03-18	Spain	Vodafone España S.A.U. [Utilities, telecoms operator]	€27,000	Insufficient fulfilment of data subjects rights. Violation of principle "Data accuracy".	Art. 5(1)(d)

Date	Nation	Entity fined	Fines [€]	Main legal basis	GDPR Article
		Complainant and former customer asked data controller to delete his data in 2015 and fulfilment was confirmed by company. Yet **data subject received over 200 SMS** from company from 2018 onwards, because complainant's mobile phone number was erroneously used for testing purposes and accidentally appeared in other customer files belonging to other customers than the complainant. €45,000 fine reduced to €27,000 due to prompt payment and admission of responsibility.			
2019-03-07	Hungary	Bank [Financial services]	€1,560	Violation of principle "Data accuracy".	Art. 5(1)(d)
		Bank mistakenly sent SMSs about subject's credit card debt to telephone number of third party. The data subjects who received the SMS were wrongly notified to erase the data. Bank **continued to send SMSs to incorrect phone numbers**. Fine is 0.0016% of bank's annual profit.			
2019-03-04	Hungary	Unnamed financial institution [Financial services]	€3,200	Insufficient fulfilment of data subject rights (information to be provided and right of erasure). Violation of principles "Purpose limitation" and "data minimisation".	Art. 5(1)(b) & (c), Art. 6(4), Art. 13(3), Art. 17(1),
		Data controller denied **subject's request for correction and erasure** of persona data. Company claimed legitimate interest in processing data to enforce a debt claim against customer. DPSA ruled phone number is not necessary for purpose of debt collection, as creditor can communicate by post. Retaining phone number of debtor violated principles of data minimisation and purpose limitation. Fine is 0.025% of company's annual net revenue.			
2019-03-01	Cyprus	State Hospital [Healthcare]	€5,000	Insufficient fulfilment of data subject rights (right of access).	Art. 15
		Hospital **failed to fulfil patient's request for access to her medical file**, because records could not be identified/ located by data controller.			

Date	Nation	Entity fined	Fines [€]	Main legal basis	GDPR Article
2019-02-28	Czech Republic	Online game operator [Media & entertainment]	€582	Insufficient measures to secure data processing.	Art. 32
	Data controller **failed to protect personal data, incl. game account IDs, email and IP addresses.** Insufficient measures could have caused unauthorised or unlawful processing and exposed data to accidental loss, destruction or damage.				
2019-02-28	Hungary	Mayor's Office of the city of Kecskemét [Public services & administration]	€3,100	Insufficient legal basis for data processing. Violation of principle "Lawfulness, fairness and transparency".	Art. 5(1)(a), Art. 6
	Data controller **disclosed personal data of whistle-blower.** Employee of an organisation that Mayor's Office supervised reported a public interest complaint directly to DPSA against his employer. After organisation learned of complaint, it sought data in order to investigate, and Mayor's Office accidentally revealed complainant's name. DPSA deemed it aggravating that the data breach enabled organisation to fire whistle-blower.				
2019-02-26	Bulgaria	Telecom service provider [Utilities, telecoms operator]	€27,100	Insufficient legal basis for data processing. Violation of principle "Lawfulness, fairness and transparency".	Art. 5(1)(a), Art. 6
	Company repeatedly registered data subject for prepaid services without the knowledge or consent. **Data subject signed no application and gave no consent to processing of his personal data.** No other legal basis was applicable. The signature on the application and the complainant's genuine signature did not match.				
2019-02-26	Czech Republic	Unknown	€776	Insufficient fulfilment of data subject rights (right of access).	Art. 15

Date	Nation	Entity fined	Fines [€]	Main legal basis	GDPR Article
		Data controller **failed to provide subject access to personal data**, though he requested multiple times.			
2019-02-22	Bulgaria	Employer [Private person]	€500	Insufficient fulfilment of data subject rights (right of access).	Art. 15(1), Art. 5(1)(b) & (c)
		Data controller **failed to fulfil employee data subject's right** in timely and complete manner.			
2019-02-20	Hungary	Debt collector [Financial services]	€1,560	Violation of principle "Lawfulness, fairness and transparency" and "Data minimisation".	Art. 5(1)(a) & (c)
		Data controller succeeded in identifying the data subject, but company refused to fulfil **data subject's request for erasure of personal data**. Debt collector company claimed it could not identify subject without requiring birthplace, mother's maiden name and other details for identification purposes. Company also claimed it is legally obligated to retain backup copies according to the Accountancy Act and internal policies. Company did not sufficiently inform data subject of these policies, so DPSA ruled controller breached transparency principle. The fine is 0.0025% of the annual profit of company.			
2019-02-18	Malta	Lands Authority [Public services & administration]	€5,000	Insufficient measures to secure data processing. Violation of "General data processing principles".	Art. 5, Art. 32
		Data controller's **website allowed public access to over 10 gigabytes of personal data via a simple Google search** due to insufficient security measures. Most leaked data were highly sensitive, *e.g.* correspondence between subjects and the Lands Authority. Maltese DPSA is authorised to impose administrative fine for breach by a public authority or body, up to €25,000 for each violation and a daily fine of €25 for each day violation persists.			
2019-02-18	Portugal	Unknown	€20,000	Insufficient fulfilment of data subject rights (right of	Art. 15

Date	Nation	Entity fined	Fines [€]	Main legal basis	GDPR Article
				access).	
	Data controller **denied right to access** recorded telephone calls.				
2019-02-15	Cyprus	Politis Newspaper [Media & entertainment]	€10,000	Insufficient legal basis for data processing. Violation of principle "Data minimisation".	Art. 5(1)(c), Art. 6
	Newspaper **published two police investigators' names & photos** as well as photograph of third in hard copy and electronic format. Subjects complained of inconvenience, unnecessary, unlawful detention of one subject. DPSA ruled journalistic purpose could be achieved by referring only to personal initials and/or faces could be blurred and/or photographs could be taken from a distance to anonymise data subjects.				
2019-02-13	Germany (Sachsen Anhalt)	Private person	€2,629	Insufficient legal basis for data processing. Violation of "General data processing principles".	Art. 5, Art. 6
	Private person sent **e-mails in which the personal email addresses of all recipients were visible.** Total number of email addresses exposed over several months was up to 1,600.				
2019-02-05	Germany (Baden-Württemberg)	Private person	€2,500	Insufficient legal basis for data processing. Violation of "General data processing principles".	Art. 5, Art. 6
	Private person sent emails from July to Sept 2018 in which personal **email addresses were visible to all recipients.** DPSA found mailing list contained up to 153 identifiable personal mail addresses.				
2019-02-04	Czech Republic	Car renting company [Transport & logistics]	€1,165	Insufficient legal basis for data processing. Violation of	Art. 5(1)(a), Art. 6(1)(f), Art. 13

Date	Nation	Entity fined	Fines [€]	Main legal basis	GDPR Article
				principle "Lawfulness, fairness and transparency".	
	Company **used GPS to track their car fleet, but no privacy notice of tracking was provided**. DPSA found no information provided satisfying Art. 13 and Art. 6 (1)(f) could not be legal basis under the circumstances. DPSA ruled Art. 5(1)(a) was violated.				
2019-02-04	Czech Republic	Credit brokerage [Financial services]	€1,165	Insufficient measures to secure data processing. Violation of principle "Integrity and confidentiality".	Art 5(1)(f), Art. 32
	Data controller **failed to provide security of personal data**, incl. protection from unauthorised or unlawful processing and accidental loss, destruction or damage, for insufficient technical/organisational measures.				
2019-02-01	Germany (Hamburg)	Unknown	€20,000	Insufficient breach notification to DPSA. Insufficient breach notification to data subject.	Art. 33 (1), Art. 34 (1), Art. 83 (4) (a)
	Data controller submitted **late notification of data breach** and failed to notify data subjects affected.				
2019-01-29	Germany (Saarland)	Private person	€118	Insufficient legal basis for data processing.	Art. 6
	Data controller **disclosed personal data to a third party** via a social media account.				
2019-01-21	France	Google Inc. [Information technology & services]	€50,000,00 0	Insufficient legal basis for data processing. Violation of principle	Art 4(11), Art. 5(1)(a), Art. 6, Art. 7

Date	Nation	Entity fined	Fines [€]	Main legal basis	GDPR Article
				"Lawfulness, fairness and transparency".	Art. 13, Art. 14
Complaints were filed by Austrian NGO "None Of Your Business" and French NGO "La Quadrature du Net" on 25 and 28 May 2018 over **creation of Google account during set-up and configuration of mobile phones using Android**. DPSA ruled company provided insufficient transparency and information, and lacked legal basis. The consent extracted was not "specific" and "unambiguous".					
2019-01-17	Bulgaria	Bank [Financial services]	€500	Insufficient legal basis for data processing. Violation of principle "Lawfulness, fairness and transparency".	Art. 5(1)(a), Art. 6
Bank **processed personal data of student without legal basis**.					
2019-01-15	Germany (Baden-Württemberg)	Unknown [Healthcare]	€80,000	Insufficient measures to secure data processing.	Art. 9, Art. 32
Data controller **accidentally published health data in digital publication** due to insufficient internal control.					
2019-01-10	Czech Republic	Employer [Private person]	€388	Insufficient legal basis for data processing.	Art. 6
Data controller **failed to delete personal data on request of former employee, which got published on Facebook**. DPSA imposed fine because employer did not delete data relating to former employee.					
2019-XX-XX	Germany (Mecklenburg Vorpommern)	Police Officer [Public services & administration]	€2,300	Insufficient legal basis for data processing.	Art. 6
Police officers **used witness's personal data** to contact minor in person. In first case, they contacted minor by SMS for photo shooting (€800 fine); in second, they contacted witness on WhatsApp (€1,500 fine).					
2019-XX-XX	Germany (Nieder-	Unknown	€294,000	Violation of principle "Data	Art. 5(1)(c)

Date	Nation	Entity fined	Fines [€]	Main legal basis	GDPR Article
	sachsen)			minimisation".	
	Company **unnecessarily stored and retained personnel data** and **collected excessive data** in personnel selection process, during which also health data were demanded.				
2019 -XX-XX	Germany (Hamburg)	Hamburger Verkehrsverbund GmbH (HVV GmbH) [Transport & logistics]	€20,000	Insufficient breach notification to DPSA. Insufficient breach notification to data subject.	Art. 33(1), Art. 34(1)
	Customer informed public transport company of security gap on its website (https/www.hvv.de), caused by update glitch for Customer e-Service (CES), which **allowed third parties logged on who owned HVV Card** to link their CES account to at least one active contractual relationship. By changing URL, website displayed personal data of other customers with HVV Card. Data controller failed to report data breach to DPSA timely.				
2019 -XX-XX	Germany (Hamburg)	Hamburger Volksbank eG [Financial services]	Unknown	Insufficient fulfilment of data subject rights (right to object).	Art. 21
	Bank sent customer newsletter with advertising content by email, after customer expressly **objected to advertising letters**.				
2019 -XX-XX	Germany (Saarland)	Restaurant [Hospitality & leisure]	€2,000	Violation of principle "Data minimisation".	Art. 5(1)(c)
	Restaurant used **video surveillance cameras on customer areas and kitchen**, contrary to data minimisation principle. DPSA rejected claim that it helped to prevent theft.				
2019 -XX-XX	Germany (Brandenburg)	Unknown company	€50,000	Insufficient fulfilment of data subject rights (general and right of access).	Art. 12, Art. 15, Art. 28(9)
	Data controller delegated duty of fulfilling right of access to third-party data processor. Third party corresponded with data subjects under its own logo and in English, so that data subjects did not understand who was responsible for data processing. Data controller **violated transparency principle and failed to fulfil duty to provide information on subject's request**. Data controller **could**				

Date	Nation	Entity fined	Fines [€]	Main legal basis	GDPR Article
	**not provide written contract** to DPSA contrary to Art. 28(9).				
2019-XX-XX	Slovakia	Unknown	Unknown	Insufficient measures to secure data processing. Violation of principle "Integrity and confidentiality".	Art. 5(1)(f), Art. 32
	Data controller **disposed of documents** containing personal data in municipal garbage dump.				
2019-XX-XX	Slovakia	Unknown	Unknown	Insufficient fulfilment of data subject rights (right of access).	Art. 15
	Data controller **failed to comply with subject's request to access** his audio recordings.				
2019 -XX-XX	Slovakia	Unknown	Unknown	Insufficient measures to secure data processing. Violation of principle "Integrity and confidentiality".	Art. 5(1)(f), Art. 32
	Data controller took **insufficient data security measures** (no further information available).				
2019-XX-XX	Slovakia	Unknown	Unknown	Insufficient legal basis for data processing. Violation of principle "Lawfulness, fairness and transparency".	Art. 5(1)(a), Art. 6 (1) (a)
	Data controller **published personal data on City website** in fulfilling disclosure duties under Freedom of Information Act. DPSA ruled City published personal data unlawfully and without subject's consent.				

217

Date	Nation	Entity fined	Fines [€]	Main legal basis	GDPR Article
YEAR 2018					
2018-12-20	Austria	Private person	€2,200	Insufficient legal basis for data processing. Violation of principle "Lawfulness, fairness and transparency" and "Data minimisation".	Art. 5(1)(a) & (c), Art. 6(1), Art. 13
	Private person used CCTV at home without notifying data subjects. **Video surveillance covered areas intended for public use of residents of complex**: parking lots, footpaths, courtyards, gardens and access areas. Video covered areas of adjacent property. Surveillance was not limited to areas under exclusive power of data controller. Video recorded hallway of house and filmed residents entering and leaving surrounding apartments, interfering in personal life without right to object to recording their image data.					
2018-12-18	Hungary	Unknown	€3,200	Insufficient fulfilment of data subject rights (general, right of access and right to restrict processing).	Art. 12(4), Art. 13, Art. 15, Art. 18(1)(c),
	Data controller failed to (1) **provide data subject with CCTV footage**, (2) store footage for **use by data subject**, and (3) **inform data subject of right to complain** to the supervisory authority.					
2018-12-17	Germany (Hamburg)	Kolibri Image Regina und Dirk Maass GbR [Media & entertainment]	€5,000	Insufficient data processing agreement.	Art. 28(3)
	Company sent request to Hessen DPSA asking how to handle service provider who declined processing agreement. After no answer was received, query was forwarded to the locally responsible Hamburg DPSA, which then fined company as data controller for **lack of processing agreement**. Note: Company states they will challenge the decision in court as they claim service provider does not act as data processor.					

Date	Nation	Entity fined	Fines [€]	Main legal basis	GDPR Article
2018-12-09	Austria	Betting place [Media & entertainment]	€4,800	Insufficient fulfilment of data subject rights (information to be provided). Violation of principle "Lawfulness, fairness and transparency" and "Data minimisation".	Art. 5(1)(a) & (c) Art. 6, Art. 13
	Data controller's **video surveillance camera recorded facility's footpath with insufficient notice to public.** Surveilling public space so as to capture data subjects on large scale is unlawful.				
2018-12-04	Bulgaria	Bank [Financial services]	€500	Insufficient legal basis for data processing. Violation of principle "Purpose limitation".	Art. 5(1)(b), Art. 6
	Bank **called customer for unpaid bills of neighbour**, who responded with "right to be forgotten" request. Receiving no answer from bank, he requested again. Still, bank failed to take action in statutory time limit. He complained to DPSA, which fined bank for processing his personal data, which was not linked to his consumer credit agreement. Purpose of data processing in this case differed from what was agreed at contract making. Bank should have asked for additional consent from data subject.				
2018-11-28	Austria	Kebab restaurant [Hospitality & leisure]	€1,800	Insufficient legal basis for data processing. Violation of principles "Data minimisation" and "Storage limitation".	Art. 5(1) (c) & (e), Art. 13, Art. 14
	Restaurant used **CCTV with insufficient notice** to public and 14-day storage period was too long. Fine was reduced by court to €1500.				

Date	Nation	Entity fined	Fines [€]	Main legal basis	GDPR Article
	Note: The Austrian DPSA published a special article with general advice on Dashcams and CCTV recordings in its newsletter.				
2018-11-21	Germany (Baden-Württemberg)	Knuddels.de [Media & entertainment]	€20,000	Insufficient measures to secure data processing.	Art. 32(1)
	Personal **data of 330,000 data subjects was accessed in cyberattack** of July 2018, incl. passwords and email addresses. The company notified a data breach in July 2018 to the DPSA and fully cooperated. It gave insights on internal structures, which showed that passwords had been stored unencrypted.				
2018-11-19	Spain	Vodafone España S.A.U. [Utilities, telecoms operator]	€5,000	Violation of principle "Data accuracy".	Art. 5(1)(d)
	Company **wrongfully charged customer, then reported his personal data to a solvency registry/creditworthiness file** (BADEXCUG). DPSA ruled this unlawful, requiring company also to reimburse subject for costs.				
2018-10-25	Czech Republic	Unknown	€388	Insufficient fulfilment of data subject rights (right of access).	Art. 15(1)
	Data controller **failed to provide personal data** requested by data subject.				
2018-09-27	Austria	Car owner [Private person]	€300	Insufficient legal basis for data processing. Violation of principles "Lawfulness, fairness and transparency" and "Data minimisation".	Art. 5(1)(a) & (c), Art. 6
	Private person **misused two dashcams**. No privacy notice was provided and they recorded traffic in public places.				
2018-08-22	Portugal	Centro Hospitalar Barreiro Montijo [Healthcare]	€400,000	Insufficient measures to secure data processing. Violation of principle	Art. 5(1)(f), Art. 32

Date	Nation	Entity fined	Fines [€]	Main legal basis	GDPR Article
				"Integrity and confidentiality".	
	Hospital's insufficient technical/organisational measures **failed to secure their database of patient information.**				
2018-07-17	Portugal	Public Hospital [Healthcare]	€400,000	Insufficient measures to secure data processing. Violation of principle "Integrity and confidentiality".	Art. 5(1)(f), Art. 32
	Hospital **personnel accessed patient data through false profiles.** Its profile system had 985 registered doctor profiles yet only 296 doctors worked there. Doctors had unrestricted access to all patient files, regardless of specialism.				
YEAR	UNKNOWN				
XXXX-XX-XX	Czech Republic	UniCredit Bank Czech Republic and Slovakia, a.s. [Financial services]	€3,140	Insufficient legal basis for data processing.	Art. 6
	Bank opened **personal account for data subject without consent or knowledge**, whose personal data was available to bank, as subject was managing employer's company account. Bank failed to provide DPSA with contract to prove contractual relationship with data subject.				
XXXX-XX-XX	Czech Republic	Alza.cz a.s. [Information Technology & Services]	€588	Insufficient legal basis (consent).	Art. 6, Art. 7
	Company obtained copy of photographic ID of data subject with consent, but did **not fulfil his consent withdrawal but continued processing his personal data.**				
XXXX-XX-XX	Czech Republic	Entrepreneur [Private person]	€980	Insufficient measures to secure data processing.	Art. 32
	Operator of online game fell victim to several DDoS attacks causing malfunction of servers. Cyberattacker blackmailed operator that attacks would not stop until he pays ransom. Attacker also offered to create upgraded firewall				

Date	Nation	Entity fined	Fines [€]	Main legal basis	GDPR Article
		protection to operator's servers. Operator agreed and paid attacker. Operator implemented attacker's new code which excelled the old one but contained "backdoor". **Attacker used it to steal all data from server about players and upload these to his website**. DPSA ruled that operator took insufficient security measures.			

Toolkit 5

Inventory of
European Data Protection bodies

Every EEA Member State has a national data protection regulatory authority. These are listed here. (Reference: European Data Protection Board, Members website at https://edpb.europa.eu/about-edpb/board/members_en (accessed July 2020)).

Figure 18: European-wide Data Protection bodies

EU Data Protection body	Authority's full title and acronym	Authority's website and contact details
EU	European Data Protection Board (EDPB)	Postal address: Rue Wiertz 60, B-1047 Bruxelles/ Brussel Office address: Rue Montoyer 30, B-1000 Bruxelles/ Brussel Dr Andrea Jelinek, EDPB chair Website: https://edpb.europa.eu Email edpb@edpb.europa.eu Please see list with contact details of the EDPB members at: https://edpb.europa.eu/about-edpb/board/members_en (accessed July 2020).
EU	European Data Protection Supervisor (EDPS)	Postal address: Rue Wiertz 60, B-1047 Bruxelles/ Brussel Office address: Rue Montoyer 30, 6th floor, B-1000 Bruxelles/ Brussel Wojciech Wiewiórowski, European Data Protection Supervisor (appointed by joint decision of the European Parliament and the European Council on 5 December 2019 for a term of five years) Website: https://edps.europa.eu/ Email: edps@edps.europa.eu Telephone: +32 2 283 19 00

Toolkit 6

Inventory of EEA national
Data Protection Supervisory Authorities
(DPSAs)

The table below details all EEA Member States DPSAs. The figures for the number of sanctions and the total value of fines cover the period from 25 May 2018 to 24 May 2020. (Reference: European Data Protection Board, Members website at https://edpb.europa.eu/about-edpb/board/members_en (accessed July 2020)).

Figure 19: EEA Member States Data Protection Authorities
Note: This list includes all EEA nations

Authority country	Authority's full title and acronym	Authority's website and contact details
Austria	Austrian Data Protection Authority (Österreichische Datenschutzbehörde) (DSB)	Address: Österreichische Datenschutzbehörde Barichgasse 40-42, 1030 Wien Dr Andrea Jelinek, Director Website: http://www.dsb.gv.at/ Email: dsb@dsb.gv.at Telephone: ++43 1 52152 2550
Belgium	Belgian Data Protection Authority (Autorité de la protection des données / Gegevensbescher-mingsautoriteit) (APD-GBA)	Address: Autorité de protection des données / Gegevensbeschermingsautoriteit Rue de la Presse 35 – Drukpersstraat 35, 1000 Bruxelles – Brussel Mr David Stevens, President Website: https://www.autoriteprotectiondonnees.be/ (French) and https://www.gegevensbeschermingsautoriteit.be/ (Dutch) Email: contact@apd-gba.be Telephone: +32 2 274 48 00
Bulgaria	Commission for Personal	Address: Commission for Personal Data Protection

Authority country	Authority's full title and acronym	Authority's website and contact details
	Data Protection (Комисия за защита на личните данни) (CPDP/ KZLD)	2 Prof. Tsvetan Lazarov Blvd., Sofia 1592 Mr Ventsislav Karadjov, Chairman of the Commission for Personal Data Protection Website: https://www.cpdp.bg/ Email: kzld@cpdp.bg Telephone: +359 2 915 3580
Croatia	Croatian Personal Data Protection Agency (Agencija za zaštitu osobnih podataka) (AZOP)	Address: Croatian Personal Data Protection Agency Selska Cesta 136, HR - 10 000 Zagreb Mr Zdravko Vukić, Director Website: http://www.azop.hr/ Email: azop@azop.hr Telephone: +385 1 4609 000
Republic of Cyprus	Office of the Commissioner for Personal Data Protection (Γραφείο Επιτρόπου Δεδομένων Προσωπικού Χαρακτήρα)	Address: Commissioner for Personal Data Protection, 1 Iasonos Street, 1082 Nicosia P.O. Box 23378, CY-1682 Nicosia Ms Irene Loizidou Nikolaidou, Commissioner for Personal Data Protection Website: http://www.dataprotection.gov.cy/ Email: commissioner@dataprotection.gov.cy Telephone: +357 22 818 456
Czech Republic	Office for Personal Data Protection (Úřad pro ochranu osobních údajů) (UOOU)	Address: Office for Personal Data Protection Pplk. Sochora 27, 170 00 Praha 7 Ms Ivana Janů, President Website: https://www.uoou.cz/ Email: posta@uoou.cz Telephone: +420 234 665 444
Denmark	Danish Data Protection Agency (Datatilsynet)	Address: Danish Data Protection Agency Carl Jacobsens Vej 35, 2500 Valby Ms Cristina Angela Gulisano, Director Website: http://www.datatilsynet.dk Email: dt@datatilsynet.dk Telephone: +45 33 19 32 00
Estonia	Estonian Data Protection Inspectorate (Andmekaitse Inspektsioon) (AKI)	Address: Estonian Data Protection Inspectorate 39 Tatari St., 10134 Tallinn Ms Pille Lehis, Director General Website: http://www.aki.ee/en/

Authority country	Authority's full title and acronym	Authority's website and contact details
		Email: info@aki.ee Telephone: +372 6828 712
Finland	Office of the Data Protection Ombudsman (Tietosuojavaltuutetun toimisto) (OM)	Address: Office of the Data Protection Ombudsman Ratapihantie 9, 00520 Helsinki P.O. Box 800, FI-00531 Helsinki Mr Reijo Aarnio, Ombudsman Website: http://www.tietosuoja.fi/en/ Email: tietosuoja@om.fi Telephone: +358 29 566 6700
France	French Data Protection Authority (Commission Nationale de l'Informatique et des Libertés) (CNIL)	Address: Commission Nationale de l'Informatique et des Libertés 3 Place de Fontenoy, TSA 80715, 75334 Paris Cedex 07 Ms Marie-Laure Denis, President of CNIL Website: http://www.cnil.fr Contact: https://www.cnil.fr/fr/webform/contacter-la-redaction-du-site-cnilfr Telephone: +33 1 53 73 22 22
Germany	The Federal Commissioner for Data Protection and Freedom of Information (Der Bundesbeauftragte für den Datenschutz und die Informationsfreiheit) (BfDI) Please note that Germany also has a DPA in each of the 16 Federal States.	Address: The Federal Commissioner for Data Protection and Freedom of Information Graurheindorfer Straße 153, 53117 Bonn Mr Prof. Ulrich Kelber, The Federal Commissioner for Data Protection and Freedom of Information Website: http://www.bfdi.bund.de Email: poststelle@bfdi.bund.de Telephone: +49 228 997799 0
Germany (Federal States/ Bundesländer)	The competence for complaints is divided among several data protection supervisory authorities in Germany. Competent authorities can be identified according to the list provided under "Anschriften und Links" at https://www.bfdi.bund.de/anschriften. Examples of German Federal State DPAs that have issued financial penalties under the GDPR include: ▪ Baden-Württemberg (homepage at https://www.baden-wuerttemberg.datenschutz.de)	

Authority country	Authority's full title and acronym	Authority's website and contact details
		▪ Berlin (homepage at https://www.Datenschutz-Berlin.de) ▪ Brandenburg (homepage at https://www.lda.brandenburg.de) ▪ Hamburg (homepage at https://datenschutz-hamburg.de/) ▪ Mecklenburg-Vorpommern (homepage at https://www.datenschutz-mv.de) ▪ Niedersachsen (homepage at https://www.lfd.niedersachsen.de) ▪ Nordrhein-Westfalen (homepage at https://www.ldi.nrw.de) ▪ Rheinland-Pfalz (homepage at https://www.datenschutz.rlp.de/) ▪ Saarland (homepage at https://www.datenschutz.saarland.de) ▪ Sachsen Anhalt (homepage at https://datenschutz.sachsen-anhalt.de)
Greece	Hellenic Data Protection Authority (Αρχη Προστασιας Δεδομενων Προσωπικου Χαρακτηρα) (HDPA)	Address: Hellenic Data Protection Authority Kifisias Av. 1-3, PC 11523 Ampelokipi Athens Mr Konstantinos Menoudakos, President of the Hellenic Data Protection Authority Website: http://www.dpa.gr Email: contact@dpa.gr Telephone: +30 210 6475 600
Hungary	National Authority for Data Protection and Freedom of Information (A Nemzeti Adatvédelmi és Információszabadság Hatóság) (NAIH)	Address: National Authority for Data Protection and Freedom of Information Szilágyi Erzsébet fasor 22/C, H-1125 Budapest Dr Attila Péterfalvi, President of the National Authority for Data Protection and Freedom of Information Website: http://www.naih.hu/ Email: privacy@naih.hu Telephone: +36 1 3911 400
Iceland (EEA country)	Data Protection Commission (An Coimisiún um Chosaint Sonraí)	Address: The Icelandic Data Protection Authority, Rauðarárstígur 10, 105 Reykjavík, Iceland Ms Helga Þórisdóttir, Commissioner Website: https://www.personuvernd.is or https://www.dpa.is Email: postur@dpa.is Telephone: +354 510 9600
Ireland	Data Protection Commission (An Coimisiún um Chosaint Sonraí)	Address: Data Protection Commission 21 Fitzwilliam Square South, Dublin 2, D02 RD28 Ms Helen Dixon, Data Protection Commissioner Website: http://www.dataprotection.ie Email: info@dataprotection.ie

Authority country	Authority's full title and acronym	Authority's website and contact details
		Online: https://forms.dataprotection.ie/contact Telephone: +353 76 110 4800
Italy	Italian Data Protection Authority (Garante per la Protezione dei Dati Personali) (Garante/ GPDP)	Address: Italian Data Protection Authority Piazza Venezia 11, 00187 Roma Mr Antonello SORO, President of Garante per la protezione dei dati personali Website: http://www.garanteprivacy.it Email: protocollo@gpdp.it Telephone: +39 06 69677 1
Latvia	Data State Inspectorate (Datu valsts inspekcija) (DSI)	Address: Data State Inspectorate Blaumana str. 11/13-15, 1011 Riga Ms Jekaterina Macuka, Director of Data State Inspectorate Website: http://www.dvi.gov.lv/ Email: info@dvi.gov.lv Telephone: +371 6722 3131
Liechtenstein (EEA country)	Data Protection Authority, Principality of Liechtenstein (Datenschutzstelle Fürstentum Liechtenstein)	Address: Data Protection Authority, Principality of Liechtenstein, Städtle 38, 9490 Vaduz Dr Marie-Louise Gächter, Commissioner Website: https://www.datenschutzstelle.li Email: info.dss@llv.li Telephone: +423 236 6090
Lithuania	State Data Protection Inspectorate (Valstybinė duomenų apsaugos inspekcija) (VDAI)	Address: State Data Protection Inspectorate A. Juozapaviciaus str. 6, LT-09310 Vilnius Mr Raimondas Andrijauskas, Director of the State Data Protection Inspectorate Website: https://www.ada.lt/ Email: ada@ada.lt Telephone: + 370 5 279 14 45
Luxembourg	National Commission for Data Protection (Commission Nationale pour la Protection des Données) (CNPD)	Address: Commission nationale pour la protection des données 15, Boulevard du Jazz, L-4370 Belvaux Ms Tine A. Larsen, President of the Commission Nationale pour la Protection des Données Website: http://www.cnpd.lu Contact portal: https://cnpd.public.lu/fr/support/contact/contact-prive.html

Authority country	Authority's full title and acronym	Authority's website and contact details
		Telephone: +352 2610 60 1
Malta	Office of the Information and Data Protection Commissioner (Uffiċċju tal-Kummissarju għall-Informazzjoni u l-Protezzjoni tad-Data) (IDPC)	Address: Information and Data Protection Commissioner Second Floor, Airways House, High Street, Sliema, SLM 1549 Mr Saviour Cachia, Information and Data Protection Commissioner Website: http://idpc.gov.mt/ Email: idpc.info@idpc.org.mt Telephone: +356 2328 7100
Netherlands	Dutch Data Protection Authority (Autoriteit Persoonsgegevens) (CBP)	Address: Dutch Data Protection Authority Bezuidenhoutseweg 30, P.O. Box 93374 2509 AJ Den Haag/The Hague Mr Aleid WOLFSEN, Chairman of the Autoriteit Persoonsgegevens Website: https://autoriteitpersoonsgegevens.nl/nl Telephone: +31 70 888 8500
Norway (EEA country)	Norwegian Supervisory Authority (Datatilsynet)	Address: Norwegian Supervisory Authority, Tollbugata 3, 0152 Oslo Mr Bjørn Erik THON, Director-General Website: https://www.datatilsynet.no/ Email: postkasse@datatilsynet.no Telephone: +47 22 39 69 00
Poland	Personal Data Protection Office (Urząd Ochrony Danych Osobowych) (UODO)	Address: Urząd Ochrony Danych Osobowych ul. Stawki 2, 00-193 Warszawa Mr Jan NOWAK, President of the Personal Data Protection Office Website: https://uodo.gov.pl/ Email: kancelaria@uodo.gov.pl; zwme@uodo.gov.pl Telephone: +48 22 531 03 00
Portugal	Portuguese Data Protection Authority (Comissão Nacional de Protecção de Dados) (CNPD)	Address: Portuguese Data Protection Authority Av. D. Carlos I, 134 - 1.º, 1200-651 Lisboa Ms Filipa Calvão, President, Comissão Nacional de Protecção de Dados Website: http://www.cnpd.pt Email: geral@cnpd.pt Telephone: +351 21 392 84 00

Authority country	Authority's full title and acronym	Authority's website and contact details
Romania	The National Supervisory Authority for Personal Data Processing ("ANSPDCP") (Autoritatea Naţională de Supraveghere a Prelucrării Datelor cu Caracter Personal) (ANSPDCP)	Address: The National Supervisory Authority for Personal Data Processing B-dul Magheru 28-30, Sector 1, 010336 Bucureşti Ms Ancuţa Gianina Opre, President of the National Supervisory Authority for Personal Data Processing Website: http://www.dataprotection.ro/ Email: anspdcp@dataprotection.ro Telephone: +40 31 805 9211
Slovakia	Office for Personal Data Protection of the Slovak Republic (Úrad pre ochranu osobných údajov Slovenskej republiky) (PDP)	Address: Office for Personal Data Protection of the Slovak Republic, Hraničná 12, 820 07 Bratislava 27 Website: http://www.dataprotection.gov.sk/ Email: statny.dozor@pdp.gov.sk Telephone: + 421 2 32 31 32 14
Slovenia	Information Commissioner of the Republic of Slovenia (Informacijski pooblaščenec) (IC)	Address: Information Commissioner of the Republic of Slovenia, Dunajska cesta 22, SI-1000 Ljubljana Ms Mojca Prelesnik, Information Commissioner of the Republic of Slovenia Website: https://www.ip-rs.si/ Email: gp.ip@ip-rs.si Telephone: +386 1 230 9730
Spain	Spanish Data Protection Authority (Agencia Española de Protección de Datos) (AEPD)	Address: Agencia Española de Protección de Datos, C/ Jorge Juan, 6; 28001 Madrid Ms María del Mar España Martí, Director of the Spanish Data Protection Agency Website: https://www.aepd.es/ Email: internacional@aepd.es Telephone: +34 91 266 3517
Sweden	The Swedish Data Protection Authority (Datainspektionen)	Address: Datainspektionen Drottninggatan 29, 5th Floor, Box 8114, 104 20 Stockholm Ms Lena Lindgren Schelin, Director General of the Data Inspection Board Website: http://www.datainspektionen.se Email: datainspektionen@datainspektionen.se Telephone: +46 (0)8 657 61 00

Authority country	Authority's full title and acronym	Authority's website and contact details
United Kingdom	Information Commissioner's Office (ICO)	Address: Information Commissioner's Office Wycliffe House, Water Lane, Wilmslow, Cheshire SK9 5AF Elizabeth Denham, Information Commissioner Website: https://ico.org.uk/ Live chat: https://ico.org.uk/global/contact-us/ Telephone: +44 303 123 1113
United Kingdom – Northern Ireland	Information Commissioner's Office (ICO/NI)	Address: The Information Commissioner's Office – Northern Ireland, 3rd Floor, 14 Cromac Place, Belfast BT7 2JB Ken Macdonald, Head of ICO Regions Website: https://ico.org.uk/about-the-ico/who-we-are/northern-ireland-office/ Email: ni@ico.org.uk Telephone: +44 28 9027 8757 or +44 303 123 1114
United Kingdom – Scotland	Scottish Information Commissioner (ICO/S)	Address: The Information Commissioner's Office – Scotland 45 Melville Street, Edinburgh EH3 7HL Ken Macdonald, Head of ICO Regions Website: https://ico.org.uk/about-the-ico/who-we-are/scotland-office/ and http://www.itspublicknowledge.info/home/ ScottishInformationCommissioner.aspx Email: scotland@ico.org.uk Telephone: +44 303 123 1115
United Kingdom – Wales	Welsh Information Commissioner (ICO/W)	Address: Information Commissioner's Office – Wales 2nd Floor, Churchill House, Churchill Way, Cardiff CF10 2HH Iaith Gwaith, Welsh Language Commissioner (no regional Commissioner) Website: https://ico.org.uk/about-the-ico/who-we-are/wales-office/ and http://www.comisiynyddygymraeg.cymru/ Email: wales@ico.org.uk or post@welshlanguagecommissioner.wales Telephone: 0330 414 6421

Other publications on topics and trends in the industry available on Amazon and extended distribution channels include the following –

This second Blue Paper lays out the legal position of the GDPR on data security and data breaches. The included Data Breach Accountability Framework helps data controllers and processors develop a defensible compliance position and strengthen their legal, technical, and organisational procedures and processes as per the GDPR. It also furnishes a GDPR Sanctions Directory, a comprehensive repository of 503 administrative fines imposed by national Data Protection Supervisory Authorities.

A Data Breach Accountability Framework: How to reduce the risk of GDPR sanctions (Professional Publication) (GOLD RUSH Publishing, London). ISBN-13: 978-1908585141.

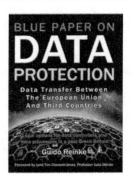

This Blue Paper furnishes robust legal options for data professionals and policy options for law-makers concerning data transfers between the EU and third countries. Key resources include an assessment of legal options and a brief overview of the EU Data Protection Regulation, the UK Data Protection Act 2018, the EU Charter of Fundamental Rights, and the Council of Europe's Convention 108+. This Paper also furnishes a synopsis of the UK's challenges in defining its future data relationship with the EU thanks to its regime of mass surveillance and data sharing with non-EU countries.

Data Transfer between the European Union and third countries: Legal options for data controllers and data processors in a post-Brexit Britain: (Professional Publication) Union (GOLD RUSH Publishing, London). ISBN-13: 978-1908585103.

This Official Publication of the Data Transfer Blue Paper is designed for politicians and scholars. It covers the same topics as the Professional edition, which includes an assessment of legal options, policy recommendations with key considerations for legislators and politicians to achieve the best possible outcomes for businesses and citizens, and an overview of existing legal privacy frameworks and of the challenges of data transfer between the EU and the UK.

Data Transfer between the European Union and third countries: Legal options for data controllers and data processors in a post-Brexit Britain (Official Publication) (GOLD RUSH Publishing, London). ISBN-13: 978-1908585110.

This book offers the first comprehensive impact assessment across the 35 *acquis* EU policy domains. The assessment ranges from the four freedoms of the Single Market – free movement of goods, services, capital and person – to essential matter like companies and competition, financial services, information society, consumer protection, energy, science & research, employment, security & defence, and more. It also provides background information and a vision of Britain and the EU in 2026.

Brexit: A Political Crisis for Europe: Impact Assessment and Lessons Learnt for the European Union (GOLD RUSH Publishing, London). ISBN-13: 978-1908585097.

This book with more than 2500 entries brings clarity to a domain which is widely considered to be complex, unstructured, and in constant flux. It is a compendious guide to the laws, regulations, standards, and recommendations applicable to compliance programmes. The Regulatory Compliance Matrix has been a bestseller in the category business law on Amazon for several months.

The Regulatory Compliance Matrix: Regulation of Financial Services, Information and Communication Technology, and Generally Related Matters (GOLD RUSH Publishing, London). ISBN-13: 978-1908585059.

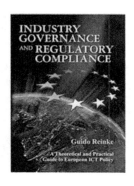

This book contains detailed guidance on how to participate in the making and comply with the output of regulatory regimes. It provides evidence for the Industry Governance Theory, which is a new take on regulatory governance that gives insight into industry's pro-active role and predominating influence in shaping European public policy. The book also introduces new tools such the Regulatory Compliance Maturity Model, the Policy Influence-Timing Model and the Stakeholder Action Matrix.

Industry Governance and Regulatory Compliance: A Theoretical and Practical Guide to European ICT Policy (GOLD RUSH Publishing, London). ISBN-13: 978-1908585028.

ABOUT THE AUTHOR

Guido Reinke is as a Data Protection Officer with a business assurance and regulatory compliance background. He has advised firms on how to design and implement global privacy frameworks. After working for the European Commission, he took employment with regulated industries and at Big Four professional services firms. He holds a LL.M. from Queen Mary University of London School of Law and a PhD in Politics and International Relations from the University of London, and has lectured on Regulatory Governance at the London School of Economics. He is also author of a Blue Paper on data transfer between the EU and third countries, a Brexit Impact Assessment bestseller and other compliance publications.

SOME FINAL PRIVACY THOUGHS BY CELEBRITIES

I have as much privacy as a goldfish in a bowl.

Princess Margaret Rose Windsor, Countess of Snowdon

I don't want to write an autobiography because I would become
public property with no privacy left.

Stephen Hawking, English theoretical physicist, cosmologist and author

Privacy means people know what they're signing up for, in plain English, and
repeatedly.
I'm an optimist, I believe people are smart, and
some people want to share more than other people do.
Ask them. Ask them every time.
Make them tell you to stop asking them if they get tired of your asking them.
Let them know precisely what you're going to do with their data.

Steve Jobs; American business magnate, entrepreneur and co-founder of Apple

Privacy is dead,
and social medial holds the smoking gun.

Pete Cashmore, founder and CEO of Mashable

Relying on the government to protect your privacy
is like asking a peeping Tom to install your window blinds.

John Perry Barlow, American poet and essayist

Privacy is not something that I'm merely entitled to,
it's a absolute prerequisite.

Marlo Brando, American actor and film director

Getting information from the Internet
is like
taking a drink from a hydrant.

Mitchell Kapor, founder of Lotus Development Corporation